Tribal Rugs

Tribal Rugs

JAMES OPIE

Nomadic and
Village Weavings
from the
Near East and
Central Asia

Laurence King

Appreciations and Acknowledgments

First published 1992 by
Laurence King Publishing

Copyright © 1992 James Opie

This paperback edition first published in
1998 by Laurence King Publishing, an
imprint of Calmann & King Ltd, 71 Great
Russell Street, London WC1B 3BN

A catalogue record for this book is available
from the British Library.

ISBN (p/back) 1-85669-125-X

Line drawings by Sue Bellucci
Cover designed by Mark Vernon-Jones
Designed by Richard Foenander
Typeset by SX Composing Ltd., Essex
Printed by Kyodo Printing Co (S'pore) Pte Ltd

Title spread:
Kirghiz nomadic encampment

Without the weavers there would be neither rugs nor books about rugs. I hope it is obvious that this volume is fundamentally a tribute to their work.

Rug dealers remain the primary source of information about tribal rugs. I benefited from contacts with dealers throughout the world, including many who provided plate materials. Rug collectors and auction firms that specialize in old and antique rugs were equally generous.

Editorial help came from many sources. Spencer Gill served as editor throughout the bulk of this many-yeared project, rendering continual support. Jannan Meyer's editorial advice was of critical help in early chapters. Murray Eiland's contributions were numerous, touching on editorial, historical, ethnological and technical matters. This book in its final form could hardly have taken shape without him. Morteza Ghashghai provided valuable information. Jon Thompson read several chapters, made important suggestions, and shared his insights. *Oriental Rug Review* and *HALI* contributed to the process by publishing my articles on design origins and other themes. My wife Catherine has helped me at every step since we met in 1988, shining light into many otherwise dark places. My secretary Sarah and many friends commented constructively and rendered moral support. During the project's final months, few pages escaped the skillful pen of my editor, Sophie Collins. Her help was essential.

Museums made key plates available. They include the Hermitage Museum in St Petersburg, the Metropolitan Museum of Art in New York, the Textile Museum in Washington D.C., the Victoria and Albert Museum in London, the Islamic Museum in Berlin, the Los Angeles County Museum of Art, the Museum of National Antiquities in Stockholm, and the Vakiflar Museum in Istanbul.

Scholars who shared their knowledge of specific subjects include P. R S. Moorey of Oxford University, a prominent scholar in the field of early Iranian metalwork; Emma Bunker, now associated with the Denver Art Museum, who has written extensively about zoomorphic-style art; John Haskins, late Professor Emeritus at the University of Pittsburgh, a leading student of the Pazyryk rug; and Lois Beck of Washington University in St Louis, whose speciality is south Persian anthropology. Fredrik Barth was generous in permitting use of both pictures and quotations from *Nomads of South Persia*. Peter Andrews provided several valuable photographs, as did Udo Hirsch and Parviz Tanavoli, and Dennis Anderson gave substantial help in photographing rugs. Salam and Mohamed Zuhairy of Archive Photo (Portland, Oregon) worked under considerable pressure to restore several photographs. The help that all of these individuals provided was indispensable and, at times, inspiring. Any factual or interpretative errors have no bearing on their work and are solely the responsibility of the author.

Line drawings throughout the book are the product of Sue Bellucci, who also organized the sequence of plates and the initial design plan. She breathed life into otherwise abstract ideas.

My son and daughter, David and Alexandra, were patient and supportive through the years of preoccupation with "the book."

I also wish to thank those individuals who, on exposure to primary proposals, never believed them for a moment, thereby forcing me to dig ever deeper into the subject.

This enterprise, so important for me personally, would not have been possible without the financial support of several customers. Among these are my dear friend James Rinehart, an anonymous and longstanding friend in Alaska, and a collector of great personal warmth and kindness, the late Timothy String.

Thank you.

Contents

Introduction

Tribal Rugs explores one of mankind's oldest surviving forms of artistic expression, encompassing knotted and flatwoven rugs, kilims, bags, and related objects from tribal and village populations of Asia. Only a tiny portion of this tradition's immense creative output has survived to the present day. Some of what remains was woven primarily to trade or sell. Other pieces, unrelated to commerce, served functions in daily tribal life; these examples represent the art in its purest form. Rarely in human history have articles destined for hard use in a subsistence way of life reached such levels of complexity and beauty. In stark contrast with the violent histories of the tribes which produce these objects, the weavings themselves reveal an artistic heritage of remarkable sensitivity.

Nomads were a conspicuous, colorful presence in Iran and Afghanistan when I first visited those countries in 1970 and 1973 respectively. Tents dotted the landscape in both countries. Through a decade of regular trips, I often rubbed shoulders with tribal people in camps as well as in cities and towns, where they came to buy and sell. Seasonal migrations on foot or by donkey and horseback were part of the normal pattern of life for several million tribespeople. In the southern city of Shiraz, a major commercial and artistic centre in Iran, the kaleidoscopic street scene was enhanced by the sight of tribal women, clothed in multi-layered dresses of vibrant hues, and bedecked with silver jewelry. Some decorated their foreheads with gold coins. These brightly dressed women from the Qashqa'i Confederacy set themselves decisively apart from their urban counterparts, who were covered from head to toe by black *chadors*. I often met Qashqa'i women in wool shops, where more prosperous weavers came to buy yarn. Portions of these rooms were packed chest-high with thousands of undyed skeins. I was fascinated by these women who came there to choose balls of choice yarns. Everything about them bespoke separateness, not only toward me – a male and a foreigner – but also toward the surrounding Persian culture. Simply by their bearing they held themselves apart, without ever conveying any hint of subservience. Seeing them stride through the bazaars with pride and determination, one could only wonder if they deliberately hid evidence of the desperate times their people were experiencing, and which virtually all Asian nomadic tribes have endured since the mid-nineteenth century. Nomadic herdsmen and their settled relatives have increasingly found themselves at odds with state institutions throughout this violent period, first in Russian-controlled areas, then in Persia, and, most recently, in Afghanistan, eastern Turkey, and eastern Iraq.

In the course of research for this book, opportunities arose to approach these women with such questions as "Do you weave throughout the year, or seasonally?" "Do you dye your own yarns or pay to have this done?" "How many days of the year do you break camp and migrate?" Many of my questions related to the origin and meaning of tribal rug motifs and designs. I soon realized that my curiosity about these subjects was not understood or shared by the women. Hearing my questions, weavers in camps and villages occasionally said, "Why would anyone want to know *that*?" They took for granted aspects of tribal culture that, from a western perspective, had to have meaningful histories and explanations.

Fresh from Europe and America, where ever-advancing technologies rule out any return to the past, I was keenly aware of the precarious position of pastoral nomads. The confident strides of Qashqa'i women in the Shiraz bazaar did not convey the whole picture. The acquisition of western inventions, coupled with the hardening policies of governments towards both nomadic and settled tribespeople, was hastening their assimilation, if not their total subjugation. Their zenith as truly separate cultures was well behind them. The survival of this way of life was now in question.

The primary causes of this crisis were not difficult to determine. The increasing accuracy and destructiveness of weapons available to leaders of powerful nations have broken a prolonged balance which formerly saw organized tribal groups holding their own in the face of the continual ebb and flow of centralized governments. As events in Iraqi Kurdistan early in 1991 revealed so brutally, there are no longer any mountains so steep or valleys so secluded that tribal communities can find a place to hide.

As tribal *khans* struggled to retain some influence in the course of the twentieth century, individual tribes and larger confederacies lost ever more ground in their centuries-old contest with central authorities. An ancient and resilient link in tribal history and, indeed, in human history was being

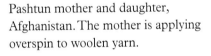

Pashtun mother and daughter, Afghanistan. The mother is applying overspin to woolen yarn.

broken before our eyes. This link spanned the vast period following pre-historic man's domestication of goats and sheep and the development of civil-izations to the modern period, with its worldwide network of political and economic relationships.

I wanted to see the remains of traditional tribal life in Iran and Afghan-istan and explore in depth an ancient craft that expressed the artistic side of this existence: tribal rugs. From the beginning, I was challenged to learn about the origin of the oldest designs. The primary focus of my study has been woven motifs containing vestiges of ancient influences. The very best of these objects remain a largely overlooked treasure in the history of Asian art.

The opening chapter of this book introduces essential traditions of nomads and their adaptation to shifting pressures and needs. Chapter 2 in-troduces the search for design origins by exploring relevant styles of ancestral tribal art. Chapter 3 summarizes what is known about the world's oldest in-tact rug, the Pazyryk. These first three chapters set the stage for under-standing two essential divisions: rugs containing traditional folk motifs (Chapter 4), and those containing designs borrowed from urban, non-tribal sources (Chapter 6).

Chapter 5 presents evidence that an initially small number of ancient motifs changed over the millennia, expanding into a vast repertoire of forms, an ever-changing vocabulary of motifs. Woven images from the most isolated nomadic tribes in Iran enable us to find unexpected relationships within a broad family of motifs. These have endured in both tribal and village sur-roundings from Anatolia to Afghanistan and from the Caucasus to southern Iran. Chapters 7–17 focus on individual tribes, tribal confederacies, and vil-lage-dominated regions. Relevant structural features are discussed as they arise.

This book encompasses both nomadic and village weavings from Iran, Anatolia (Turkey), Afghanistan, and areas farther to the north and east in Central Asia. The time span embraced reaches back over two millennia. Yet, most of the nineteenth-century rugs that appear in the plates have been on the market within recent years. The availability of objects of such extra-ordinary quality remains an appealing feature of this field.

It is important to emphasize that tribal weaving is an art practiced by women. While men organized migrations, tended animals, planned fresh raids, or looked back on past adventures, the creative spirit and deft fingers of girls and women kept this art form alive. In 1898, Otis Mason wrote:

Women, more than men, have enriched . . . tribal mythologies with elements from other sources. Captured and carried from place to place, they have taken with them their stories which, by removal from their indigenous soil, have assumed the form of myth.[1]

Rug designs, like folk myths, have been altered and reshaped in dozens of directions in the course of their long history among Asia's tribal popu-lations. They constitute an ancient puzzle, fragments of which have survived into our own era.

The gradual loss of artistic vitality in tribal weavings cannot be dated definitively to any decade within the past century. By 1980, this once widespread Asian folk art had declined to the level of an uninspired commercial craft. Fortunately, the 1980s saw the beginnings of an unexpected revival in the use of vegetable dyes. This movement gains steam as we approach the end of the century. I have seen new vegetal-dyed Qashqa'i weavings of amazing vitality. Perhaps there is hope, therefore, that in reference to a few tribes, this study is not totally a matter of "looking back," but one which looks forward, as well.

Part I
Tribal Culture and Art History

The Tribal Way of Life

1

Long after the last nomadic family surrenders to the overwhelming temptations and influences of modern industrial culture, tribal rugs will remind us of an extraordinary and ancient way of life. Pastoral nomadism began to evolve after one of mankind's most significant breakthroughs: the domestication of grazing animals, including cattle, goats, and sheep. Some students of prehistory surmise that scattered shepherd families gradually abandoned village homes in favor of portable dwellings and a lifestyle adapted to the grazing requirements of large herds. Self-sufficiency was a central aspect of this new way of life, but some economic support came from urban populations, who provided a market for wool and livestock. Systems for allotting pasture rights among families and clans gradually evolved and patterns of leadership emerged – some of whose outlines can be found in biblical accounts. Aside from their accomplishments in social and economic spheres, early nomads made works of art, including ritual objects, decorated tools, and containers. Although our knowledge of prehistoric weaving traditions is minimal, this craft, too, must have been practiced and refined from an early date.

People whose lives focused unswervingly on raising flocks of sheep and goats inevitably engaged in selective breeding, leading to higher-quality fibers. Basic weaving and felt-making techniques, known since prehistoric times, were brought to more refined levels after improved fibers became available in dependable quantities. When dyeing technologies took a corresponding leap, the decorative potential of woven objects assumed a new place in both urban and tribal culture.

Tribespeople and villagers were and are highly sensitive to qualitative variations in the materials around them. I recall noticing, in an Afghan village market, the strict system used by nut growers in laying out their wares; I counted, for example, seven different grades of pistachios. The fine quality of wool in many older weavings suggests that wool was formerly sorted and classified in a similar manner.

Nomads who formed coherent tribes never roamed from place to place simply out of an urge to wander. They moved purposefully, according to the seasons, in order to find suitable pasture for their animals. The same creatures whose feeding needs dictated the essential patterns of migratory life also made this lifestyle possible. Sheep and goats provided meat, milk, and cheese. Their wool and skins were fashioned into clothing, shelter, bedding, and containers. Donkeys and camels carried tents, cooking equipment, and other belongings. Animal dung served as fuel. Many nomadic bags decorated with animal figures reflect a special affection and regard for these creatures as vital participants in the nomadic way of life. This life was strenuous and even coarse in many respects, but rich in a sense of belonging: to a family, to a tribe, and to the earth itself.

If animals were the most vital possessions of nomads, grazing lands were their overpowering need. To find grass, mountain-dwelling nomadic herdsmen took their animals up into higher elevations in the spring, where melting snow revealed plentiful grass. In the late autumn, when snow threatened, they moved back to the lowlands. These treks varied in length from tribe to tribe, with some groups traveling distances in excess of four hundred miles.

Of great importance to many of these nomadic groups were their traditional migration trails, known to some groups as "the tribal road." These routes periodically changed hands due to invading tribes who seized desirable pastures, absorbing previous residents or pushing them into less hospitable terrain. Through all of these disruptions and the mixing of ethnic bloodlines, the tribal road endured. However, by the early 1990s, the tribal road had begun to change. The tracks of four-wheel-drive vehicles have begun to replace the hoofprints of donkeys, even in the most remote areas.

It is difficult for us in the West to comprehend the appeal this way of life holds for its adherents, given the hardships of long migrations. In the past, some members of the Bakhtiyari tribe walked barefoot for long distances on ice and snow during parts of their spring migration. Some groups crossed swollen rivers, scaled mountain ranges, and traversed desert expanses, all in the ordinary course of a year. By surmounting these difficulties, tribespeople saw themselves as superior to untested town-dwellers.

Conflicting needs and perspectives caused an uneasy breach between nomads and town residents. Given the legendary brutality of many nomadic tribes, the prejudice of settled populations was natural. Yet some exchanges between nomadic and settled cultures were necessary and mutually desirable. From the viewpoint of nomads, these contacts became increasingly essential with the passage of centuries. Although early nomads in some regions smelted their own metals, gradually, the acquisition of metal objects depended solely on trade. During recent centuries, guns and gunpowder

1.1 The women's colorful dresses and the characteristic hats worn by the men identify this family as Qashqa'is from southern Iran.

were procured by barter or purchase. Occasionally, they were confiscated from defeated government forces. It was common for nomads to grow much of the grain they needed on land within winter grazing districts, but some grains were purchased or bartered for. Unless they were available locally, salt and spices were purchased in towns – as were luxuries such as gold and silver jewelry. This was also true of some dye materials used in weaving. In return, nomads sold and traded their animals or animal skins, as well as butter and wool. And at an unknown point in their long history, they also began selling their primary art objects: tribal rugs.

Pile rugs made for sale or trade were a byproduct of ancient and varied weaving traditions among nomads. We in the West tend to look at all tribal weavings as decorative objects that coincidentally were useful to their makers, rather than as useful objects which happened to be decorative.[1] The tribal way of life called for the invention of several types of woven objects, beginning with the most fundamental tribal textile, strips of tenting material, which, when sewn together, form the very homes in which members of many tribes live. These tents are made exclusively by women. However, not all tribes rely on tents *per se* for shelter. Throughout Central Asia and in cooler regions of Iran and Turkey, *yurts* were and still are preferred by some tribes. These circular structures are formed by assembling a portable wooden frame and then covering it with large pieces of felt. Therefore, these felt-covered *yurts* also depend on wool fibers, transformed by hand labor. Another primitive weaving type, the reed screen, shelters tents and yurts from wind and dust. Some screens are elaborately decorated with traditional rug and kilim designs.

Nomads have created a great variety of containers to hold and safeguard everything they own. These vary from enormous double saddlebags, carried by camels or donkeys, to tiny single bags, designed to hold precious possessions, such as a single copy of the Koran. There are bags for water bottles, bags for drop spindles, bags made solely to hold large spoons, and bags for carrying salt. The list goes on: cradles to support babies, large box-like containers, and grain sacks. Flat-woven pieces include many types of kilim (from the Persian word, *gelim*). These vary in their size, decorative treatment, and function. The largest kilim in a tribal dwelling is a dust cover over goods piled at the rear of the tent. Rudimentary flatweaves serve as curtains to separate the men's and women's sections. The considerable variety of woven forms developed for use on animals included halters, straps, horse-covers, and tasseled weavings attached to the rumps of donkeys.

The local names applied to most indigenous nomadic weavings are unfamiliar to anyone outside the tribes themselves and a handful of ethnologists and students of tribal culture.[2] Gradually, rug collectors and dealers have mastered such Persian terms as *jajim, sofre, chanteh* (small single bags) and *malband* (pack-animal bands). However, each region and linguistic grouping uses different nomenclature, the sum total of which, if gathered together, would fill many pages. Small rugs and cushion covers known in Turkey as *yastik* are called *balisht* among Baluch weavers near the Iranian-Afghan border. The word *mafrash* describes quite different articles, depending on whether the object is from a Turkoman group in Soviet Central Asia or a Turkic-speaking group in Iran, such as the Shahsavan. Moreover, the weaving type that Shahsavan tribespeople call *mafrash* is known as *rakhtekhab-pich* among Lurs and Bakhtiyaris. Adding to the complexity of this study are corresponding differences in the names given to specific motifs. "Ram's horns" in one locale are "animal heads" elsewhere. Such variations, even in the limited context of a single region, can lead to considerable problems of interpretation by foreign scholars.

Structural elements and decorative embellishments which adorn scores of weaving types are as varied as the items themselves. Unfortunately, names

applied in the West to aspects of structure and technique frequently bear 13
little relationship to terms used by nomadic women. Most readers will understand what is meant by "symmetrical knot" or "*soumak*" (extra-weft wrapping), but nomadic weavers in Anatolia, Iran, or Afghanistan would not.
They have their own names.

TRIBES, SUB-TRIBES, AND VILLAGERS

Another problem of terminology relates to the word "tribe." It can suggest a
large confederation composed of a heterogeneous cluster of smaller, more
homogeneous groups. This describes the Qashqa'i and Bakhtiyari tribal confederacies in Iran, both of which were major tribal powers in the past
century. In other contexts, "tribe" implies a single, closely-knit unit. Between these extremes are such peoples as the Tekke Turkomans, living
primarily in regions to the west of the Caspian Sea. The Tekke tribe is one of
many groups within the loosely related Turkoman peoples. Like other Turkoman tribes, such as the Salors or Yomuds, the Tekkes speak a Turkic language.[3] If we were to approach a contemporary Tekke weaver and ask her to
describe her tribal affiliation, she might say "Tekke," but would be just as
apt to mention a smaller division within the group, possibly even a village
name. Or she might respond by referring to the larger framework of tribes of
which Tekkes form a part, and respond "Turkmen" (Turkoman). We see,
therefore, that a weaver can belong to several tribes at once, depending on
one's use of the word "tribe."

Another example is the broad array of groups in western Iran, eastern
Iraq, and southeastern Turkey who call themselves "Kurds." Their language, Kurdish, is related to Persian (Farsi), in the Indo-European language
group.[4] Most of those born into Kurdish culture clearly think of themselves
as Kurds. However, a Kurdish weaver would be inclined to refer to her tribe
by a more specific name, such as "Jaff" or perhaps an even smaller unit such
as "Guran." Within these sections are still smaller clans. Therefore, such
terms as "tribe," "sub-tribe," and "section" rarely have fixed references.
Their meanings change according to the contexts in which they appear.

Very few names by which we presently identify Asian nomadic populations have been in use for more than fifteen hundred years, suggesting the
significant measure of flux that characterizes tribal life. In many cases,

1.2 An Iranian Bakhtiyari chief meets
with others leaders during the 1924
spring migration.

1.3 Baluch camp, Iran.

several racial groups have mixed within a single tribe. For example, Turkoman tribes include both Mongolian and Indo-European peoples. Consequently, in some cases our use of the word "tribe" needs to take ethnic combinations into account.

Moreover, membership of a nomadic tribe does not always imply a year-round nomadic way of life. Millions of nomads live in villages for part of the year, or settle permanently without abandoning their tribal allegiances and identities. Some live in villages populated by members of their group; others in ethnically-mixed towns and cities.

LARGE-SCALE TRIBAL MIGRATIONS

Pastoral nomadic life favors relatively small shifts in camp sites in the short term but may entail far-flung displacements over longer periods. Consequently, only a few tribes known to us for their weavings have occupied their present lands for more than one thousand years. Climatic changes, military successes and failures, and broad, historic migrations caused tribes to fragment, gain and lose members, and even disappear from the historical record. These movements may also involve modifications in language and alteration of the tribal names by which they are known.

Such considerations complicate the task of ascribing accurate labels to certain weavings. It is partly for this reason that I place less emphasis on specific attributions than on broad families of designs. Still, the need for a reasonable degree of precision in nomenclature cannot be avoided. At times, efforts to achieve such precision lead to difficulties. For example, several tribal groups within the south Persian Qashqa'i Confederacy were speakers of Turkic languages who came into southern Iran within the past four hundred years. Other segments of the same confederacy are of Luri background (native Iranians). Some of these Luri factions spoke their own language, Luri, which is related to Persian. Their form of nomadism developed slowly under local geographical and ecological conditions which varied substantially from circumstances in the Turkic-controlled steppes. Lurs within the Qashqa'i Confederacy often married within their group, and their rug designs throughout the nineteenth century often reflect Luri traditions. Nonetheless, they recognized the authority of Turkic-speaking Qashqa'i khans, to whom they paid taxes in the form of animals. Luri-dominated groups appear on old lists of tribes within the Qashqa'i Confederacy. In terms of their political loyalties, their participation in the Qashqa'i Confederacy made "Qashqa'i" a functional label for these particular people. However, in an ethnic sense, they were Lurs. Now the question arises: are we to label rugs woven by such sub-tribes according to their political loyalties (in this case Qashqa'i) or according to their ethnic roots (Luri)? There are no fixed answers to these questions, and each author approaches problems of this kind according to his or her own viewpoint, knowledge, and preferences. We shall encounter similar questions (and some answers) in later chapters.

MARRIAGE CUSTOMS AND OTHER COMMUNAL TRADITIONS

Many first-person reports by westerners with experience in rug-producing countries recount tales of brides being purchased or stolen, of protracted bargaining sessions over young women, and centuries-old blood feuds. One such account, related to marriage, appeared in *S. W. Persia, a Political Officer's Diary 1907–1914*, by Sir Arnold Wilson.

One very handsome tall youth of 23 had long desired the hand of the daughter of a Kadkhuda [minor chief] of a rival and not always unfriendly tribe, who asked too high a price. One day, with a dozen of his father's retainers, the youth made a raid upon the camp of his future father-in-law during the absence of all the able-bodied men. He seized his bride, put her across his saddle, and, guarded by his henchmen, rode away with her amid the piercing screams of her mother, her sisters, and the maidservants. No blood was shed, and he left in the tent a bag of money containing what he regarded as a fair price for her.

1.4 An *asmalyk*, a decorative pile weaving for the lead camel in a Turkoman wedding procession.

There was much talk of war between the two tribes, but public opinion was in his favour; it was a "good match"; such a marriage would help to keep the peace between the two tribes concerned. It was felt that her father had asked too much. The youth treated her well; he was regarded as a bit of a hero among men, and she a heroine among women. Her father-in-law was delighted and gave her many gold pieces and a flock of young goats. That was eight months ago: all was now forgiven and he was about to become a father. She was the joy of his life; the embodiment of female virtue and beauty, and also good at making fine carpets.[5]

The customs of a bride-price and dowry are common among many peoples of the world. Among Asian nomadic tribes the interesting factor, from our point of view, is the role played by rugs in these negotiations. They demonstrated an important and marketable skill that could be relied upon for income. At the same time, dowry pieces offered tangible evidence of a young woman's aesthetic sensibilities, enhancing her stature. Several illustrations in the Turkoman chapter show superb weavings made specifically for wedding ceremonies. While dowry traditions have weakened in the course of the twentieth century, few contemporary tribal marriages take place without rugs being offered as gifts.

Weaving was, however, more than a source of income or a means of artistic expression. Women enjoyed a sense of community while working together on weaving projects. The old tradition of singing during this work still continues in some areas. Heavy combs used for packing wefts into place have small pieces of metal loosely attached which make a jingling sound. In the hands of tribal women, these tools are transformed into musical instruments, keeping steady rhythms as a background for songs and chants.

At their highest level of development, weaving traditions served as focal points for a quality of communal life that no longer exists in Asia or elsewhere. The following comments of G. I. Gurdjieff, who financed his

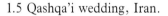

1.5 Qashqa'i wedding, Iran.

remarkable travels in Asia by dealing in oriental rugs, were related by his pupil, P. D. Ouspensky,

He spoke of the ancient customs connected with carpet making in certain parts of Asia; of a whole village working together at one carpet; of winter evenings when all the villagers, young and old, gather together in one large building and, dividing into groups, sit or stand on the floor in an order previously known and determined by tradition. Each group then begins its own work. Some pick stones and splinters out of the wool. Others beat out the wool with sticks. A third group combs the wool. The fourth spins. The fifth dyes the wool. The sixth or maybe the twenty-sixth weaves the actual carpet. Men, women, and children, old men and old women, all have their own traditional work. And all the work is done to the accompaniment of music and singing. The women spinners with spindles in their hands dance a special dance as they work, and all the movements of all the people engaged in different work are like one movement in one and the same rhythm. Moreover each locality has its own special tune, its own special songs and dances, connected with carpet making from time immemorial.[6]

"ISOLATION" IN TRIBAL AND VILLAGE LIFE

The Qashqa'i women whom I watched bargain in the bazaars of southern Iran represented points of contact between tribal people and towns and cities throughout Asia. One dealer in Shiraz remarked, "Tribespeople are proud of their life up in the mountains, but they also love coming to the bazaar." Such contacts were and are part of the continuous inter-dependence of nomadic and urban populations, especially among tribes who migrate near cities or large towns and complement the large measure of independence enjoyed by nomads. Although the degree and frequency of contacts with settled populations vary from tribe to tribe, relatively few nomads, even in the past, have lived in complete isolation from the surrounding culture.

Among the channels of contact between urban cultures and nomadic tribes were the tribal chiefs and other élite members of the tribe. For a number of centuries, khans who migrated seasonally with their tribes also lived part of the year in city residences. As Morteza Ghashghai,[7] my closest friend in the Qashqa'i family, confirmed, the ruling Qashqa'i family was always considerably more urban-oriented than the tribespeople they led. Bridging urban and tribal cultures was an important aspect of a khan's practice of statecraft and politics. For the last few generations, Qashqa'i khans have owned automobiles, traveled abroad, and received formal educations. Because of their position as role models, tribal leaders inevitably served as a conduit for urban influences into the tribes. Several heads of confederacies have been only nominally related to the people they led. The clearest example is the Khamseh Confederacy of southern Iran, headed for some decades by a Jewish commerical family in Shiraz.

Wealthy tribal families who established joint residence in urban and tribal surroundings had a discernible impact on some tribal rug designs. Keenly aware of the lastest urban styles, leading families have sometimes paid weavers from their tribe to produce copies of finely patterned urban carpets. Morteza Ghashghai remembers his mother's success in persuading local Qashqa'i weavers to reproduce a motif that was popular in central Europe during the 1930s and early 1940s. The weavers worked according to her directions, without any resistance to her instructions. We can assume that this was a normal situation in leading tribal families.[8]

These considerations have an important bearing on our understanding of many tribal designs. We shall find material confirming the urban basis of several patterns in Chapter 6. Both Chapter 10 and Chapter 17, dealing with the Qashqa'i and Turkoman tribes respectively, also include evidence that numerous rugs from both groups, including examples enjoying market popularity as truly "nomadic" weavings, were actually made for sale, rather than for use in nomadic tents. Many rugs and commercially-inspired bag fronts reflect underlying urban design influences beneath layers of "tribalization."

Tribally related village rugs frequently represent a complex mixture of influences. As was the case with some designs in the Pazyryk rug and with thousands of surviving examples from more recent centuries, many weavings from these sources are folk versions of city designs. These developments depended largely on the influence of commercial and aesthetic currents, radiating outward from cities and towns. On the other hand, villagers in some areas sustained ancient design traditions by remaining on or beyond the periphery of urban influences in the rug trade. The fact that villagers do not migrate helps explain the conservatism of many traditional village patterns. This was certainly the case in parts of Anatolia, the Caucasus, and areas in the Zagros mountains in Iran.

The suggestion that village rather than nomadic weavers both invented and preserved the very oldest designs has been advanced by several authors.[9] A nomadic source for several ancient designs shown in Chapter 4 is possible. In my opinion, nomads played an important role in both developing and spreading several of the oldest patterns. From an early period in this process, village women helped sustain them in local weaving traditions.

TRIBAL CHIEFS

Tribal chiefs number among history's least respected figures; the names of such leaders as Genghis Khan and Attila are bywords for cruelty. In many ancient chronicles tribesmen were simply called "barbarians." What else could one call horse-mounted tribes whose chiefs made drinking vessels out of their enemies' skulls? Asia suffered under hundreds of tyrant khans, and Europe lived through successive waves of terror perpetrated by Huns, Goths, and Turks.

During the twentieth century, chiefs have maintained their position by exercising negotiating skills, rather than by bloodletting. This change came about as centralized states increased their ability to control all populations within their borders by military means, thereby squeezing nomads and their leaders into a corner. Ultimately, no surviving hereditary chiefs have been a match for the complex political, economic, and military changes that have taken place over the past one hundred and fifty years.

One of the outstanding chiefs of our own era, and arguably the last great tribal khan, was Nassr Khan Qashqa'i, a descendant of Jani Khan, founder of the Qashqa'i Confederacy in the late eighteenth century. Due to the influence of descendants of Jani Khan, the family name, Qashqa'i, came to be applied to the entire body of tribes that this family ruled. The last Qashqa'i *il khan* (paramount chief), Nassr Khan, died in exile in the United States in 1984. His story is inextricably tied to the changing power balance between tribes and the central government in Iran. To understand this story, one must first understand the special role of khans in the politics of Iran.

The position of *il khan*, as well as other major posts in tribal organizations, was handed down from generation to generation. Usually the oldest son took the place of his father, but younger brothers or cousins sometimes challenged this system. Intrigues were common. Shahs had a major role in the selection of several historically important khans. They accomplished this by legitimizing and stabilizing the reigns of prominent tribal families in exchange for a measure of indirect authority over scattered tribes. An essential element of this endeavor was the granting of large tracts of land to selected tribal leaders and formally confirming their right to the title of khan. Without the cooperation of khan families, shahs would have needed to apply constant military force to obtain taxes and conscripts for the army. During the long era of mounted cavalry, difficulties inherent in conducting military operations in remote tribal settings placed the central government at a considerable disadvantage. Local nomads knew the terrain, including ideal places to hide or from which to attack. By granting authority to khan families, shahs attempted to cement alliances with powerful elements within tribes. To gain this advantage shahs had to relinquish some of their direct authority, as well as any claims to pasture lands that were, at best, difficult to manage profitably from a distance. Khans knew very well how to extract wealth from their positions, especially their control over pastures. The latter were allocated through a chain of command down to the rank and file members of the tribe. After the system was firmly established, a family's use of a pasture depended on a combination of tradition and annually renewed permission from a minor leader who, in turn, derived his authority from the khan above him, and so on, up to the paramount chief. The same chain of command reaffirmed the *il khan's* leadership. It was, in essence, a feudal system.

From the viewpoint of the tribespeople beneath him, the khan was both a helpful factor (mediating on their behalf, overseeing migrations, allocating pastures, and so on) and, at the same time, an antagonistic one (collecting taxes, conscripting soldiers, and limiting access to pastures). From the view-

1.6 Nassr Khan, pictured in the 1940s, the last *il khan* of the Qashqa'i Confederacy, itself the last powerful tribal confederation in Iran.

point of the shah, the ideal khan was a junior partner in power. In reality, many khans exploited any opportunity to augment their own autonomy, wealth, and authority, when and as they could get away with it. Weak shahs appeared on the scene from time to time, offering a heyday of independence for nomadic tribes and their leaders. Sooner or later, however, weak shahs were replaced by stronger figures. New pressures would be brought to bear on uncooperative khans, new deals would be made, and the whole complex system continued.

At the bottom of the political pyramid, the ordinary members of the tribe needed clear-cut access to pastures during the spring-summer grazing season as well as in autumn-winter. At the top, shahs sought effective control over all populations within their borders. This system of interlocking and competing self-interest often broke down at one or another point. If khans were too weak, they were of no value to the central government. The collection of taxes and other obligations would go by the board. However, if a particular khan and his family became too strong, they could act independently of the central government and even threaten it. The Qashqa'i family became such a threat.

Reza Shah, father of the last shah, was the first Persian monarch to confront challenges of this nature with modern weapons. In the process he discovered that the balance of military force was so much in his favor that he could dispense with the former arrangement of sharing power with khans and move quickly toward a system of totally centralized authority, enforced by the army. After outlawing nomadism during the 1930s and banning traditional tribal dress, Reza Shah proceeded to forbid the use of tents and yurts in Iran. Leading Qashqa'i khans were forced to leave the country, and several were assassinated. These and related developments drove Nassr Khan and other members of his family into the first of several long exiles. Unable to migrate, thousands of Qashqa'i commoners and their herds starved to death. Nassr Khan was initially powerless to help them. However, when the British and Soviet governments forced Reza Shah to abdicate in 1941, Iran's centralized political structures all but dissolved. Naturally, Iran's nomads greeted the development with jubilation. Old people sang as they loaded their belongings onto donkeys, re-establishing their migratory way of life.

The Qashqa'i, like other nomadic tribes, faced staggering problems. Many families had lost all of their animals to starvation. Without animals, how could they live? Nassr Khan called a meeting of chiefs and other members of the Qashqa'i élite, many of whom were very wealthy. Together they arranged a partial redistribution of flocks within the tribe.[10] Every family began the spring migration with a donkey and a herd sufficient for survival. In a few years the Qashqa'i Confederacy was strong again.

A new, if brief, era of centralized leadership emerged among the Qashqa'i, one in which the khan no longer represented a meeting point between the government and the tribes but operated as an effective and popular leader, pursuing the welfare of his people as well as his own personal and family interests. During the 1940s and 1950s, Nassr Khan enjoyed widespread popularity among his people. His service as an active leader lasted until Shah Mohammad Reza Pahlavi, backed by the C.I.A., fully consolidated his own power in the 1950s.

One of the Shah's most effective tactics in combating the power of tribal khans was his famous land reform program, instituted in 1962. Ostensibly this policy brought relief to landless peasants, breaking the choke-hold of wealthy landlords, which included tribal leaders. One of its actual accomplishments in the sphere of tribal life was to sever an essential link in tribal power structures. Without control over substantial pastures, the Qashqa'i *il khan* could no longer effectively grant or withhold grazing rights. The paths and schedules of migratory tribes were placed under Iranian army administration, with a colonel assigned to oversee tribal leaders who formerly had dealt directly with Nassr Khan. Migrations depended on government permits. By means of his network of reforms, the Shah undercut an important bloc of potential rivals: the leaders of Iran's nomadic populations.

In spite of these measures, Nassr Khan and his brother Khosrow Khan were still perceived as threats – which in fact they were. Their opposition to the Shah was unambiguous. The Shah might have resorted to assassination or execution in order to remove them permanently from the scene, but this was not usually his style. Such a solution would have carried the disadvantage of further consolidating opposition within the Qashqa'i family and their sizeable following. Both Nassr Khan and Khosrow Khan were therefore exiled, and other leading nomadic families were forbidden to enter southern Iran. Khosrow Khan, a vigorous and widely loved individual, lived in Europe, where he gained some financial support from the sale of Persian rugs. When the 1979 revolution began to topple the Pahlavi government, Nassr Khan was living in the United States. The two brothers returned to Iran by separate routes. Tens of thousands of tribespeople greeted Nassr Khan as a triumphant caravan of cars and jeeps carried him into Qashqa'i territory. This exultant response to his return was a final but short-lived tribute to Asia's last great tribal chief. After responding to the revolution with enthusiasm and making open statements of his support for Ayatollah Khomeini, he had second thoughts. Uncomfortable with his inability to exert any influence on the direction of the revolution, he waged an unsuccessful resistance against the new government. [11] When this failed, Nassr Khan managed, with help from Iranian Kurdish leaders, to escape from Iran. His brother, Khosrow Khan, exercising his characteristic independence, remained in southern Iran. After a lifetime devoted to resisting central govern-

1.7 Kurdish tribesmen loading saddlebags filled with grain.

ments, he was publicly executed in Shiraz, a demonstration of power which left a profound impression on the Qashqa'i family. Their influence on Iranian political affairs collapsed.

This dismal cycle ran a similar course long ago among Turkomans in Central Asia, both before and during the Soviet period. Czarist Russian troops defeated Tekke tribesmen in a decisive battle in the 1870s. Soviet collectivism further disrupted patterns of Turkoman leadership during the twentieth century, driving thousands of families to escape into northern Iran and Afghanistan. Many leaders disappeared under Stalin's tyranny or were stripped of power.

Farther to the southwest, Kurds, eager for a Kurdish homeland, have suffered humiliations and constraints in Iran, Turkey, Iraq, and Syria. Tens of thousands of Iraqi Kurds died during an insurrection in 1991. Long-standing pressures on Kurds in Turkey, where they were misnamed "mountain Turks" in the media, erupted in violent local disturbances in southeastern districts near the border with Iraq. Campaigns for an autonomous homeland continue.

To the east, nomads in Afghanistan were able to avoid the intrusion of international pressures until the Soviet Union's unprovoked invasion of their country in the early 1980s. At the time of writing, very few khans in Asia wield enough influence to protect their people's way of life. Barring unforeseen political developments, only the indulgence or indifference of secure governments offer hope for easier times ahead. A handful of tribes are holding their own. Many groups in Iran and Afghanistan still function as pastoralists, with some elements of hereditary political structures. Modified forms of traditional nomadism can also be found in China, in Mongolia, and in republics in Central Asia which were formerly within the Soviet Union. Dramatic political restructuring in the former Union and its constituent republics, initiated in 1991, opens the door for liberalizations that could favorably affect tribal groups in some areas. Nonetheless, it is likely that large, politically coherent units under effective chief khans have permanently vanished.

THE SWIFT DECLINE OF AN ANCIENT TRADITION

While the nomadic way of life is in the process of disappearing, its most important artistic tradition, too, has suffered a decline. It is generally acknowledged that tribal rugs produced since the First World War are not equal in quality to those woven in earlier times. The breaking point came in the last century among some tribes.

In searching for the causes of this rapid qualitative decline, many rug collectors point to the development of synthetic dyes as a critical turning point. Others speak of the disruptive role of commercial incentives which have gradually displaced tribal traditions. In my opinion, both of these are aspects of a single phenomenon. Asian tribal weaving can be viewed as the last healthy phase in an extremely long cultural cycle, originating in prehistoric times. The high level of nomadic and village weaving declined steadily as overpowering economic and political developments forced the final manifestations of this cycle toward the status of picturesque anachronisms. Pressures from external markets, always a factor in the work of some tribal weavers, finally became overwhelming. Bit by bit, the art of rug making was torn from its traditional roots. With the spread of western products, including time-saving synthetic dyes, the cultural ties connecting tribal weavers to their ancient artistic heritage were gradually weakened.

It is distressing but imperative to acknowledge that tribal and village weaving, as practiced for over two thousand years, reached a critical cross-roads as western industrial civilization spread and gained supremacy during the nineteenth and twentieth centuries. In my opinion, it is too late to stimulate artificially the kinds of broad cultural support that must exist for a folk craft such as rug weaving to achieve the status of true art. Hints of an earlier splendor can still be discerned in production from scattered areas, and recent attempts to encourage and revive local traditions, particularly in Turkey, may spread to Iran and other countries. The program in Turkey was explicitly designed to reintroduce the use of vegetable-dyed yarns and to encourage the maintenance of local weaving traditions. This project, under the acronym DOBAG, resulted in attractive rugs and, at the same time, rendered moral and financial support to local societies.[12] However, the rebuilding or stimulation of tribal and village rug weaving as an indigenous art form, arising as a spontaneous local cultural expression, faces overwhelming barriers. Traditions that gave rise to woven products of the quality seen in these pages have fallen before the Goliath of industrial civilization.

To understand and fully appreciate what has been lost, it is useful to examine the historical foundations of tribal weaving. This requires us to look back to a time when nomads and their village-dwelling kin were both creators and collectors of important art.

The Roots of Nomadic Art

2

Several motifs that tribal weavers have incorporated in their designs retain features of an ancient artistic style. This style made frequent use of real and mythological animals and birds, and of parts of these creatures, including heads, antlers, and horns. Art historians have given this style various names, depending on factors of time, place, and stylistic emphasis. In its broadest meaning it can be called "zoomorphic." An appreciation of some motifs found in more recent tribal weavings depends on an awareness of this ancestral art. In the absence of such a perspective, we could easily underestimate the aesthetic breadth and depth of nomadic life. Archeological finds within recent years confirm that early nomads produced and commissioned art objects of enduring importance in the study of Asian art.

Zoomorphic styles of various kinds took root on all continents, beginning at the time of paleolithic cave paintings. The list of European peoples that featured animal images in some stage of their art includes, but is not limited to, the early Greeks, Etruscans, Celts, Goths, Vikings, Germans, and Slavs. Vestiges of these traditions have continued into our own time in animal figures on coats-of-arms and royal insignia, as well as in the folk art of many regions. Marija Gimbutas has recorded the survival of early animal images in materials from the Baltic region,[1] and Bruce Chatwin has noted strong relationships between imagery in the Ipiutak native culture of Alaska and animal figures in north Asian art.[2] Many other examples could be cited in folk art found throughout Eurasia.

A particular form of zoomorphic art, called "animal-style,"[3] is found throughout the vast Eurasian steppe zone stretching from the southern Ukraine eastward into Mongolia. In the first millennium B.C., this region included areas controlled largely by a variety of Indo-European nomadic groups, including Scythians, Sakas, Sarmatians, Massagetae, and other ethnically and/or linguistically-related peoples. Examples of their art, which was dominated by stylized animal figures, have been found in first-millennium B.C. archeological sites in the Caucasus Mountains. A similar bronze art tradition with some ties to both Near Eastern and steppe nomad motifs thrived in the Zagros Mountain range in western Iran, in and near the province of Luristan.

During the 1970s, I found ancient zoomorphic-style objects for sale in antique shops in both Iran and Afghanistan, often in the hands of street traders. These men sat on pieces of cloth surrounded by wares from widely separated cultural epochs. Forgeries of coins and minor statuary from the time of Alexander were favorite items, but authentic finds also cropped up. Once in the city of Ardebil, in northwestern Iran, I spent an hour with a man whose inventory included wristwatches (both working and broken), false teeth, rubber bands, razors in varying states of distress – and a handful of three-thousand-year-old bronze bracelets. Several were "animal-style," with animal heads at each end.

Such ancient artifacts excited my interest in Scythian and other Eurasian nomadic art. Readings in this subject prepared me for a memorable encounter in Isfahan late in the 1970s, when an antique dealer showed me an impressive collection of ancient artifacts, the accumulation of a lifetime devoted to collecting. A handsome, balding man with a neatly trimmed mustache, he cheerfully answered my questions about Persian miniatures and other works which hung on the walls of his shop. Because I had not yet recognized the importance of early nomadic art and the relevance of some examples to my main interest, tribal rugs, during earlier visits I overlooked genuinely ancient materials which he kept in glass display cases. These included early bronzes, carved seals and small stone sculptures. By 1977, my interest in the origin of rug designs had touched other fields of art history. I focused attention on areas such as the Caucasus, the Central Asian steppes, and Luristan. In this last area lived remote tribes most able to withstand direct pressures from both invading groups and urban societies.

The art of early nomadic peoples had a fundamental purpose: the conveying of mythological and allegorical ideas. A visual "shorthand" developed by using a single image, or even part of an image, to represent primary figures in local mythologies. One aspect of this usage, as found in early steppe nomad art, was noted by a specialist in this area, Veronique Schlitz. The following passage is taken from her chapter "Animals in Art and Religion" in *The World Atlas of Archaeology.*

The art of the steppes is a coherent system of signs and operates like a language. For these peoples . . . it must have occupied the place of written language. Like language it has its vocabulary which consists of details selected from the bestiary, its syntax . . . and also its stylistic devices. Besides the constant use of metaphor, there are other linguistic devices, such as metonymy, which reduces the animal to one of its parts.[4]

This approach to symbolism enhanced my appreciation of the animal-style objects that I encountered in my travels in Iran and Afghanistan, including examples owned by the antique dealer in Isfahan. During a five-day stay in

2.1 Carved wooden griffin head from the Pazyryk Valley; fourth or third century B.C.

2.2 Animal pole-top decoration from the Bronze Age; Anatolia, late third millennium B.C.

2.3 Fantastic tattooed animal on the body of a tribal chief or shaman. From Barrow 2 in the Pazyryk Valley, southern Siberia, fourth century B.C. (After Rudenko).

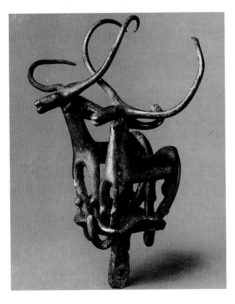

Isfahan in 1977 I frequently visited his shop to study his collection. It turned out that he had a strong interest in early nomadic gold work.[5] He owned several small objects similar to that shown in Illustration 2.5 and a handful of other items from the steppes. But the heart of his collection was an abundant sampling of bronzes from Luristan.

Luristan and nearby provinces are among several regions in which ancient motifs have clearly survived in tribal weaving traditions. The earliest surviving representations of these forms were cast in bronze and are known as "Luristan bronzes."[6] The makers of these objects were tribespeople living in the Zagros, a range of mountains on Iran's western flank. Students of this region's culture agree that the lifestyle of its nomadic tribes today closely resembles patterns of nomadism which developed in ancient times, when tribes in the Zagros region provided horses for the armies of Sumer and Babylonia. Wool from Elam, a kingdom that included portions of the Zagros during several stages of its history, was traded or sold to neighboring states. "Transhumance" (the seasonal moving of shepherd societies and their flocks), livestock breeding, and the gathering of acorns as a dietary staple have been features of tribal life in Luristan for at least four thousand years. The region provides important research sites for studies devoted to early stages of Asian village life and early attempts to domesticate sheep and goats.

A number of ancient bronzes for which the region is famous served originally as decorated harness bits. Illustration 2.7 shows a complete horse's bit. Along with objects of this type, the antique dealer's display cases included several animal figures with multiple heads (Illustration 2.8).

Among the saddlebags I purchased in the Isfahan bazaar on my last visit there in 1978 was a Luri piece that contained an unexpected image: an animal with a head at each end of its body. The piece originated among a migratory Luri tribe whose descendants still live in Bakhtiyari Province, an administrative district where nomadic Lurs and Bakhtiyaris continue to migrate. (The tribal name "Luri/Bakhtiyari" is useful for Luri products from this district.) I had seen this same two-headed design in a number of rugs, but never in a weaving from an area which also included this image in its ancestral fine art (Illustration 2.8). It struck me that these two-headed motifs may have entered the repertoire of tribal weavers in Iran at the same time that bronzes of the same design were made. If so, two-headed animals represent a direct and unbroken line of woven motifs spanning more than two-and-a-half thousand years.

What does the two-headed animal mean? At present, we can only speculate. Veronique Schlitz's statement about the "vocabulary" of steppe-nomad artisans may offer a starting point. Like words, designs are subject to abbreviations and contractions. The two heads at either end may be related to animal-combat scenes by suggesting a struggle of opposing forces – much as

2.4 A steppe-nomad plaque of the "animal style"; Altai region, fourth century B.C. From the collection of Peter the Great.

2.5 Scythian-style deer, with legs folded under the body. Late first millennium B.C.

2.6 A bronze finial or standard, featuring threatening animals. From a Luristan burial, eighth or seventh century B.C.

2.7 Functional tribal art. A bronze bit with cheek plaques. From Luristan in western Iran, eighth or seventh century B.C.

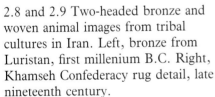

the two seemingly identical poles of a magnet have opposing positive and negative fields.

The two-headed animal is one of the most striking ancient images to be found in tribal rugs. It appears not only in Iranian art but also in other cultures, even in such distant places as Lithuania, which complicates the question of where ancestral Iranian tribes learned this motif. The design may have originated locally or could have been imported into the Zagros. In either case, it is not far-fetched to suggest that early Zagros artists who worked in perishable materials such as wood and wool yarn used some of the same designs found in local bronzes. According to this viewpoint, once the pattern was rooted in a native textile tradition, it passed unchanged from generation to generation among relatively isolated nomads. Such long-term stability was more likely with simple forms than with highly detailed motifs. Even in the cultural isolation of remote valleys in the Zagros, complex patterns containing subtle iconographic references could not survive unchanged over a time span exceeding two-and-a-half thousand years. For even one motif to survive unchanged is remarkable.

Evidence presented later in this book, again focusing on this part of Iran, raises the possibility that other old patterns have survived among pockets of nomads from an ethnic background known as "Indo-Iranian." Although we lack chronological evidence in the form of successive textile samples, a cluster of motifs appear to have survived here for many centuries. A secluded nomadic culture which resisted foreign elements and, consequently, outside artistic influences, was an ideal environment in which early design forms could be perpetuated, even into the nineteenth and twentieth centuries.

If textiles were buried in ancient Luristan graves, they were destroyed in

2.8 and 2.9 Two-headed bronze and woven animal images from tribal cultures in Iran. Left, bronze from Luristan, first millenium B.C. Right, Khamseh Confederacy rug detail, late nineteenth century.

the course of reckless searches for saleable bronzes by grave robbers. Unless protected by an extremely dry or extremely cold climate, ancient weavings have only a slight chance of surviving in recoverable states. Nonetheless, we can hope that some fragments of evidence may yet be found when systematic archeological research resumes in Luristan.

Given the extraordinary variety of designs in traditional tribal and village weavings, no single geographical area could conceivably provide a single, comprehensive answer to the question of design origins. There is no evidence of an unabridged body of ancient tribal motifs from a single source-culture surviving *en masse* and unchanged in tribal weavers' repertoires. Yet each discovery in this study adds another piece to the extraordinary enigma of tribal rug designs. Nomadic weavings from Luristan and other portions of the Zagros Mountains contain helpful pieces of the puzzle.

Further evidence in Chapters 4 and 5 will illustrate ways in which other ancient designs survived with few alterations among nomadic and village weavers. Before continuing this theme in connection with specific motifs, we shall examine the world's oldest intact tribal rug, the Pazyryk. More than any other weaving in our study, it suggests the artistic attainments that enriched ancient tribal life.

The Pazyryk Rug

3

In the summer of 1949 Sergei Rudenko, a noted Russian archeologist, unearthed an astonishing find, a twenty-four-hundred-year-old pile rug of complex design in an unprecedented state of preservation.[1] The rug's environment throughout its long history had been ideal: a tribal tomb which climate and fortuitous circumstances had converted into an enormous block of ice. The "Pazyryk," as it is called, is one of the most unlikely discoveries in the history of archeology and will remain a key object in the study of Oriental rugs of all types, including tribal rugs.

Students of the early stages of rug making operate under a considerable handicap. Virtually all tangible evidence, so helpful in any study, has decayed into dust. Although a few scraps of pile weaving are older than the Pazyryk,[2] the latter has the advantage of being nearly complete. However, its extraordinarily good condition is not the Pazyryk's sole claim to renown. Designs in the rug and the locale in which it was buried guarantee it a prominent place in any discussion of early pile weavings from either urban or tribal surroundings.

The rug is named after the Pazyryk Valley in the Altai Mountains, one of several mountain chains in southern Siberia, west of Mongolia and somewhat north of the center point of the Eurasian land mass. Given its remoteness and its cold, forbidding climate, such a spot seems an unlikely place for nomadic burial grounds. But the Altai range is not far from northern portions of the steppes above western China, the homeland of a succession of "barbarian" nomadic tribes. Indo-European groups constituted the core of early steppe nomad populations in this region. Mongolian and other eastern peoples gradually exerted greater influence, leading to the domination of the steppes by Turkic tribes early in the first millennium A.D.

Although the freezing Siberian winters facilitated the rug's survival, the summer thaw is sufficiently warm to have permitted ancient nomadic tribes to travel there to bury their fallen chiefs and shamans. Milder summer weather also allowed twentieth-century Russian archeologists to trek in with their teams, remove boulders covering a series of tombs, and extract burial goods by means of a simple expedient: they melted the ice with boiling water.

Rudenko was not the first to disturb these graves; thieves had plundered them of any gold objects shortly after burial. Fortunately, they left behind a considerable body of art treasures made of wood, felt, and woven cloth. From the viewpoint of art historians seeking to reconstruct the surroundings in which the rug was buried, these objects are priceless. They include a large

3.1 The Pazyryk rug (fourth or third century B.C.), the forerunner of later examples that mixed traditional folk motifs with formal urban patterns. Design and technique suggest an origin in or near Central Asia, probably an oasis.

3.2 The early stages of excavation at one of the Pazyryk sites.

and spectacular felt wall hanging featuring a goddess theme, a four-wheeled cart, Chinese silk textiles, and elaborately carved wooden harness equipment (Illustration 4.32).

However self-serving their motives, the thieves unknowingly did posterity a favor by cutting into the tomb. The rupture permitted water to fill the chamber, and the frigid winter temperatures locked the grave into a permanent deep-freeze. A great mound of boulders, intended to deter grave robbers, served to insulate the crypt throughout the entire year, permitting us to enjoy and study these extraordinary artifacts more than two thousand years after their burial.

In studying the Pazyryk, Rudenko noticed unmistakable Persian influences in some of its design. He and other scholars initially assumed that the rug was, in essence, Persian and had been traded or carried to a region far from its point of origin. This assumption has been challenged from several points of view. Understanding the network of new conclusions that gradually emerged necessitates a thumbnail sketch of the geographical spread of Iranian art of the sixth to fourth centuries B.C., which is known as the Achaemenian period, after the ruling dynasty. Initially centered in southern and western Iran, Achaemenian influences had spread into Persian-controlled parts of Central Asia by the mid-fourth century B.C., when the rug was buried.[3] Trade, military alliances, and service in Persian armies had left a Persian stamp on oasis towns, much as areas of Europe and Asia adopted features of American culture following the Second World War. Bearing such factors in mind helps explain how a rug containing both urban Achaemenian and nomadic features appeared so far from Persia itself.

Inquiries into who buried the rug, who wove it, and what the weaver or weavers' motives may have been took on greater complexity as findings accumulated. Evidence involved studies of motifs,[4] dyes,[5] the rug's structure,[6] and steppe nomad ethnological histories.[7] When combined, conclusions from these separate lines of research led scholars to conclude that the rug was made somewhere in a northeastern outpost of the Persian empire, possibly in Central Asia, relatively close to where it was buried. A town or oasis tied to Persian economic and political currents was a natural crossroads for the urban and nomadic design themes found juxtaposed in the Pazyryk.

Rudenko noted in particular one motif with strong Achaemenian associations, the horses and mounts in the primary border (Illustration 3.5), which correlate strikingly with horse-and-groom relief carvings at the ancient city of Persepolis (Illustration 3.4). This resemblance cannot be disputed. However, later scholars have pointed to differences between the bas-relief horse-and-groom scenes at Persepolis and those in the Pazyryk's border. None of the grooms are mounted in the Persepolis scenes; each walks next to his horse. In the rug, however, half the grooms are on horseback. This may

3.3 Border detail of the Pazyryk Rug.

3.4 A bas-relief on a temple at Persepolis resembles horse-and groom figures in the rug's main border. Sergei Rudenko, who discovered the Pazyryk, was the first to notice clear Persian influences.

3.5 Unlike the Persepolis bas-reliefs, some tribesmen pictured in the Pazyryk border are on horseback, one of several "tribal" details in the design.

seem a small design alteration, but it is the kind of change that occurs when a formal scene is adopted by nomads who were known for their riding skills. The saddle covers on many of the horses contain designs of a decidedly nomadic flavor (Illustration 3.7). The deer in several secondary borders correspond more precisely to provincial design styles than to urban ones. They resemble animals in the grazing posture found widely in the mid-first millennium B.C., including nomadic examples. Illustration 3.6 suggests a possible relationship between the Pazyryk deer and bronze repoussé motifs from Luristan.[8] The manner of indicating muscles is similar, and both animals carry markings on their flanks.

Apart from the connection with Persepolis bas-reliefs, some squares in the field resembling tiles also underscore the rug's ties to urban art. Numerous experts have compared these squares to stone floor carvings at Nineveh (Illustration 3.8). Altogether, such evidence confirms that the adoption of urban patterns by provincial weavers occurred during an early stage of pile weaving.

In spite of urban influences, there can be no doubt that the tribe responsible for burials in the Pazyryk Valley followed a nomadic way of life. Their graves also contained horses, buried with a wealth of equestrian gear, attesting to a horse-centered existence. It is quite possible that the nomad chief with whom the rug was buried commissioned it in an oasis town where designers and weavers were attuned to contemporary rug designs in Persepolis or other Persian cities. If so, tribal characteristics could have been added to the designs out of a natural tendency to bend formal patterns to suit local tastes.

Fundamental questions about the function and purpose of the rug remain open to debate. These considerations are necessarily tied to the question of who wove it. If the Pazyryk is, in essence, a tribalized urban weaving from a provincial Persian center in Central Asia, the makers probably had little more in mind than to copy a court pattern while adding certain features that would appeal to local nomadic taste. From the viewpoint of the weavers, symbolism in this case would be incidental to commercial motives. This point of view, to which I subscribe, is currently in the minority. Some scholars believe that the rug served as a gaming board. Others see it as a funerary object symbolizing burial customs that involved embalmed horses and

3.6 A repoussé animal figure from Luristan bears features in common with the deer in the rug's secondary borders. (Repoussé after Moorey, *Catalogue of the Ancient Persian Bronzes in the Ashmolean Museum*, Oxford. Woven stag drawing after Rudenko.)

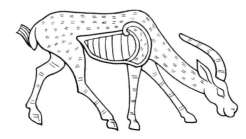
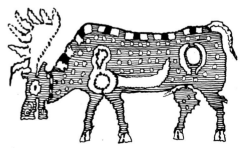

3.7 A felt saddle-cloth like those pictured on horses' backs in the Pazyryk rug.

grooms guarding a tomb's periphery.[9] Still others claim that the Pazyryk's images represent undeciphered themes relating to the afterlife. A few concede that they simply don't know what the rug's purpose was. Whether or not definitive answers will be forthcoming to the many questions that remain, the tribal lifestyle of the rug's final owner and the tribal influences in several of its motifs, allow us to view the Pazyryk as, to some extent, a "tribal" rug.

The discovery of the Pazyryk established that knotted carpet making, involving a standard arrangement of a field surrounded by borders, dates to the first millennium B.C. or earlier. The fine craftsmanship (up to 277 symmetrical knots per square inch) and remarkably uniform patterns lead us to conclude that rug making developed long before the weaving of this piece. The Pazyryk's discovery also affirms that nomads were familiar with a high quality of pile weaving, most likely as purchasers, rather than – in this case – weavers. If the chief himself purchased or traded for the rug, he was among the first of many tribal leaders to favor a style of rug combining urban and tribal features.[10]

Initially it was thought that the nomads who buried the Pazyryk were Scythians; many books on the subject repeated this conclusion. However, since the 1960s, scholars specializing in the study of steppe nomad cultures have realized that Scythians, whose habitat was much farther to the west, could not have been responsible for these Altai graves. A leading Pazyryk scholar, John Haskins, late professor emeritus at the University of Pittsburgh, headed those who conclude that a large nomadic group known to the ancient Greeks as the Massagetae, distant relatives of the Scythians, buried the rug, as well as other objects in and near the Pazyryk Valley.[11]

To my knowledge there is no convincing evidence suggesting that the motifs in the Pazyryk were repeated in later weavings. However, a number of motifs in tribal and village rugs of the nineteenth and even the twentieth centuries may be traced to sources that are even older than the Pazyryk. These images, and variations of them, have been kept alive in indigenous bags, kilims, and rugs, especially in more remote tribal habitats. Surviving ancient motifs constitute a study nearly as fascinating as the discovery of the Pazyryk itself.

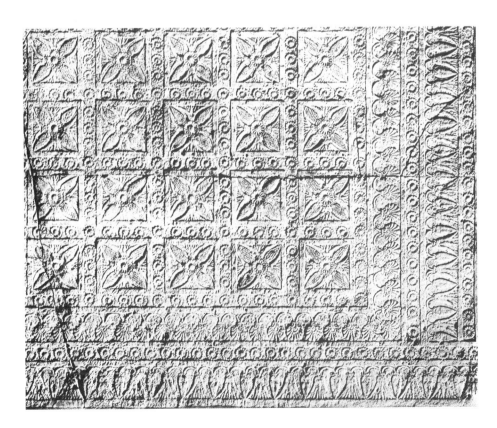

3.8 The rug's repeating field patterns have been compared to carpet-like stone floor carvings at Nineveh.

Ancient Motifs in Tribal Rugs

4

For as long as dealers have offered Oriental rugs to buyers in the West, stories about the antiquity of designs and their meanings have embellished the folklore of this field. But whereas legends are plentiful, conclusive information in this area is scant. Chinese and Tibetan rugs contain a number of ancient motifs that relate to specific eastern religious concepts. Dragon motifs in rugs from some regions carried symbolic overtones relating to folk tales and myths. Prayer arches in rugs conveyed clear Islamic references. Mathematical symbolism, known to have a prominent role in Islamic architecture,[1] was probably a feature of court-sponsored carpets but not of village and tribal patterns.

Apart from these few certainties, anyone who sets out to explore the mysterious domain of tribal rug motifs has little in the way of a guide. Even identifying the oldest motifs is difficult; interpreting them is even more so. Although few would argue that some tribal images are quite old and may have held significance for early weavers, few observers agree on which motifs are the oldest and what symbolic functions they served.

Before we can intelligently address the subject of symbolism, we must first pose some fundamental questions relating to origins. Among these questions are the following: are there truly ancient designs in tribal and village rugs? If so, what are they? Which tribes or locales preserved the oldest patterns and for the longest periods? Can we pinpoint any towns, cities or nomadic habitats where they originated? The purpose of this chapter is to provide a background for exploring these questions and obtaining a few answers. Some of the answers must remain tentative for the time being; others can be asserted unequivocally.

The first image discussed, the lion, suggests the complexity of this vein of study. Lion figures in rugs may represent an ancient design that survived locally among nomads, or they may be a transplant from urban art within the last three or four hundred years – a relatively short period of time. Acknowledging these distinctly different possibilities helps one to develop clearer standards for deciding which motifs are relatively recent and which have survived intact for as long as two millennia, and perhaps longer.

4.1 Detail of Khamseh Confederacy rug, late nineteenth century, shown on page 49.

Whimsical lion images are found on coarsely knotted south Persian rugs called *gabbeh*.[2] The use of this motif by both nomadic and urban populations has been a consistent feature of Asian art for several millennia. Parviz Tanavoli's most recent book on the subject, *Lion Rugs: the Lion in the Art and Culture of Iran*, proposes that *gabbeh* lion rugs may be an ancient cultural inheritance of the Lur tribes, from whom neighboring Qashqa'i tribes acquired the pattern. He also points out similarities between urban lion art and related forms in south Persian tribal rugs.

In response to my questions about this motif, both dealers and tribespeople in southern Iran spoke of the lion as a guardian figure, a symbol of courage. "The man of the tent," I was told, "is the *lion*. When he is gone, the rug represents him." This is clearly a contemporary folk interpretation. Ancient lion images were often symbolic in the true sense of the word, serving as astrological symbols or protagonists in heroic combat scenes.[3] Deeper levels of symbolism were presumably lost over the centuries, yet the lion image continued in Iranian art.

Undyed dark brown wefts in the Luri example (above, opposite) indicate an origin in Luristan Province, rather than from Qashqa'i or Luri weavers living in Fars Province, to the southeast of Luristan. Tough, bristly pile wool and dark-brown undyed wefts also support this attribution. The second piece (below) includes dyed red wefts and ivory warps, features that suggest an origin within the Qashqa'i Confederacy.

4.2 Lions mark the graves of Bakhtiyari warriors and aristocrats in the cemetery at Shar-i-Kord, east-central Zagros.

4.3 A lion-decorated cup or *rhyton*, Achaemenian Period, Iran, sixth to fourth century B.C.

4.4 Luri lion rug, 4ft 5in × 8ft 7in (134cm × 261cm), late nineteenth century.

4.5 Qashqa'i lion rug, 4ft 7in × 6ft 3in (137cm × 190cm), late nineteenth century.

4.6 A fifth-millennium B.C. swastika from Level 20 at Teppe Gawra, Iraq.

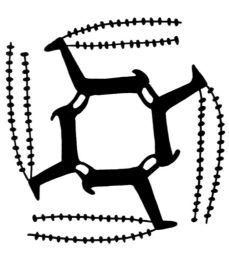

4.7 Animal figures formed swastika-like shapes in near-Eastern ceramics of the third millennium B.C.

4.8 Architectural borders may be the source of linked swastikas in tribal and urban rugs. Iran, first century A.D. From a stucco decoration at Kuh-i-Khwaja.

4.9 Bakhtiyari salt bag, 1ft × 1ft 10in (33cm × 50cm), late nineteenth century.

Many rug designs can be traced to general categories of ancient art without being identified with specific geographical regions or ethnic groups. This is true not only of individual field motifs, but also of border patterns. An example is the most abused and misused of all ancient motifs, the swastika. The name for this motif appears to come from the Sanskrit *Sv-asti*, meaning peace, well-being, or benediction.[4] Even more than the lion motif, the swastika was the common property of a variety of nations and peoples scattered throughout Eurasia and even in the Americas. Swastikas in Chinese art connote infinity or immortality.[5] Woven swastikas appear most frequently in Chinese and Tibetan rugs, but are also found in Caucasian village rugs and in kilims from the Bakhtiyari tribe.

Illustration 4.6 depicts the oldest swastika form that I have seen in archeological literature. It was found in a fifth-millennium B.C. Iraqi site.[6] Illustration 4.7 portrays a third-millennium example from Samarra, north of Baghdad, in which repeating animal figures take the shape of a swastika.[7]

Both of these nomadic Bakhtiyari weavings contain linked-swastika patterns. Similar borders appeared in classical Greek and Roman ceramics and architecture, as well as in Egyptian Coptic textiles and Persian architecture during early centuries of the Christian era. Chinese rugs of much later periods included the same borders.

4.10 Bakhtiyari animal trapping, early twentieth century.

40

Several cultures that employed swastikas also favored infinity symbols known as "endless knots." Both designs are found in Celtic art from the British Isles as well as in Chinese and Tibetan art, in Iranian art, and also in a small group of tribal weavings from the Zagros and elsewhere. The endless knot on the facing page forms the center of a medallion on a Luri/Bakhtiyari saddlebag.

The illustrations left and below include related motifs from a variety of cultures and periods. Efforts to trace the original source of this motif raise an important question: Did the motif spread from east to west, or from west to east? It is known that Indo-European nomads brought several early motifs to the fringes of northwestern China and possibly into China's heartland.[8] Whether endless knots were among these is not known. The similarity of Celtic designs to patterns found throughout Asia merits careful analysis.

Several open questions make attempts to trace the origin of Luri/Bakhtiyari endless-knot motifs especially puzzling. Could the design have come into the Zagros from China? Is it possible that textile traditions among the Copts in Egypt had an influence? Vikings also used endless knots in their art, and we know that Vikings were active around the Black Sea. Did their influence touch mountain-dwelling tribes in Iran, or did earlier movements out of Iran account for some Viking patterns? It is also possible that groups with ties to Celtic peoples lived in the Zagros from a very early date – a viewpoint held by several scholars.[9]

A few modern Luri/Bakhtiyari bags (from the 1930s) have this same design feature, showing no changes from the oldest known nineteenth-century versions. At this stage of our study, the question of when endless knots entered the vocabulary of Luri/Bakhtiyari weavers remains unanswered, but the motif's antiquity cannot be doubted.

4.11 A Chinese infinity motif, the knot of destiny, is among the eight Buddhist symbols of good fortune.

4.12 Early Chinese endless knots were embellished with animal heads, with round eyes. Chou period, seventh or sixth century A.D.

4.13 Coptic Christians wove endless knots in some textiles. Fifth century A.D.

4.14 Viking art of the eighth and ninth centuries includes endless knots with squared corners, much like the form of this pattern in Luri/Bakhtiyari weavings.

4.15 Complex knotwork panels are a hallmark of Celtic art (from a stone at Meigle, Perthshire, Scotland).

4.16 Endless knot detail from Luri/
Bakhtiyari saddlebag, late nineteenth
century, shown on page 61.

The peacock image appears in innumerable folk tales from a variety of eastern cultures over many centuries. In Indian sacred legends, Sarasvati, goddess of poetic arts, rides on a peacock, and Indra, god of rain and thunder, sits on a peacock throne.

Many folk populations re-fashioned the contexts in which legendary peacocks appeared, at times giving them a primary role in religious mythologies. One example from a Kurdish sub-group was reported by Count Bobrinskoy, a Russian anthropologist, in his book *Peacock from Heaven*.[10] Bobrinskoy recounted a pre-revolutionary hunting trip to the Caucasus Mountains, where scattered Kurds maintained a separate culture through the early decades of the twentieth century. His tale hinged on the chance hiring of Kurdish hunting guides who were followers of the Yezidi religion.

In evening talks around campfires, Bobrinskoy's guides related the fundamental ancient Yezidi legend of "Taus Malek," a radiant angel-peacock who was cast from heaven and fell to earth. A solitary Kurdish shepherd found the injured bird and cared for it. As a reward, the peacock imparted fundamentals of the Yezidi religion to this shepherd, who thereby became the first Yezidi. The essence of this faith, as related by Bobrinskoy's companions, teaches acceptance of defects in every person and every event.

Peacock images in wood, metal, pottery, and textiles have circulated widely throughout urban and provincial Asian cultures. Evidence of peacocks in the vocabularies of tribal and village weavers appears most frequently in rugs from three areas: the Caucasus, Kurdistan, and southern Persia. Qashqa'i examples, such as those adorning the large fragment from a horse cover shown at right, have more in common with Caucasian models than with neighboring Luri ones. Some tribes that were later part of the Qashqa'i Confederacy may have brought this motif with them when they moved from northwestern Iran or the Caucasus to southern Iran. Rugs from neighboring Luri and Khamseh Confederacy tribes include peacocks, but of a different style.

4.17 Qashqa'i horse cover, 2ft 2in × 3ft 7in (66cm × 112cm), and detail, left, late nineteenth century.

Trees have served as symbols in religious and folk art for thousands of years and continue to have a place in Jewish, Buddhist, Christian, and Islamic traditions and iconography. The Bodhi tree of Buddhist mythology and the palm in Christian ritual, for example, continue a preoccupation with trees dating from extremely early periods. This widespread veneration has taken myriad forms, from overt tree worship to the old Armenian practice of studying the movement of branches as a source of divine messages.[11] Massive Assyrian reliefs depicted priests next to trees, and some peoples carried tree branches with them as they approached images of their deities. Among the most enduring and widespread of symbolic trees are the Tree of Life and the Tree of Knowledge. Like all powerful symbols, they have acquired many meanings. The Tree of Life, for example, connotes a sense of being connected, of nature's beneficence, and of life forms grounded in a hidden root system but growing solidly upward.

Trees in Oriental rugs include the naturalistic depictions found in urban weavings as well as radically stylized tribal and village patterns. The Kazak rug shown opposite exemplifies the extreme simplicity of well-conceived village rugs in the southern Caucasus, often made by Armenians.

The detail below, from a south Persian rug pictured on page 175, features an archaic pattern known as an "animal-head tree," near an animal with extra heads. Baluch weavers, too, preserved "animal-head tree" variations of this type (page 240). The early emphasis of animal- or bird-heads in nomadic art among scattered Eurasian populations appears to have been adapted to early tribal rug designs, including "animal-trees."

4.18 "Animal-head tree" and multi-headed animal in a south Persian tribal rug.

4.19 Kazak, 4ft 4in × 4ft 9in (132cm × 144cm), late nineteenth century.

Ancient Motifs in Tribal Rugs

The two-headed animal motif (introduced in Chapter 2) belongs to an important category: that of long-standing motifs that survived solely in folk contexts. Such forms have been used by nomads and villagers since the first millennium B.C. or possibly earlier.

From the viewpoint of art historians, animal designs that depict unnatural forms (for example, two-headed animals, composites of various animals in one image, and works of art that combine humans and animals) differ significantly from naturalistic animal motifs. Since goats looked much the same two thousand years ago as they do today, drawings or other renderings of these animals which are more-or-less naturalistic also look the same. Consequently we cannot assume that ancient and modern art objects that incorporate images of goats are related art historically merely because the images resemble one another. There is another reasonable explanation for the similarity of ancient and modern images: they both mimic nature. However, this analysis does not hold true for animal forms that involve unnatural or invented creatures that do not exist in nature. Since two-headed animals did not occur naturally either in ancient times or in the nineteenth century, finding both ancient and modern examples of such two-headed motifs in art objects suggests that the motif may have been passed down through the centuries as a part of local tradition. This suggestion is especially strong when both early and later examples came from the same geographical area.

Similar figures are found among artifacts from several early cultures. Luristan bronzes of this type were made prior to the construction of early Persian (Achaemenian) cities, whose ruins include columns decorated with massive two-headed creatures (Illustration 4.22). Given the abundance of symbolic imagery in ancient times, we are on secure ground in assuming that these forms, too, had symbolic meaning.

Tribal cultures in and near Luristan suffered extraordinary setbacks during the late 1930s, shattering local weaving traditions. Unfortunately, little field work that was carried out in Luristan when local tribal cultures were still fully intact focused on contemporary tribal art and culture. It may now be too late to determine through field work if any meanings associated with archaic woven designs survived into the twentieth century. John Haskins, whose work on the Pazyryk rug has already been noted, wrote in 1990: "All over the Orient, from remote antiquity to the recent past, we find that a motif – once it has been accepted – never really leaves the artistic lexicon of the receptor. The motif may change, be combined or abstracted, and possibly lose its original meaning, but once adopted some vestige of it remains."[12]

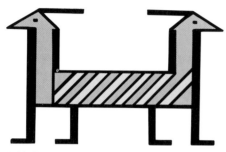

4.20 Detail of salt bag, opposite, from the Zagros region.

4.21 Luristan bronze, eighth to sixth century B.C.

4.22 Achaemenian capital, Persepolis, fifth century B.C.

47

4.23 Luri/Bakhtiyari salt bag, 1ft 7in × 2ft 2in (48cm × 66cm), first half nineteenth century.

Two-headed animal forms also appear in this rug from the south Persian Khamseh Confederacy, a collection of tribes which included Turkic, Arabic, and native Iranian elements. The animals are more complicated in this case, with stylized floral protrusions extending from their backs. This adaptation could relate to mythological two-headed animal figures in other cultures. In Lithuania, for example, two-headed horses are shown with a plant growing from their backs (Illustration 4.25).

The difficulty in interpreting folk motifs among Asian tribal groups becomes apparent when we recognize that many surviving motifs from earlier art are fragments of a formerly coherent vocabulary, the keys to which have been lost. Myths from antiquity, when available to us, are comprehensible intellectually, and they also speak to something in our emotional life, especially when they are found intact. Fragmentary pictorial legacies, including woven motifs, have lost part of their meaning. When mythologies that gave old designs their meaning are lost or unknown, the task is doubly complicated. Unless we are intimately acquainted with the cultures from which they came, such symbols are as difficult to decipher intellectually as scattered words and phrases from an ancient tribal legend.

More detailed studies, touching artifacts and legends from many cultures, could unearth useful materials.[13] Until this line of research is developed more fully, we will rarely be able to specify the meanings of individual designs. In the meantime, they provide evidence of a time when tribal cultures were so rich in symbolism that practical everyday belongings were decorated with fragments of their mythologies.

4.24 Detail from Khamseh Confederacy rug, opposite.

4.25 Gables in traditional Lithuanian homes pictured two-headed horses in association with trees and birds. Like remote areas in the Zagros, Lithuanian culture includes many archaic images, related to myths of equal antiquity.

4.26 Khamseh Confederacy, 3ft 6in × 5ft 7in (106cm × 170cm), nineteenth century.

Ancient Motifs in Tribal Rugs

The animal pictured in Illustration 4.29 is from a large Luri bag front, possibly from the early nineteenth century, shown in full on the right. It features a stylized two-headed figure on the back of an animal. Few nomadic woven motifs offer such an intriguing comparison with ancestral art.

The braided tails and the reins show that these animals are horses, a mainstay of nomadic economies in the Zagros. The Luristan bronze (Illustration 4.28) has primary features in common with the oddly-stylized images on the back of each horse. Twenty-five hundred years have altered this two-headed motif, but its association with horse imagery and its essential outlines have remained relatively constant. A human face in the bronze has become a simple pointed shape in the woven design. (For a similar treatment of heads, see the human figures in a south Persian rug shown at the bottom of page 37.) The bronze image is of the "heroic" type, in which a human struggles to control mythical animals. We can only speculate on its meaning to recent weavers within the Luri sub-tribe that continued this form.

Illustration 4.27 offers a further stylization of the two-headed figure in a Yomud Turkoman rug, shown on page 313. This and several other patterns

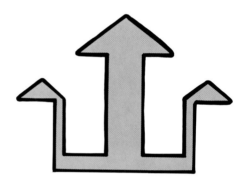

4.27 Detail from a Yomud rug, second half of nineteenth century.

4.28 Bronze from Luristan, eighth century B.C.

4.29 Horse and stylized two-headed figure, Luri tribe, Zagros region.

confirm ties between earlier Zagros cultures and Turkoman weaving traditions. The time-scale and specific cultural contexts in which these images were transmitted are an important area for future research.

Large saddlebags of this type were woven solely for tribal use throughout the 1930s and even into the 1940s. A few examples contain horse-and-rider images, stylized more drastically. See a detail at the bottom of page 123, from a bag set that was useful in confirming the Luri attribution. Pieces of this type have white woolen warps (or, rarely, undyed cotton) and red-orange double-wefts in the pile section, features of the bag front shown here.

The pile panel at the bottom of the bag, which added strength and durability at vulnerable points, confirms that the piece was the front of a large saddlebag. Such pile sections are a common feature of Luri and Bakhtiyari bags of all sizes. The upper section of the piece, including the row of horses, is in *soumak* (extra-weft wrapping).

This piece and an identical mate are among the rarest nomadic weavings to surface in recent decades.[14]

4.30 Luri bag front, 3ft 9in × 1ft 10in (114cm × 55cm), first half nineteenth century.

Ancient Motifs in Tribal Rugs

Anyone giving tribal and village rugs even passing notice has seen "S"s in both borders and fields. Ancient motifs of the same shape were explicit "two-headed dragon" symbols from widespread sources: steppe nomads, Celtic metalworkers of western Europe, Iranian artisans, Chinese craftsmen of the late Chou period (seventh and sixth centuries B.C.), and others. Most "S" shapes in tribal and village rugs lack eyes and other details of the original dragon image. One region where an older version of the design survived in tribal weavings was the Zagros.

The detail on the right shows part of a complete Luri/Bakhtiyari saddle-bag set which includes minor borders of this type. The repeating "S"s, stacked vertically, clearly terminate in heads of some kind, similar to ancient examples shown on the left, along with a single unit from the Luri/Bakhtiyari borders. One of the early examples, Illustration 4.34, is a border pattern from a Chinese bronze of the Chou period. Illustration 4.35 is of an Iranian bronze of uncertain age, possibly from the Islamic period (seventh century A.D. or later) and possibly pre-Islamic.[15] To varying degrees, all of these objects share features with each other and with individual "S" units which make up the Luri/Bakhtiyari border (Illustration 4.31).

Bodies of evidence indicating early contacts between Chinese cultures, Celtic groups, and tribal populations with roots in Iran are highly complex.[16] Evidence of early contacts between Chinese cultures and groups with roots in Iran is also complex. We cannot rule out mutual influences between the Zagros region and parts of China during the second and first millennia B.C. Future research in these areas may take account of Zagros tribal weavings, which appear to form the final link in this long chain.

It is doubtful that Luri weavers continued such an explicit border style through the 1930s without some sense of its connotations. To my knowledge, however, no-one ever questioned a nomadic weaver about this during the era when the tradition was still alive.

4.31 "S" border unit, Luri/Bakhtiyari bag, c. 1900.

4.32 Celtic brooch, early Christian era.

4.33 Horse-harness decoration, Pazyryk Valley, fifth to third century B.C.

4.34 Border from a Chinese bronze vessel, sixth century B.C.

4.35 Iranian bronze "S", uncertain period.

4.36 Opposite, detail of Luri/Bakhtiyari bag, late nineteenth century, shown on page 61.

Illustrations 4.36 and 4.37 provide a deeper look into the "S" theme in tribal and village rugs as it continued through the centuries. Illustration 4.37 includes a connected-"S" border in a famous fifteenth-century Anatolian weaving, the "dragon and phoenix" rug. Illustration 4.36 shows the same border type from a twentieth-century Luri/Bakhtiyari bag. The Anatolian version lacks eyes and horns, but the overall shape links it closely to the Luri/Bakhtiyari pattern.

Placing these side-by-side raises the question, which border came first? Disregarding the chronological age of the two weavings, which pattern is older in style? Designs found in a fifteenth-century rug would normally be considered the antecedents of closely related nineteenth- or twentieth-century work. In this case, however, the reverse appears to be true. The fifteenth-century version suggests a degenerative process which had not occurred in the Luri/Bakhtiyari border. Eyes and horns are absent in the former, thereby changing the repeating figures into simpler geometric forms. Evidence supporting this belief includes earlier "S" shapes in Asian art which include details that are present in the Luri/Bakhtiyari border but absent in the dragon rug border.

A key factor in this reasoning is the relative isolation of portions of the Zagros Mountains. In artistic development, isolation fosters conservatism. Between the sixth and the fifteenth centuries Anatolia underwent several profound waves of invasion which drastically influenced Anatolian culture. These include the Islamic expansion and domination by Turkic tribes from Central Asia. While Luristan was not spared domination by Turkic groups, the degree of impact was weaker there.

Earlier Kurdish movements into eastern Anatolia, though not clearly documented, are obvious, given the number of Kurds in modern-day Turkey. By contrast, tribal populations in the Zagros region had been relatively stable.

Some earlier rug scholars argued that Turkic groups brought the oldest body of rug motifs to Iran and Anatolia, thereby influencing local patterns. However, I suspect that borders with "S" figures, as well as many other designs, had been in use long *before* Turkic groups arrived in western Asia in substantial numbers. These native patterns gradually lost certain details. The impact of new cultural influences in Anatolia and northern Iran must have contributed to the degenerative process. Geographical barriers and a pervasive cultural conservatism protected motifs among some Zagros tribes from the same fate. Consequently, we face an unusual set of comparisons in the form of these two "S" borders, which cut across our usual sense of chronology. From this perspective, even Luri/Bakhtiyari "S"-border patterns of the 1930s are "older" than related fifteenth-century examples from less isolated areas.

4.36 Repeating "S" borders, Luri/Bakhtiyari saddlebag (see page 114).

4.37 "Dragon and Phoenix" rug with repeating "S" border, Anatolia, fifteenth century.

Birds were another widespread theme in ancient art that survived in tribal and village rugs. Notable examples include "bird rugs" from southern Persia and five-sided Turkoman "bird *asmalyks*," pile weavings made especially for weddings.

Birds have always played a primary role in folk tales as well as in some of Asia's most profound literature. The most famous and eloquent example is *The Conference of the Birds*, a philosophical and religious poem written in the twelfth century by the Persian Sufi master Farid ud-Din Attar. In the course of the poetic narrative an assembly of birds share a long spiritual pilgrimage and discover their ultimate unified self. In traditional Persian folk tales, such as "The Bird Flower-Triller," and the Turkestan story "Prince Hassan Pasha," magical birds are agents of personal transformation, living in a spirit world beyond life and death.[17] According to a quasi-historical myth, Genghis Khan was guided in an hour of need by a parrot. In some places, prayers are considered more potent if said while a bird is singing. We in the West join the majority of Asian peoples in placing birds in a separate and important mythological category: what are angels but combinations of human and bird forms? Next to trees, birds are mankind's most popular symbol.

Surrounded by many references to this image, Asian tribal weavers naturally included bird motifs in their weavings. The Tekke Turkoman example below is from Sigmund Freud's collection. Its design includes two-headed animals as secondary motifs. South Persian rugs of this type display a remarkable latitude of styles, suggesting a deeply rooted regional tradition with many variations.

4.38 Tekke Turkoman wedding trapping (*asmalyk*), 2ft 7in × 4ft 4in (79cm × 132cm); second half of nineteenth century.

4.39 Khamseh Confederacy, 4ft 2in × 6ft 4in (127cm × 193cm); nineteenth century.

4.40 An Anatolian kilim design.

4.41 Detail of a Bakhtiyari kilim, showing two figures, *soumak* technique.

We saw in Chapter 2 that parts of animals, especially animal heads and horns, were a common theme in Asian village and nomadic art for an extremely long period. We could not expect to determine the precise source for such widespread usage, the meaning of which shifted from place to place and era to era.

Tribal weavers included animal heads in their work, at times with explicit details such as eyes and horns, but often in such a stylized manner that the original implication was lost. Heads became pure shapes, called "latch-hooks" by many writers, "hooked rhombs" by others, or simply "hooks." All of these terms ignore the original source of these forms (as, no doubt, did many of the weavers). I prefer the "animal head" label.

The photograph at right includes animal heads in unexpected configurations: as repeating border elements in a large Bakhtiyari saddlebag. Illustration 4.42 shows a detail of the border, a local pattern which may relate to early art. The motifs on a Luristan bronze bar shown in 4.43 include repeating-head designs.

Illustration 4.41 shows an unusual detail from a Bakhtiyari kilim shown on page 137. The human figures' hands are fashioned to resemble animal or bird heads. The origin of this device is obscure. There could be some relationship to human images in Anatolian weavings of the type shown in Illustration 4.40.

4.42 Animal-head details, Bakhtiyari saddlebags.

4.43 Bronze from Luristan, with human and animal heads, early first millenium B.C.

4.44 Pattern from a silver cup, first millennium B.C.

4.45 Bakhtiyari saddlebags, 3ft 4 in × 4ft 6in (101cm × 137cm); first quarter of twentieth century.

Details from the Luri/Bakhtiyari saddlebag set pictured at right were shown on pages 41 and 54. The complete weaving is a fitting image with which to close this chapter. Column-like forms in the center of each field panel are noteworthy and appear to be archaic patterns. These columns are decorated with explicit animal heads which have both eyes and horns shown in the expanded detail below.

An early authority in this field adopted the term "latch-hook" for all motifs of this type because of coincidental similarities between actual latch-hooks on nineteenth-century gates and doors and stylized animal heads in Oriental rugs. Although misleading and ethnocentric, the term stuck as an aid in discussing motifs that appeared in innumerable weavings. Unfortunately, laymen, armed with a convenient label, tended to accept it without questioning the origin of these motifs, as if the name in itself meant something. The "latch-hook" convention delayed our ability to see how some superficially dissimilar forms were related and had a common origin in early Eurasian tribal and village cultures.

The name "animal-tree" could be applied to these shapes, but doing so would unduly stretch the tree metaphor. I propose the label "animal-head column" for this pattern and ones closely related to it. It is possible that these columnar shapes originated in Iran. Alternatively, they may represent more widespread Asian traditions featuring animal or bird heads, without a single cultural source. In any case, ample evidence confirms that conservative examples of this image endured in the Zagros Mountains of Iran.

The importance of these motifs hinges less on their specific origins than on their role in clarifying relationships among a broad family of tribal and village designs, to be discussed in the following chapter. It can be shown that countless generations of weavers, working throughout a vast geographical area, created large numbers of design variations based on a core network of forms.

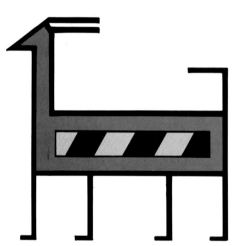

4.46 Animal motif from a south Persian horse cover.

4.47 Animal-head detail from Luri/ Bakhtiyari saddlebags, opposite.

4.48 Luri/Bakhtiyari saddlebags, 1ft 9in × 3ft 1in (53cm × 94cm); late nineteenth century.

Design Origins:
Exploring a Vast Family
of Motifs

5

Compiling a complete catalogue of all the motifs that appear in tribal rugs would take years of painstaking work. The task of tracing the origins of these motifs, while theoretically possible, could require additional decades. This chapter focuses on only one network of patterns, those that include the "animal-head" (hook) shapes introduced in Chapter 4. The manner in which these design elements developed among tribal and village weavers in one region, such as Central Asia, varied noticeably from the way they developed in other areas, including Anatolia and Iran. The Luri/Bakhtiyari animal-head columns relate to all of these variations in a manner that sheds light on the origin of hundreds of patterns.

Given the modest number of early tribal textiles preserved in dry or frozen environments, it may be impossible to reassemble the prototypes of this family of motifs. Woven patterns based on animal-head columns may have first appeared among a small population in the Zagros and then spread gradually to other tribal and village weavers. Or, conceivably, weavers over a broader area began gradually to adopt these forms, taking them from different sources. It is extremely difficult to know which of these scenarios is more likely. The time-frame in either case is pre-Islamic. My own conclusions favor a central source among tribes in Iran during the first millennium B.C. According to this model, movements of tribal populations carried the motifs from this area into neighboring regions.

The piece shown on the facing page formed the bottom and sides of a rectangular box used to carry possessions during migrations. (See page 112 for a complete example.) The animal-head columns in both the top and bottom panels differ from the example shown at the conclusion of Chapter 4 on page 61. Here we see multiple columns, side by side, rather than the single columns featured in smaller bags.

Two of the columns, shown in Illustration 5.2, on page 64, lay the groundwork for seeing several important design connections. Shaded areas highlight motifs that developed in a number of directions.

5.1 Luri/Bakhtiyari bedding bag panels, 4ft 2in × 5ft 5in (127cm × 165cm); late nineteenth century.

Design Origins

The search for design origins is analogous to the study of language origins. In both cases, attention is focused on similarities that imply relationships. Specialists in historical linguistics work to trace dialects or languages to earlier and more fundamental tongues. In the same fashion, some woven designs can be traced to fundamental forms.

The front and back of a superb Luri/Bakhtiyari bag are shown on the facing page. For an intact weaving of this type, see page 111. This piece also shows variations of the same basic multiple-column patterns.

Drawings included in this chapter suggest how certain motifs in the animal-head columns were later used individually and in time were adapted in various ways. Like the words of dispersed languages, motifs in rugs, kilims, and bags multiplied with the passage of time. While there is no concrete proof that the Luri/Bakhtiyari animal-head columns represent the *original* form, a body of evidence in this chapter suggests that the Luri/Bakhtiyari versions changed less than others. Had these examples not survived, it would be impossible to comprehend essential relationships in the broad family of motifs that contain animal-head features.

5.2 Drawing of animal-head column with details extracted on the right.

65

5.3 Luri/Bakhtiyari saddlebag (*khorjeen*) panels, 4ft 8in × 6ft 6in (143cm × 199cm); first quarter of twentieth century.

Design Origins

These two Luri weavings are of particular interest because they show sets of animal-head columns that have fundamental points in common with the patterns found in large Luri/Bakhtiyari saddlebags. The animal heads in the rug (right) have neither horns or eyes. Small secondary medallions were removed, leaving repeating primary medallions in a more compact form, without pairs of heads extending from either side on lateral arms. It is obvious, however, that the sets of columns in the rug are related to and derived from nomadic Luri weavings of the type pictured below, a *sofre*, which was used as a ground cloth. The *sofre*, in turn, is closely linked to nomadic bags. A set of transitional drawings suggests stages which lead from the more archaic bag and *sofre* patterns to field designs in the rug.

5.5 Transitional drawing suggesting ties between *sofre* animal-head columns and repeating medallions in a Luri rug, right.

5.4 Luri/Bakhtiyari *sofre*, 3ft 8in × 4ft 3in (112cm × 129cm); early twentieth century.

5.6 Luri, 5ft 9in × 6ft 3in (175cm × 190cm); late nineteenth century.

Design Origins

The drawings below show the gradual removal of a series of parts from the animal-head column, leaving the simple arms and heads. The result closely resembles repeating elements in this Anatolian kilim from the Balikesir region. I apply the term "lateral arms" to the prominent lateral forms in this piece. These elements were given local names, including "scorpions' tails" by weavers in the Balikesir district. Such local descriptions of motifs are fascinating but often have limited value in the process of learning about the origin of a form.

This kilim pattern, and hundreds of similar designs, all appear to share a common source. The value of the Luri/Bakhtiyari version in this analysis becomes apparent when it is compared not only with one specific motif, but with dozens of different patterns using the motif. As this family of motifs spread, any meanings attached to specific variations must have changed. Folk interpretations of motifs are considerably more fluid than the motifs themselves. Also, limitations that weave structures impose on the way lines can be drawn encourage the repetition of certain shapes, regardless of the cultural references they contain. Woven motifs can be made larger or smaller or can stretch in one direction or another, within limits dictated by the size of a given weaving and by constraints imposed by weaving structures. Changes of meaning are not subject to such restrictions. What we find in field work in Asia confirms this: related patterns are called by different names in neighboring areas, often irrespective of their shared family resemblances.

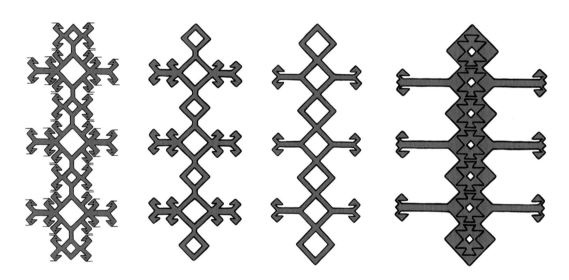

5.7 Portions of the animal-head column, when simplified slightly, indicate the origin of kilim designs with pronounced "lateral" arms.

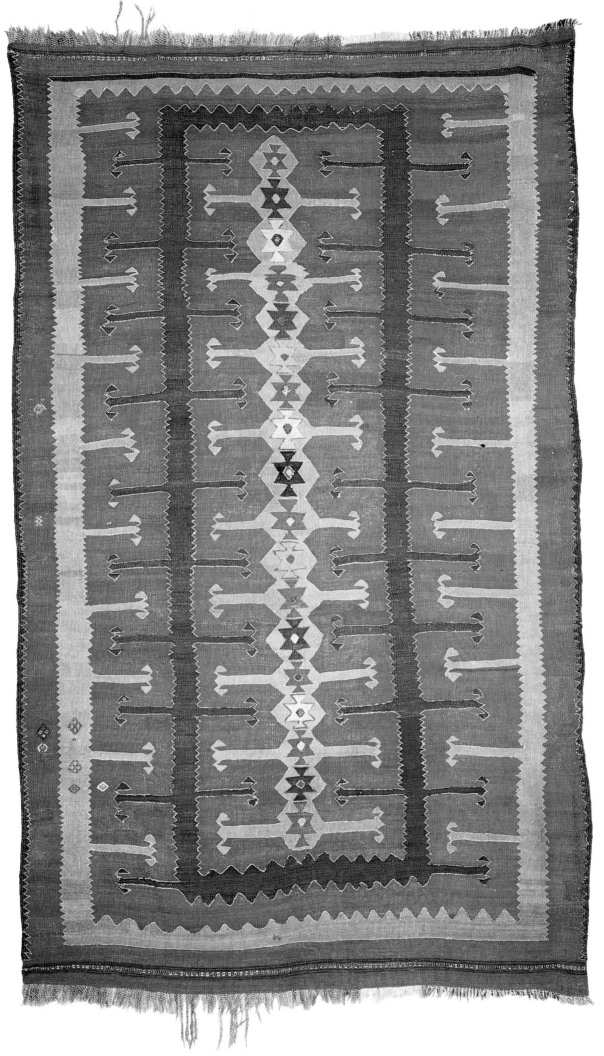

5.8 West Anatolian (Yuncu) kilim, 5ft 7in × 9ft 7in (170cm × 272cm); nineteenth century (E. Herrmann).

Design Origins

No single fragment of the animal-head columns became so widespread and varied as the central portion, which became separated as an independent motif. I propose the name "animal-head medallion" as a substitute for the "latch-hook medallion" label. The superb Caucasian prayer rug shown on the facing page employs simple animal-head medallions as repeating field motifs. Motifs of this sort could have been carried to the Caucasus region by Kurds, whose earlier homeland was in the Zagros highlands of western Iran.

The illustrations below suggest a chain of transitions leading from the medallion as it appears in a complete animal-head column to the simpler version in this Caucasian prayer rug. No horns or eyes embellish these Caucasian medallions. They float on the field as purely geometric shapes. The loss of horns and eyes represents the kind of alteration we would expect as motifs move from a nomadic setting to a more settled way of life, in which animals do not figure so prominently. Similar adaptations took place in all the areas represented in this book, including Central Asia, Anatolia, and even villages in Luristan.

At present we have no evidence that the Luri/Bakhtiyari patterns represent unaltered, *original* configurations of these forms.[1] Even in the most isolated Zagros districts, some modifications must have occurred. However, the materials examined in this chapter confirm that they are more than local variations. They allow us to formulate a coherent picture of underlying relationships among complex groups of design elements.

5.9 Animal-head medallion forms (above) are clearly derived from more complex animal-head patterns.

5.10 Kuba prayer rug, 3ft 1in × 5ft 1in (94cm × 155cm); second half of nineteenth century.

Design Origins

Three rows of drawings on the facing page relate to three different rugs. They suggest transitional stages which gradually produced distinctive medallion forms in three weavings from three regions. All were woven in the late nineteenth century, and each features a substantially modified version of the animal-head medallion. These drawings suggest a few directions in which the medallion altered. Note that designs at the bottom of the three columns bear slight resemblance to each other and, in two cases, only a limited relationship to the form at the top of the page. However, they all contain related basic shapes: stylized necks and heads. Some weavers probably understood these forms as related to animals; others did not.

Illustration 5.13 is of a medallion from a Luri rug shown on page 75. The animal heads around this medallion have lost any vestige of the horns or eyes in the naturalistic original version. In general, however, this medallion differs little from the prototype.

The central column of drawings in illustration 5.11 depicts a Turkoman medallion from a rug shown on page 74. This version offers more striking deviations from the prototype at the top of the page. The essential features of this motif include a larger medallion with a greater number of heads surrounding a compact interior medallion. Additional changes nearly obscure any resemblance to the prototype.

Illustration 5.14 is an Anatolian variation in which considerably more exaggerated changes are apparent. No solid medallion center exists, only the neck and head shapes themselves, which have an extra twist. The original Luri/Bakhtiyari medallions measure only a few inches in height. Related Anatolian kilim medallions measure nearly two feet, a modification suggesting many centuries of permutations. The kilim containing this final medallion also appears on page 75.

The purpose of these comparative illustrations is both simple and sweeping: they suggest that hundreds of tribal and village rug medallions share common ties.

5.12 Detail of 5.15.

5.13 Detail of 5.16.

5.11 Drawings suggest separate paths of development for three styles of medallion, all of which are based on animal-head forms.

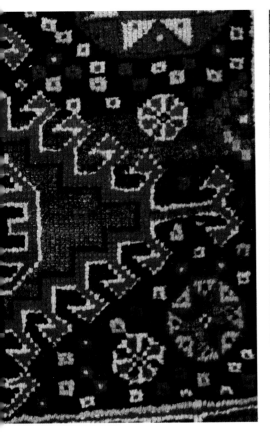

5.14 Detail of 5.17.

5.15 Yomud main carpet, 5ft 2in × 9ft 9in (157cm × 297cm); second half of nineteenth century.

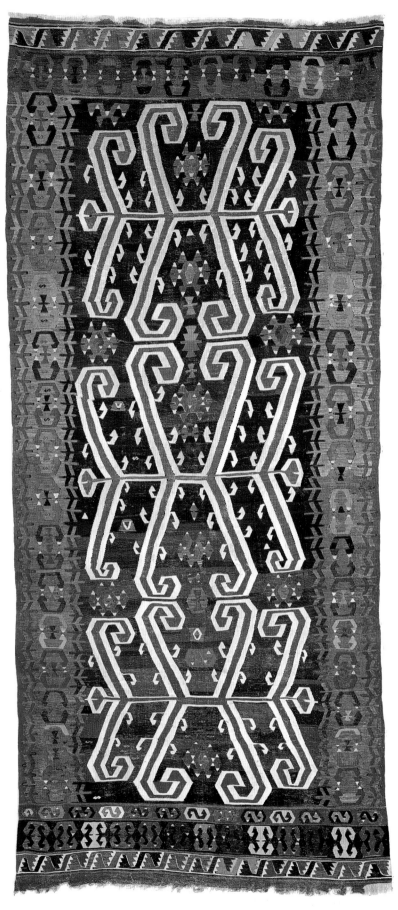

5.16 Luri, 3ft 4in × 9ft 3in (101cm × 266cm); late nineteenth century.

5.17 Central Anatolian kilim, 5ft 7in × 12ft 11in (171cm × 395cm); nineteenth century.

Design Origins

Evidence accumulates that weavers in most regions treated traditional motifs as abstract geometric forms, subject to free experimentation, rather than as fixed and unchangeable symbols. This helps explain the adaptation of field motifs, or fragments of them, as border patterns. The concentric repeating half-medallions in the border of this Kazak rug serve as an example. Their size and spacing permit a field pattern/ground shift, such that our eyes go as easily to the white background as to the field motifs. Long ago, an individual weaver must have observed that the negative space (white background) can generate new positive designs. Columns of repeating meander-motifs in the Baluch rug pictured below confirm this step.

5.18 Baluch, 4ft × 6ft 8in (122cm × 203cm); late nineteenth century.

5.19 Bordjalou Kazak, 5ft 3in × 6ft 7in (160cm × 200cm); nineteenth century.

That tribal people were adept at seeing these pattern shifts is suggested by the account of a nineteenth-century European traveler who, while visiting some Iranian nomads, showed an English magazine to his hosts. It contained a black-and-white etching depicting a London street scene. The nomads found the picture incomprehensible, partly because they were unable to tell if the essential image was conveyed by the printed black shapes, or by the white background. Learning to shift our vision as we look at these weavings brings us closer to a level of visual literacy that nomads and villagers in Asia mastered centuries ago.

Design Origins

Transitional drawings below show another portion of the animal-head column that became a separate design unit. The motif emphasized in the shaded areas underwent several changes, suggested by the final image on the right, which nearly duplicates forms in the center of repeating Kurdish medallions. Many rugs and kilims contain motifs that are even closer to the prototypical form.

Given the Kurds' long tenure in western Iran, we can envisage an early time when they wove designs that all but duplicated the patterns of neighboring Zagros tribes. Kurds in western Iran, northeastern Iraq, eastern Turkey, and elsewhere are intensely proud of their heritage. Nonetheless, Kurds did not experience the degree of isolation and conservatism which prevailed among nomadic Lurs. Kurds were in much closer contact with ethnic groups to the west and north of the Zagros and were more subject to the cross-cultural pressures that lead to changes in language, dress, and folk motifs. Therefore, in spite of their proximity to the Lurs, we would not expect Iranian Kurdish rug designs to remain quite so stable as designs among more isolated Luri weavers.

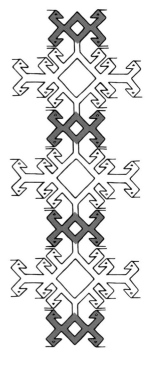

5.20 Animal-head column details developed into separate design units.

5.21 Some Luri/Bakhtiyari bags contain small medallions of this type, which include horns extending from the heads.

5.22 Kurd, 4ft 2in × 6ft 9in (127cm × 205cm); late nineteenth century.

Design Origins

Transitional drawings below isolate another distinct portion of the column, one that appears as a separate motif in many weavings, including the Shah-savan *soumak* panel shown beneath them. This figure has a central diamond and pairs of heads, both above and below, bent symmetrically. Two-headed animals in rows on either side of the field add another archaic touch.

The Shahsavan group is an important source of traditional artifacts, particularly bags and large woven boxes (*mafrash*). Turkish is the official language of the Shahsavan, and they share other features of Turkic nomad cultures. In their complexions and facial structures, some members suggest a mixture of Turkic and native Iranian peoples. Shahsavan tribespeople whom I saw near Ardebil, in northwestern Iran, near the border with the Soviet Union, only slightly resembled Turkic-speaking people in several parts of Afghanistan who identified themselves as Turkomans, Uzbekis, or Hazaras. Native Iranian groups were associated with the Shahsavan in early times. Tracing the origin of Shahsavan motifs along ethnic lines is therefore an especially difficult task. Here, the repeating border motif suggests a link with Luri/Bakhtiyari animal-head columns.

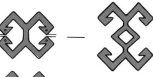

5.23 Simplified column elements relate to border units in the Shahsavan weaving shown below.

5.24 Shahsavan *soumak* panel, 1ft 9in × 1ft 8in (53cm × 51cm) and detail, right; nineteenth century.

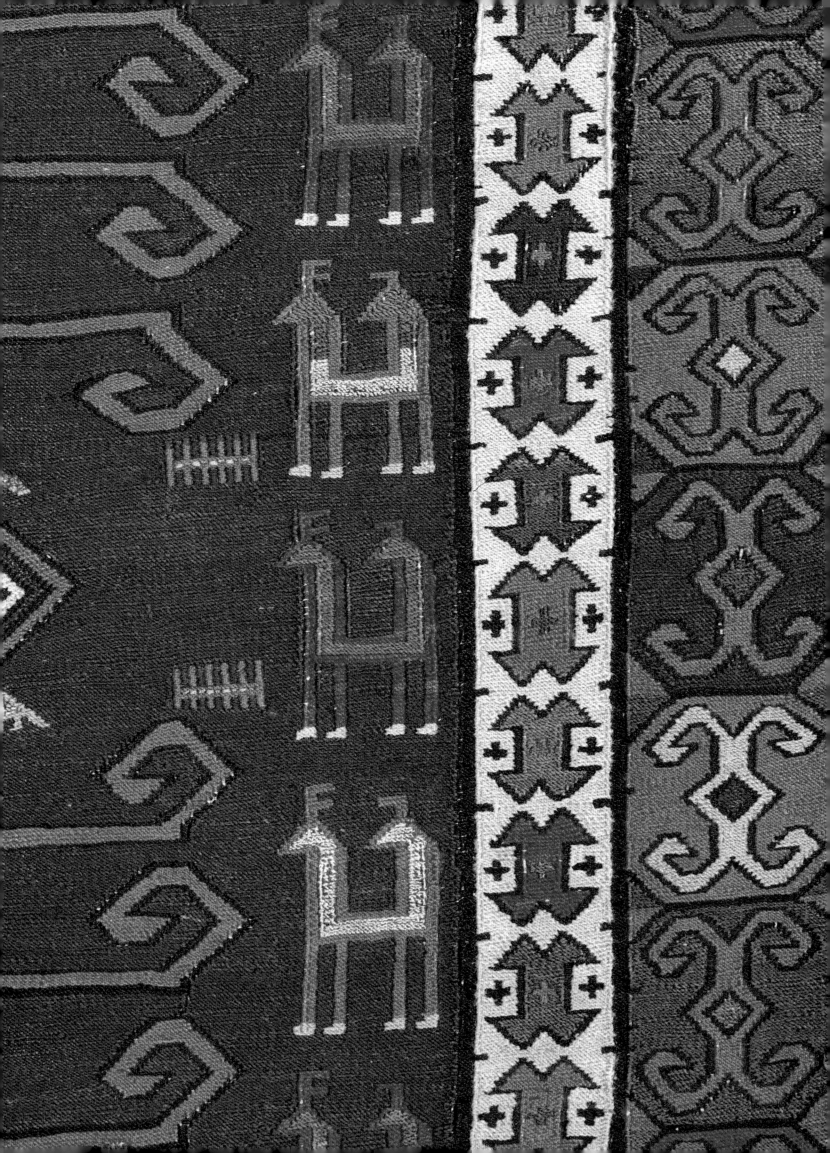

Design Origins

Successive generations of imaginative weavers treated parts of the animal-head column as pure shapes, separate from their original context. In this way, an ever-expanding array of possibilities was created. By altering the size of motifs, by repeating them, by controlling the coloring and spacing of motifs, and also by arranging a lively tension between positive and negative shapes, weavers could achieve a dramatic multiplication of patterns. The contribution of experiments with interlocking positive and negative forms must have been substantial. The structures of slit tapestry weave, especially, lend themselves to the duplication of such symmetrical and complementary shapes.

This kilim illustrates the effectiveness of such a positive/negative shift. Design-play leading to this field-pattern/ground relationship was mastered by both village and nomadic weavers.

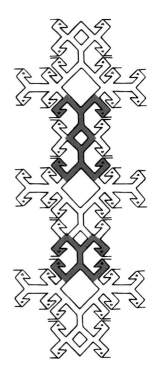

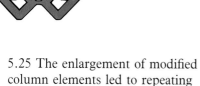

5.25 The enlargement of modified column elements led to repeating patterns as seen in the Anatolian kilim, right.

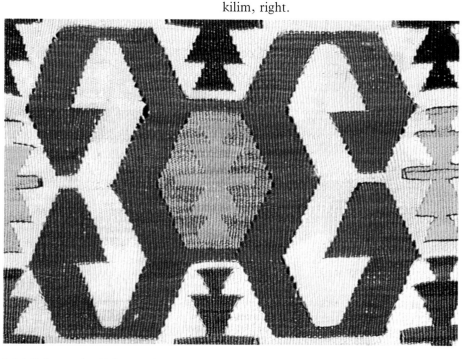

5.26 Column detail from kilim, right.

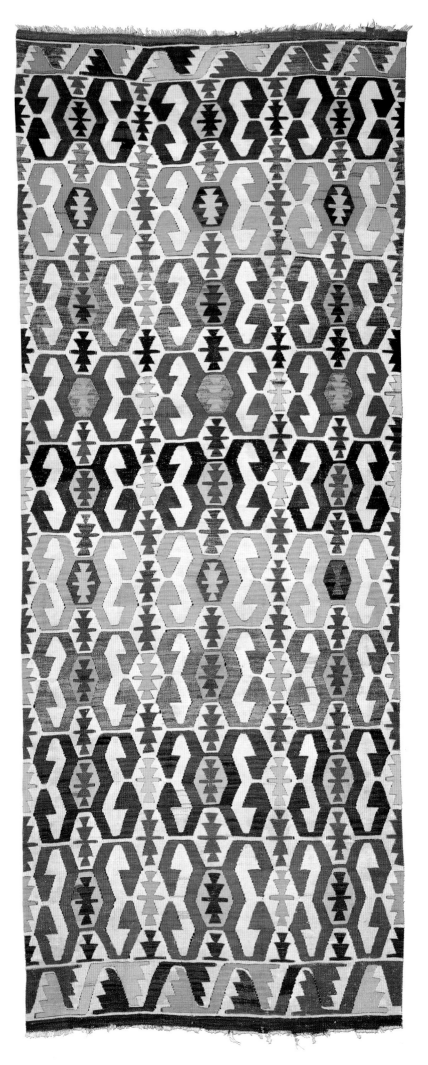

5.27 Central Anatolian kilim, 4ft 7in × 11ft 1in (140cm × 338cm); nineteenth century (E. Herrmann).

Another motif shared by both tribal and village weavers is shown in Illustration 5.28 and in the repeating field design of the Qashqa'i rug shown on the opposite page. It, too, stands as a separate motif but is closely related to the animal-head column. The design of the major border contains a separate network of adaptations.

This rug originates from the Shekarlu, a no-longer-extant sub-tribe within the Qashqa'i Confederacy. The Qashqa'i are considered a Turkic group, and the majority of Qashqa'i spoke Turkish, a branch of the Altaic language family. The Shekarlu were dominated by Luri (native Iranian) people. As mentioned in Chapter 1, these Lurs within the Qashqa'i spoke Luri, a dialect of Farsi, in the Indo-Iranian family of languages. Yet, Shekarlu members accepted Qashqa'i khans as their leaders and adopted other aspects of Qashqa'i identity.

The adoption of one group within another, thereby blurring ethnological distinctions, was a common feature of Asian tribal life. Invading tribes often absorbed a defeated people, as the Qashqa'is did members of the Shekarlu tribe. This provides some explanation of how traditional Luri rug designs entered the vocabulary of numerous Qashqa'i groups.

The weaver of this rug varied the shape of repeating field motifs at many points of her work. In spite of the strong role of tradition, tribally related village weavers who worked beyond the control of workshops improvised freely within the framework of traditional local patterns.

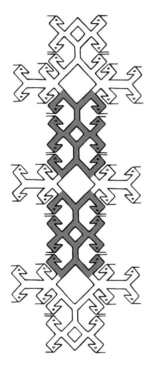

5.28 Some animal-head patterns represent more complex derivatives from column details.

5.29 Qashqa'i, 5ft 1in × 6ft 8in (155cm × 203cm); mid-nineteenth century.

Design Origins

Urban rug designs represent a separate group of influences, one that has left an indelible imprint on village weaving traditions in several areas. This was especially true of the Caucasus from the sixteenth through the nineteenth centuries. Long-standing local folk-weaving traditions were displaced in some areas by patterns devised by professional carpet designers. However, an examination of many nineteenth-century Caucasian rugs confirms that older folk motifs survived throughout successive waves of intense workshop activity.

Most of the smaller motifs in the field of this Caucasian rug are related to the family of motifs discussed in this chapter. They were simplified, rounded, or distorted in other ways. Nevertheless, an underlying correlation with animal-head elements is discernible, especially in shapes presented in Illustration 5.30. It must be emphasized that these drawings are intended to show broad relationships, rather than precise lines of descent from the Luri/Bakhtiyari patterns.

Over the centuries, diverse Asian peoples developed their own names for motifs of this type, including "ram's horns." Some designs were given different names by different groups of weavers and represent more than one lineage. It follows that one interpretation of a specific motif does not rule out other valid interpretations which coexisted and overlapped.

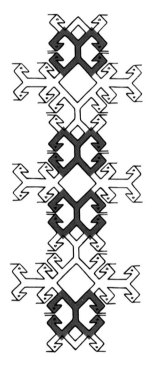

5.30 The rounding of derived forms, right, disguises their probable links to more geometric animal-head patterns.

5.31 Detail from Kazak, right.

5.32 Karachov Kazak, 4ft 11in × 7ft 6in (150cm × 228cm); nineteenth century.

Design Origins

Some designs represent such a complex series of alterations that efforts to pinpoint lines of descent can be only educated guesswork. This is especially true in Anatolia, where kilim variations became particularly intricate. Yet we can see ties with the animal-head column complex in basic features of these motifs. The repeating field medallions in this Anatolian kilim are such an example.

In his landmark book, *Kilims*, Yanni Petsopoulos makes the following observation:

It would appear that in many parts of Anatolia, a strong local tradition remained undisturbed by the fashions imposed by the Ottoman court in Istanbul, and continued to produce pieces in a much earlier style. That such a style should survive longer in kilims than in carpets is quite understandable given the fact that while the carpets were a commercial commodity, and sensitive to the demands of changing fashions in the commercial centres, kilims remained largely in the places where they were woven for local use, where there was no pressure for them to change stylistically.[2]

The question of when these motifs entered Anatolia is one of the most fascinating yet to be resolved. Ambitious efforts in the early 1980s attempted to demonstrate an ancient Anatolian source, in the form of neolithic representations of a goddess. This approach has come under severe questioning.[3] My own proposal is that Kurdish tribes in Iran and Anatolia served as a conduit for the passage of a basic tribal design vocabulary from one area to the other. Passing centuries and the creative impulses of thousands of village weavers adapted this vocabulary into shapes that were suited to different weave structures. Pile weaves allowed the shapes to be rounded; flatwoven slit tapestry weaves favored straighter lines.

5.33 Designs from some regions suggest more drastic derivatives from original patterns.

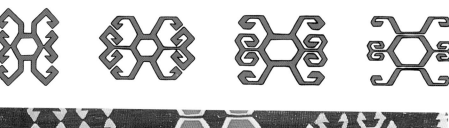

5.34 Detail of kilim, shown right.

5.35 Western Anatolian kilim,, 5ft 6in × 11ft 2in (168cm × 340cm); nineteenth century.

Design Origins

The survival of archaic forms within the Luri/Bakhtiyari group has only recently been recognized. No ivory-ground nomadic bags from this group were shown in rug literature before 1976, when *Lori and Bakhtiyari Flatweaves*, by Amedeo de Franchis and John Wertime, was published. The importance of animal-head shapes had been recognized by V. G. Moshkova and others, but in general, efforts to trace the origin of common forms focused on Turkoman weavings. This short chapter introduces an engaging new direction of study, one that many readers will be able to continue independently. Given the marvelous diversity of patterns in tribal and village rugs, new variations will always be coming to light.

The family of motifs examined in preceding pages constitutes one of the most complex networks of folk patterns in the history of Asian art. Careful comparisons of design variations among specific tribes can often shed light on the early histories of the tribes themselves. Tribal rugs, long neglected as a serious academic study, have significant contributions to make toward a fuller understanding of Asian history and art.

The story of tribal rugs is noted for two opposing tendencies that are present in all processes: stability and change. Tribal movements, invasions, and displacements contributed to gradual alterations. Improvisation born of the weavers' own creativity was another primary factor. However, one other influence, extraneous to folk cultures, had a substantial impact on designs, at times totally disrupting local traditions. The next chapter addresses an important aspect of tribal rug studies: the role of urban rug patterns in tribal design vocabularies. As I suggested in Chapter 1, understanding the influence of urban designs in the history of tribal rugs is of fundamental importance in achieving a balanced perspective.

5.36 & 5.37 Luri/Bakhtiyari *chanteh* (single bag), 1ft 2in × 1ft (35cm × 30cm) and detail, right; first quarter of twentieth century.

Urban Influences in Tribal Rugs

6.1 Mogul mille-fleurs rugs inspired later Qashqa'i copies, as seen right. 3ft 7in × 5ft 3in (112cm × 160cm); eighteenth century.

Although ancient folk traditions account for many tribal and village motifs, urban rug patterns also exerted a substantial influence on the building of design vocabularies. Virtually every tribe under discussion copied urban designs at some point in their history. Tendencies on the part of villagers to copy workshop designs were especially strong during periods of economic vitality, but the process was probably always going on, if only by momentum. This factor is obvious in regard to a number of patterns, especially *botehs* (paisleys), and many *Herati* variations (named after the city of Herat in Afghanistan, where this pattern was popular). In other cases, the tribal adaptation of urban motifs is less obvious.

This important phenomenon began before the era of the Pazyryk rug, which itself contains a mixture of tribal and urban features. Evidence suggests a similar blending in the wake of urban weaving artistry during and after the Sassanian period of Iranian history (between the third and the late sixth century A.D.). Tribal weavers were also influenced by developments in urban carpet art during the Timurid period, following Tamerlane's invasion of Iran late in the fourteenth century, during the Safavid dynasty (the sixteenth and seventeenth centuries), and throughout the period of the Byzantine and Ottoman empires in Turkey.

The clearest examples of urban patterns in tribal rugs are fairly recent. Prominent among these are Qashqa'i mille-fleurs patterns. The Qashqa'i rug pictured on the right surely owes its inspiration to Indian carpet art of the seventeenth and eighteenth centuries, which in turn had been influenced by Persian forms. How did such a formal, even foreign, pattern become incorporated in tribal rugs? It is known that Qashqa'i troops accompanied the Persian monarch Nadir Shah in his invasion of India in the second quarter of the eighteenth century. A Qashqa'i leader could have returned to southern Persia with booty in the form of a Mogul carpet, which he then had copied. Whatever the truth of the matter, the transplanted style survives under the tribal name "Qashqa'i."

6.2 Qashqa'i workshop rug, 4ft 2in × 5ft 6in (127cm × 168cm); late nineteenth or early twentieth century.

Most books on tribal rugs underestimate the influence of urban designs in tribal weaving.[1] The discovery that motifs once perceived as tribal emblems owe their origin to workshop designs can be deflating. However, the ability to recognize the merging of separate influences is an important step in efforts to understand and appreciate tribal rugs.

A striking example of tribalization is found in numerous Qashqa'i rugs and saddlebags, as well as in work from a neighboring tribal group, the Khamseh Confederacy. Tracing this pattern – a medallion with attached twin pendants – from its urban roots reveals a long sequence of gradual changes. These demonstrate that formal designs, having been learned by tribal women, changed so drastically that later versions appeared to be thoroughly tribal.

The pendants in the Qashqa'i rug shown on the facing page are of central interest here, given changes that occurred to motifs of this type over a period of time, in both their appearance and in their place in rugs and other weavings. Clarifying the beginning stages of a process of degeneration, two illustrations below show pendant forms from a sixteenth-century Tabriz carpet (Illustration 6.3) and a related Khamseh Confederacy pendant from the mid-nineteenth century (6.4). Both forms have features in common with the Qashqa'i pendants in the ivory-ground rug but represent more original or less corrupted manners of drawing these forms.

Under the direction of weaving workshop owners, Qashqa'i and Khamseh Confederacy village weavers copied such designs probably after being shown urban rugs of this style. Some Qashqa'i copies feature knot-counts in excess of 250 knots per square inch, rivaling the density of city carpets. They have other features intended to enhance their marketability, including the use of silk wefts and fully depressed knots, wherein adjacent warp threads are immediately above or below each other. The examples shown on the next two pages suggest that processes of tribalization advanced dramatically once these formal patterns reached Qashqa'i women in smaller villages, as well as in nomadic camps where knot-for-knot copies were the exception.

6.3 A sixteenth-century Tabriz pendant form.

6.4 A mid-nineteenth century Khamseh Confederacy pendant.

6.5 Qashqa'i workshop rug, 6ft 9in × 10ft 2in (210cm × 310cm); mid-nineteenth century (E. Herrmann).

The chief modification in these pendant forms involved their position in the design: from being subordinate to the central medallion, they became the primary field motif. They also underwent considerable stylization, resulting in a gradual restructuring of their shapes. The two graceful projecting stems, seen in Illustrations 6.3 and 6.4, became four symmetrical and angular "arms," especially in the Qashqa'i *wagireh* (sample rug) shown in 6.7.

Such major adaptations characterize the work of many tribal weavers. Village women working on their own looms freely adapted patterns observed in rugs from commercial studios, on display in bazaars. Nomadic weavers, seeing the work of their village counterparts, tried their hand as well. They did so for one reason: to sell their wares. Even some saddlebags and other pieces which collectors have tended to view as separate from market influences were, in fact, commercial weavings. Some supposed "bag fronts" were probably made in workshops and never formed part of a bag.

The appearance of certain motifs in saddlebags or small weavings has suggested to some western rug experts that these motifs not only were tribal but also served a heraldic function. This viewpoint gradually came to be questioned, leading to the realization that tribal weavings influenced by commercial workshops are separate from nomadic articles with traditional designs.

6.6 Detail, Qashqa'i rug, late nineteenth century.

6.7 Qashqa'i *wagireh* showing a highly stylized medallion. 1ft 11in × 2ft 10in (58cm × 86cm); first quarter of twentieth century.

6.8 Qashqa'i, 3ft 2in × 4ft 4in (97cm × 132cm); late nineteenth century.

Urban Influences in Tribal Rugs

Overwhelming evidence confirms the adoption of many urban patterns from the sixteenth century onward in tribal and village weaving. Proof of earlier stages of this process is limited and includes gaps which can as yet be filled only by educated guesses. Occasionally, tribal weavings that appear on the market or in rug literature can help to fill one of these gaps, especially if we recall that urban motifs, once acquired by tribal weavers, change in predictable ways. They become simpler and more geometric in their lines and often appear in the company of older non-urban motifs.

Such is the case with the Turkoman weaving shown on the facing page, a piece that points to a much earlier era of tribalization. The two illustrations below show roundel motifs, a hallmark of Sassanian textile art as well as related Byzantine and Chinese styles.

Beginning during or before the sixth century A.D., weaving workshops in Iran produced tapestry weaves featuring birds or animals within circles, a fashion copied by professional weavers over a wide area. The piece shown in Illustration 6.10 was found in China and is probably Chinese work of the T'ang dynasty (seventh to early tenth centuries A.D.). Illustration 6.9 shows a related seventh- or eighth-century Iranian pattern featuring a mythological creature, the *Senmurv*, presumably related to the poet Attar's *Simurgh* (literally meaning "thirty birds") in *The Conference of the Birds*.[2] The transfer of these early roundels into a nomadic weaving should alert us to the possibility that other ties existed between urban woven art and early Turkoman rugs.

6.9 A roundel from an Iranian textile, seventh or eighth century. Related Turkoman designs could have been acquired through trade contacts.

6.10 Animal-decorated roundel from a Chinese workshop, T'ang dynasty.

6.11 & 6.12 Yomud *torba*, 3ft 4in × 1ft 8in (102cm × 51cm) and detail; first half of nineteenth century.

Urban Influences in Tribal Rugs

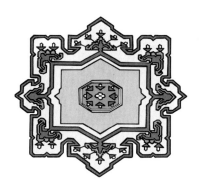

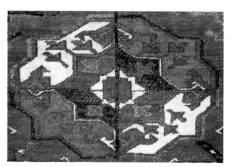

6.17 A Tekke gul c. 1880.

The origin of the Tekke gul and several related Turkoman guls is one of the most interesting riddles in the larger puzzle of design origins. The inspiration for these forms is usually considered to be tribal in origin, related to archetypal emblems. However, a quite different possibility exists: that the Tekke gul represents a mixture of old tribal elements and tribalized Anatolian urban forms. The series of drawings on the left does not attempt to reproduce a complete sequence of stages of a tribalization process, but suggests its general outlines. Illustrations 6.13 to 6.16 show four drawings, and 6.17 reproduces a typical Tekke Turkoman gul. Three of the line drawings, 6.13, 6.15 and 6.16 were taken from published rugs. Illustration 6.14 is a hypothetical transitional form. Illustration 6.13, an urban medallion, represents a type of medallion which, in my opinion, began a tribalization process among Turkoman weavers, possibly employed in workshops in Central Asia. The rug that contains this medallion was ascribed by Balpinar and Hirsch to the seventeenth century.[3] The transitional gul shown as 6.15 is from a rug in the same collection.[4] The link between 6.15 and Turkoman guls is obvious, but what is not obvious is the line of influence. It seems entirely possible that the development of these motifs parallels the evolution of four-armed Qashqa'i motifs, discussed earlier in this chapter. That is, Turkoman weavers, guided by the owners of weaving workshops, adopted a successful and attractive urban medallion which, through processes of change, adaptation, and the addition of older tribal elements, acquired a more tribal appearance.

Various Turkoman sub-tribes produced guls related to the Tekke gul, treating them in a relatively fluid manner. As variations on this motif developed among different Turkoman sub-tribes, these peoples could be identified according to which version they produced. The sharing of guls gave rise to complex theories in order to explain a process that may well have been all too simple. Weavers living close to each other automatically copied related forms, including those that had been adapted from urban medallions. Their daughters copied these motifs, making slight changes from generation to generation. The "Tekke gul" is still changing today in the hands of Soviet, Iranian, Afghan, and Pakistani weavers.

Surely some extremely old designs were known to Turkomans. Some of these feature animal-head medallions, two-headed animals (called "Tauk Nauska" in Turkoman rug literature), related bird or animal motifs, or forms that evolved from them. Later in this book we shall examine the proposal that these early forms may have been acquired directly or indirectly from tribes who migrated eastward from Iran and whose descendants were absorbed by Turkomans and other Turkic groups in Central Asia.

According to the proposal just outlined, Turkomans acquired formal

6.13 A central medallion from an east Anatolian rug, in the Vakiflar Museum, Istanbul, ascribed to the sixteenth or seventeenth century. The darker areas show primary features that became tribalized. Note the anchor-like shapes that extend from eight points in the inner portion of the medallion.

6.14 Transitional drawing. The outlining shapes are now more angular. Dart-like forms begin to point toward the center of the medallion. The anchor-like forms with outlining shapes are more geometric.

6.15 From a rug in the Vakiflar Museum, Istanbul. The outlining of the medallion (gul) has become even more angular. Small dart-like forms point toward the center, and the anchor-like shapes are severely geometric.

6.16 The round symmetry of the central medallion has given way to a flattened oval effect in this drawing of a Tekke gul. Darts are multiplied and anchor-like figures still have outlining forms, which have acquired animal-head features.

designs from workshops for the same commercial reasons that Qashqa'i weavers acquired them during and after the seventeenth century. Depending on where they lived and perhaps on individual preferences, both Qashqa'i and Turkoman women might choose between working in a controlled workshop or at home. During favorable economic periods, they were assured of reasonable success in the marketplace, so long as their work met contemporary standards. Nomads could also participate in this enterprise, having the advantage of raising their own wool. This form of commerce was therefore perfectly adapted to either village or nomadic life, both of which had suitable resources in the form of labor and raw materials.

The tribalization of urban patterns could not have mattered to rug dealers in the seventeenth and eighteenth centuries, any more than it did to rug dealers in the nineteenth century. Their job was to buy and sell, not to oversee the purity of designs. Some variations in patterns may have been viewed as desirable. The manner in which Turkoman guls developed in repeating patterns may have enhanced their saleability.

By the early twentieth century, gul patterns had been tentatively attributed to certain tribes by several authors. By the 1960s, serious rug buyers insisted on more exact terminology than "Bokhara," "Princess Bokhara," and the like. The taste for greater accuracy was satisfied with a mixture of up-to-date field work and more speculative concepts regarding "tribal emblems" and the antiquity of various Turkoman guls. Clearly, the sorting of fanciful and factual interpretations is an ongoing process, especially in connection with Turkoman rugs.

In some regions, the consistent problem of misreading tribalized urban forms as ancient tribal designs may have been an indirect result of political pressures. This appears to be the case in Turkey, where Turkic dialects and Turkic contributions to art history were emphasized as an adjunct of state policy. Scholars within the former Soviet Union labored under other handicaps, including isolation from colleagues abroad.

In common with Qashqa'i rugs of a more commerical type, many Turkoman rugs reveal a consistent emphasis on high knot counts, good wool quality, and design uniformity. All were important factors for tribal weavers, their agents, and employers who sought to compete with city workshop products. In both the Qashqa'i and Turkoman tribal families, these traits carried over into the weaving of bag fronts and other items. Some of the most finely woven examples may be carefully controlled workshop products. With some notable exceptions, tribal weavers were not purists. When exposed to strong market preferences, they tended to adapt to them.

An experience of my own supports this outlook. In 1974 I was introduced to a family of Qashqa'i women engaged in a family enterprise of weaving kilims from camel's hair and undyed wool. The mother and her three daughters completed one piece each week. Admiring their work, I agreed to buy all the kilims they wove for a period of eighteen weeks. The mother (and spokeswoman) asked if there were special designs I preferred, and suggested several possibilities. These included both traditional motifs (goats and camels) and tribalized urban patterns (stylized roses). As their customer, the decision was in my hands.

Our efforts to identify indigenous traditional designs need to be tempered by the realization that commerical workshops played an important role in the introduction of new patterns and motifs, the adaptation of these elements, and the refinement of weaving techniques and structures. There are scores of other tribalized urban motifs that could be included in this discussion. As decorative objects, this class of rugs and bag fronts exemplify a successful blending of careful craftsmanship, fine materials, and mastery of complex patterns. Compared to indigenous nomadic weavings, many are tribal in name only.

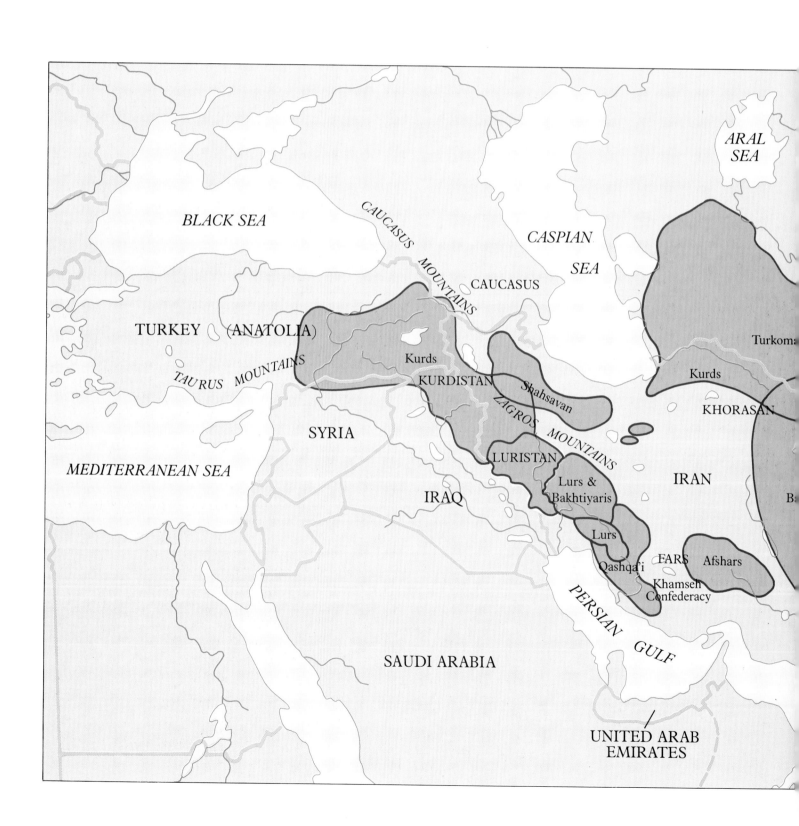

BLACK SEA

CAUCASUS MOUNTAINS

CASPIAN SEA

ARAL SEA

CAUCASUS

TURKEY (ANATOLIA)

TAURUS MOUNTAINS

Kurds

KURDISTAN

Shahsavan

ZAGROS MOUNTAINS

Turkoma

Kurds

KHORASAN

SYRIA

LURISTAN

Lurs & Bakhtiyaris

IRAN

B

MEDITERRANEAN SEA

IRAQ

Lurs

Qashqa'i

FARS

Afshars

Khamseh Confederacy

PERSIAN GULF

SAUDI ARABIA

UNITED ARAB EMIRATES

Kazakhs

beks

Kirghiz

CENTRAL ASIA

AFGHANISTAN

PAKISTAN

Part II
The Tribes and Their Weavings

Our study thus far has taken us from the Altai Mountains of Siberia to the rocky slopes of the Zagros. We have seen purely traditional weavings as well as urban-influenced rugs from several tribal districts. This second section examines rugs from specific tribes and regions. From this point forward, a region-by-region and tribe-by-tribe approach offers the best opportunity to see the products of each group in the context of its specific history and culture. Maps locate each group geographically.

The first eight tribes discussed in this section reside in Iran, or did so earlier in their history. These include native Iranian (Indo-European) tribes, Turkic-speaking groups, and some Arabs. The discussion then turns to rugs and kilims from Anatolia. With the exception of Kurdish and "Yürük" work, most Anatolian weavings are not "tribal" in any strict sense, but are the work of village weavers, with roots touching traditional tribal patterns. Many Anatolian village pieces contain few if any urban influences. A short look at selected examples helps clarify processes that promoted the multiplication and spread of traditional patterns. A sampling of rugs from the Caucasus in Chapter 16 serves the same purpose. The final chapter is devoted to Central Asian tribes, particularly the Turkomans.

The first Iranian tribes addressed are those whose traditional designs shed the greatest light on early motifs, the Lurs, Bakhtiyaris, and Kurds. I consider their homeland, the Zagros Mountains, as the likely source of core motifs that were shared and adapted by tribal and village weavers over a vast area. This point of view is advanced as a working hypothesis within a broader framework directing attention not only to the Zagros, but to Indo-European tribes spread over a wider area. All tribes and districts under discussion participated in the enlargement and spread of motif vocabularies.

The Lurs

7

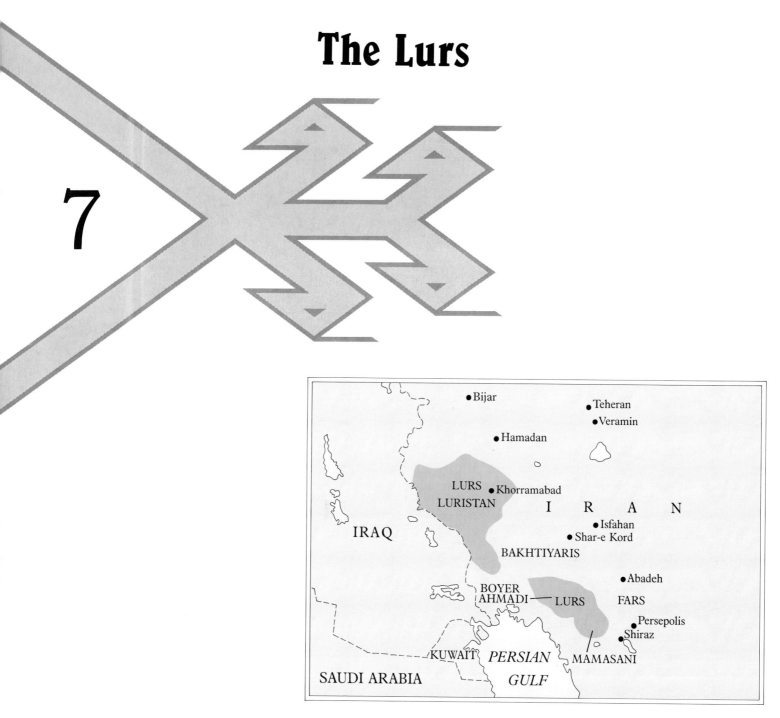

Primary groups of Lurs live in two main areas; Luristan, to the west, and in Fars province, to the south. Some Luri people live near Veramin, southeast of Teheran, and many others were absorbed into other south Persian tribes.

The map shows two Luri-dominated areas: Luristan proper, on Persia's western frontier, and a separate area to the southeast between Bakhtiyari and Qashqa'i territories. A partition of territories between Lurs and their Bakhtiyari cousins forced a division into these two zones. Technically, the Bakhtiyari are part of the Luri group, but their importance and separate identity lead most writers to treat them separately. Ethnologists list several Luri sub-groups as components of both the Khamseh and Qashqa'i Confederacies. Lurs are also part of the tribal mixture living near Veramin, south of Teheran. Rough estimates of their total population run as high as 3,000,000, including village-dwellers.

Historical references to Luristan date to the seventh or eighth century A.D., or perhaps slightly earlier, well after the "Luristan bronzes" (see page 26) were fashioned. Earlier names for the area, or parts of it, included Elam

7.1 Detail of Luristan rug shown on page 120.

and Gutium (land of the Guti tribes), as well as other designations mentioned in Assyrian and Babylonian commercial and political documents.

Nomadic Lurs share characteristics with other mountain-dwelling populations throughout the world, including reticence in their contacts with outsiders. Lord Curzon, writing in the late nineteenth century, made this comment about early inhabitants of Luristan: "From the earliest days we read of this mountain country as a wild and inaccessible region, inhabited by formidable tribes. They set at nought the authority of the Medes and Persians; they defied Alexander."[1] In the more restrained words of P. R. S. Moorey, a leading scholar in the field of early Iranian metalwork, "The formidable topography encouraged the separate development of local communities . . . [but] widespread semi-nomadism forestalled complete isolation."[2]

In spite of geographical and cultural obstacles, Medes and Persians imposed their control over the Zagros, although pockets of nomads may have retained their own cultural features. Luri (or Lori), the language of Luri and Bakhtiyari nomads, has two major divisions. Both are conservative forms of Farsi, brought to the Iranian plateau by Persians. A Zoroastrian from Tehran told me that his father could communicate with Luri villagers by speaking Dari, the ancient Zoroastrian language, related to Old Persian.

From the fifth to the end of the first millennium B.C., clusters of tribes from other areas found refuge in Luristan's protected environment, bringing their own culture with them. The Zagros was under the control of Elamites and Akkadians for extended periods. Both Babylon and Assyria exerted their military and economic influence, and Zagros tribes served as mercenaries in Sumerian, Babylonian, and Assyrian armies. One important local tribe, the Guti, dominated Babylon late in the third millennium.[3]

The fall of the Achaemenian empire at the hand of Greeks in the fourth century B.C. brought greater isolation to remote Zagros nomads. The remains of Sassanian buildings and bridges, constructed sometime from the third to the end of the sixth centuries A.D., suggest that Luristan was of some importance in the minds of Sassanian rulers. Later shahs built little and taxed as much as possible, including the exaction of payments by nomads in the form of sheep and goats. Muslim Arabs invaded Iran in the seventh century A.D. and their faith was at least nominally adopted by the entire Luri population. (One twentieth-century traveler observed that some tribesmen showed only a minimal familiarity with essential Islamic beliefs,[4] and

7.2 Bronze from Luristan, eighth to seventh century B.C.

7.3 A scene in Luristan. Rivers that make the region inaccessible during spring floods are readily crossed in summer. 1920s photograph.

other writers have reported the survival of ancient rites such as "blood brotherhood.") In the course of overrunning and dominating Persia in the tenth century, Turks also occupied Luristan; however, they left minimal traces.

During recent centuries nomadic Lurs wove rugs, kilims, and bags on simple horizontal looms, secured by wooden stakes driven into the ground. While direct evidence of ancient weavings in their locale is scant, such basic weaving methods probably date to early periods there. Archeological sites in Luristan do not yield the stone loom weights, used on primitive upright looms, suggesting the use of horizontal looms. Village weavers, too, normally used floor looms in recent periods.

If we were to question tribespeople in various Lur-dominated areas about their tribal affiliations, their answers might be "Luri" (of the Lurs) or perhaps "Mamasani," "Boyer Ahmadi," or other Luri tribal divisions, each with its own territory and minor cultural differences. The Boyer Ahmadi and Mamasani live closer to Qashqa'i territories in northwestern Fars Province, well to the southeast of Luristan. Tribes in that area are known collectively as "Kuhgilu" or "Kugilueh."

It is possible to distinguish rugs woven in Luristan proper, where dark-brown undyed wefts are the rule, from Boyer Ahmadi and Mamasani Luri rugs, which feature red or red-orange wefts. To distinguish between Boyer Ahmadi and Mamasani work requires the help of local dealers, some of whom are very knowledgeable about the weavings of their own neighborhoods.

Symmetrical (Turkish) and asymmetrical (Persian) knots are found in pile weavings from Luri villages, but symmetric knots are the overwhelming rule in pieces of nomadic origin. The oldest known Luri weaving I have seen, shown on pages 50-51, has a symmetrically knotted pile panel. The use of symmetrical knots may date to an extremely early period in this locale, before Turkic groups learned this knot. Consequently, the label "Turkish knot" is misleading on historical grounds. Nomadic Bakhtiyaris and Kurds also use the symmetrical knot, and probably have throughout their long histories.[5]

Enough is known about the nomadic weavings of this group to accord

7.4 Luri weavers at work on a horizontal loom. Warps are dark wool or goat hair; 1930s.

7.5 Luristan bronze, eighth to seventh century B.C.

them a special place in the study of tribal rugs. By circumstances of both geography and cultural history, Luri nomads and their close relatives, nomadic Bakhtiyaris, remained closer to ancestral designs than any other tribes in Asia. Few other tribes show so little interest in producing items for the marketplace. Such refinements as high knot counts and thoroughly planned designs were never a hallmark of nomadic Luri work. (It is true, however, that village weavers in the area tried their hand at copying "*mina khani*" and other urban patterns.[6])

Lightweight items – kilims, *gabbeh* rugs, and saddlebags were necessary items in the form of nomadism that prevailed in the Zagros. Due to the need to travel lightly, heavy pile rugs were less suitable. Consequently, motives behind pile rug weaving were mixed. Some rugs were made for domestic use. Many were woven to sell. All in all, the romantic mental picture that rug collectors in the West developed regarding tribal weaving traditions is more appropriate to Lurs than to any other group. However, they, too, wove rugs for external markets.

From our point of view, Luristan's rugged terrain, which still bars easy access from Iraq, is a two-edged sword. Relative isolation fostered integrity of style, but it also impeded fieldwork which might have brought the value of archaic Luri designs into prominence much sooner. It is unsettling to realize that we missed, by only a few decades, the opportunity to study the oldest and least-adulterated nomadic designs while they were still "alive" in isolated nomadic habitats.

7.6 A Luri tribesman, c. 1938. His tattered clothing and disheartened bearing suggest the anguish of countless nomads during Reza Shah's forced-settlement period.

The possibility of such a study was severely impeded by the terrible displacements that nomadic groups suffered during the 1930s, when Reza Shah attempted to modernize Iran by a combination of decree and military force. Due to a lack of cohesive leadership, remote Lurs suffered even more than neighboring Bakhtiyari and Qashqa'i tribes. Hunger was severe; some tribespeople starved to death. Documentation of this disaster was fragmentary and after-the-fact.[7] To date, no writers have focused attention on the effect of this period on folk-weaving traditions. Nomadic bags from the 1940s and 1950s are still on the market in some numbers, since Lurs have continued to abandon nomadism. The aesthetic quality of these objects is by no means equal to similar pieces from the 1920s and 1930s. It appears that the disasters of the 1930s represent a watershed in modern Luri history from which the tribe never fully recovered. This was less true with Bakhtiyari tribes. Their wealth and coherent political structures permitted them a more complete recovery after Reza Shah's abdication in 1941.

As we saw in Chapter 2, the term "Luri/Bakhtiyari" is a reliable name for many nomadic bags for which more definitive labels would be open to question. It also refers to weavings from Lur groups in Bakhtiyari Province,[8] including many of the ivory-ground bags with classic animal-head columns. I have included most pieces carrying the Luri/Bakhtiyari attribution in this chapter, rather than treating them as a separate group.

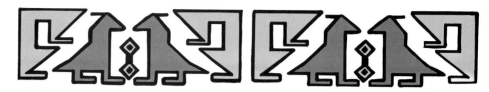

7.7 Border detail from the ivory-ground saddlebags shown opposite.

The large *soumak* saddlebag set shown opposite contains a clear, complete arrangement of animal-head columns. Minor borders are modified repeating-"S" meanders. A confronting-animals motif, shown in Illustration 7.7, is part of the main border. This is ancestral to several border patterns found in the work of other Iranian tribes, including the Khamseh Confederacy and Baluch tribes. (See page 202.)

The salt bag shown below features an especially clear field pattern/ground shift, enabling us to focus readily on a secondary network of patterns. As is often the case with Luri and Bakhtiyari bags, a knotted pile band completes the bottom of the piece.

7.8 Luri/Bakhtiyari salt bag, 1ft 6in × 2ft 1in (48cm × 64cm); first quarter of twentieth century.

7.9 Luri/Bakhtiyari saddlebags, 3ft 1in × 4ft 11in (94cm × 150m); 1920s.

The Lurs

These two articles are more closely related in function than their appearance initially suggests. The piece pictured on the right is shown exactly as it came off the loom some decades ago. It was never cut and bound into the form of a *rakhtekhab-pich*, the name Lurs give to a bedding bag, known by some Turkic-speaking tribes as *mafrash*, although this was clearly its intended purpose. The central ivory rectangle with simple crosshatching was to be the bottom panel. The pair of five-sided shapes at the bottom were woven as end pieces. In their final, box-like form these would be attached on three sides by cotton or goat-hair threads.

Design similarities as well as wool texture suggest that both these weavings came from precisely the same sub-tribe within the larger Luri family of tribes. The precise location of this sub-tribe is uncertain, but they appear to have lived in Bakhtiyari Province rather than in Luristan. Both objects were probably made in the 1920s, a period of considerable independence for Luri nomads.

7.10 Luri/Bakhtiyari *rakhtekhab*, 2ft high × 3ft 10in long × 2ft wide (61cm × 117cm × 61cm); 1920s.

7.11 Luri/Bakhtiyari, 3ft 8in × 7ft 10in (112cm × 239cm); 1920s.

The Lurs

These two examples are intended to emphasize the remarkably different ways in which individual weavers interpret the same designs, thereby giving distinctive connotations to their work. The opened bag panel shown to the right suggests such words as "primitive," "vigorous," and "unsophisticated." The salt bag, on the other hand, evokes an opposite set of ideas: "sensitive," "precise," "fastidious," and even "elegant."

Note the fine rendering of the "S" border in the piece pictured below, as well as the perfect spacing of all field and border units. All the animal heads in both pieces have clear horns and color blocks indicating eyes. In their different ways both pieces are consummate expressions of tribal art.

7.12 Luri/Bakhtiyari salt bag, 1ft 6in × 1ft 9in (46cm × 53cm); early twentieth century.

7.13 Luri/Bakhtiyari bag (opened), 3ft 5in × 4ft (104cm × 122cm); late nineteenth century.

Dealers and auction houses commonly label kilims of the type shown here "Qashqa'i." However, the dark warps (seen as fringe) and the more primitive treatment of patterns point to a Luri source, probably in Fars Province. By way of comparison, Qashqa'i kilims are often more refined in their patterns. Qashqa'i warps are commonly thinner and, as a rule, ivory in color. Patterned kilim ends of the type seen in the piece shown on the right do not necessarily confirm a Luri attribution, given their frequent use in work from Qashqa'i sub-tribes, which contained some Luri people.

Design similarities in Luri and Qashqa'i kilims, saddlebags, and many rugs reveal the extent to which Qashqa'i tribes absorbed Luri elements during past centuries, thereby acquiring traditional Luri patterns. Not surprisingly, no urban inspiration is present in either of these two kilims.

7.14 Luri kilim; late nineteenth century.

7.15 Luri kilim, 5ft 10in × 9ft 8in (178cm × 295cm); late nineteenth century.

The Lurs

The animal heads that surround three large medallions in this Luristan rug include dots of color, representing eyes. Soumak-woven threads in the medallion detail on the right indicate the same feature, as well as horns. The exact stages that led to such large-scale medallions are lost in the early history of these patterns, but it is possible to reconstruct a plausible development. Weavers must have started with smaller weavings decorated with smaller medallions, surrounded by fewer heads. Inevitably, the task of making larger rugs with similar designs arose, requiring an aesthetic decision: repeat many small medallions or increase their size? There is evidence that both solutions were tried, as some tribal weavings of this type feature oversized medallions, and others are based on an infinite repeat of smaller units. The size of the heads themselves were the same in each category, but their numbers multiplied as medallion size increased. This process could conceivably have begun before the Christian era, or perhaps in the course of the first millennium A.D. By the fifteenth century, a period represented by many examples, related rug designs in Anatolia had already undergone substantial changes and fragmentations. Patterns among nomadic weavers must have remained more stable in parts of the Zagros.

The ivory-colored motifs in the center of the three medallions are found in many Qashqa'i weavings, as well as in rugs from the Talish area in the Caucasus. This design has features in common with the "endless-knot" motif, discussed in Chapter 4. (See page 40.)

Note that partial medallions extending from the side borders have features in common with half-medallions in the kilim shown on the previous page.

7.16 & 7.17 Luristan, 5ft 4in × 7ft 8in (163cm × 234cm), and detail; late nineteenth century.

The unusually wide border in the rare Luristan rug shown below contains both one- and two-headed animals. Most "S" shapes in the border include lines indicating horns. The field is based on tree forms interspersed with animal and bird designs. A relationship with certain Caucasian and Shahsavan patterns is apparent in the stylized trees, as well as bird shapes in the field, one-third from the bottom.

Narrow borders are a feature of many old Luri rugs, including the superlative piece pictured opposite. Pairs of confronting animals decorate the flanks of stylized lions in the field. Several rows of *boteh* (paisley motifs) in the upper field may be an adapted urban motif, as is true of most large-scale *boteh*. Scores of small animals populate the borders. The improvisational approach to patterns in both these rugs is a frequent feature of Luri work.

7.18 Luristan, 5ft 5in × 9ft 1in (165cm × 277cm); second half of nineteenth century.

7.19 Luristan, 4ft 1in × 9ft 3in (124cm × 282cm); second half of nineteenth century.

The animals pictured in the bottom row of this nineteenth-century *soumak* Luri bag front are clearly related to those examined on pages 50–51 of Chapter 4. Illustrations 7.20 to 7.22 show a series of related horse-and-rider forms; Illustration 7.20 is familiar from Chapter 4; 7.21 is from the *soumak* bag front shown on the right; 7.22 (opposite page) is a detail from a 1940s bag from the southeast corner of Luristan, southeast of Khorramabad. This horse and stylized rider pattern has evidently been a feature of local textile culture for an extremely long period. (See the Luristan bronze pictured on page 50.) Although the two-headed figure on the back of the late-nineteenth-century horse in Illustration 7.20 is more crudely rendered than the one in the later example, 7.22, in general, the three figures reveal a steady deterioration. Only the earliest example, 7.20, shows the two-colored braided reins extending from the horse's mouth to the stylized rider. The drawing of the horse in this oldest example is refined and balanced. The drawing of the late-nineteenth-century example is angular but appealing. Fifty or sixty years later, the overall appearance of the forms is more or less intact, but the artistry with which they are expressed has declined significantly. The forced-settlement period of the late 1930s appears drastically to have accelerated a descent that had been under way for many decades.

Although recent weavings are usually of less interest from the aesthetic viewpoint, they can be useful in our efforts to trace the tribal and geographic origins of earlier designs. They also confirm the opinion of many writers that tribal weaving standards declined irreversibly when traditional modes of pastoral nomadism were overturned.

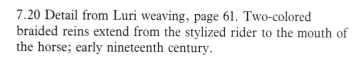

7.20 Detail from Luri weaving, page 61. Two-colored braided reins extend from the stylized rider to the mouth of the horse; early nineteenth century.

7.21 Detail from Luri bag front, opposite page, above; late nineteenth century.

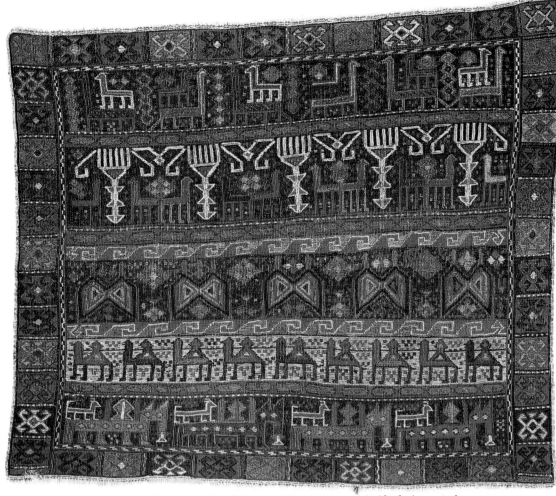

7.23 Luri bag front, 2ft 6in × 2ft 11in (76cm × 89cm); second half of nineteenth century.

7.22 Detail from a 1940s Luri saddlebag (not shown), woven near Khorramabad; mid-twentieth century.

Gabbeh rugs are another traditional Luri weaving form – one that Qashqa'i weavers appear to have learned from their contacts with native Iranian groups. Writings on this subject by Parviz Tanavoli, Sekandar Amanolahi, Georges Bornet, and others, have brought examples of this remarkable native art into prominence. The term *"gabbeh"* refers to a general style of weaving, not to a tribe or sub-tribe. Designs in these weavings have a bold, strongly "folk" flavor. Numerous wefts between rows of knots speed the process of weaving typical examples of this type. Occasionally, examples reveal only two or three wefts.

The first literary reference to *gabbehs* was in the sixteenth century in a decree from Shah Tahmasp concerning the welcome due an important guest:

We have ordered a silk tent to be set up for the kitchen near the royal pavilion and the private quarters, covering the ground with silken carpets from Khorasan, and gabbehs.[9]

The example shown here is not typical, if the word "typical" can be applied to a category so diverse and full of surprises. It is one of the oldest I have seen, possibly from the mid-nineteenth century or earlier, and belongs to a group of pile weaves that imitate kilim designs. This piece has as many as ten wefts between adjacent rows of knots. The use of ivory warps is a characteristic of most Qashqa'i rugs, but is also found occasionally in Luri pieces. Irregular design features are consistent with nomadic Luri work.

By the late 1970s, *gabbehs* had been "discovered," and tribal weavers were making most of their output for the marketplace. Dealers wisely encouraged them to improvise freely, and one occasionally finds remarkably inventive designs among newer models. Luri and Qashqa'i weavers accounted for most *gabbehs* produced in the past century, with some contributions from Bakhtiyari and Khamseh Confederacy weavers.

7.24 & 7.25 Luri(?) *gabbeh*, 4ft 6in × 6ft 9in (137cm × 206cm) and detail, left; mid-nineteenth century or earlier.

The Lurs

Luri "bird rugs" constitute a rare and appealing sub-group. Most south Persian examples of this type are the work of weavers within the Khamseh Confederacy. Luri versions are sufficiently different from those of the Khamseh to suggest that a united tradition, once shared by several native Iranian tribes, began to fragment several centuries ago and to develop regional characteristics. Chapter 12 will show a related pattern among the Afshars, one that may have been learned from neighboring Khamseh weavers. Several birds in the piece pictured on the right have yet-smaller birds perched on their heads. This, too, could be an archaic design feature. Field patterns in the rug shown below include human figures, several types of animals, and "animal-tree" details which may have been inspired by Luristan bronze art.

7.26 Luristan bird rug, 5ft 3in × 8ft 4in (160cm × 254cm); last quarter of nineteenth century.

7.27 Luristan bird rug, 5ft 4in × 10ft 1in (162cm × 307cm); 1890s.

The Lurs

The long-standing Islamic prohibition against human images in art had little effect on Luri motifs. Apart from birds and animals, human figures are common in their work. This is especially the case with regard to rugs from Luristan proper, but is also true of Luri work from farther south, into Fars Province. The presence of red wefts in the piece shown on the right points to an area in Fars or perhaps the southeast corner of Luristan. This piece was probably woven by a Mamasani and Boyer Ahmadi weaver in Fars.

Red wefts in the classic Luri rug pictured below (left) also imply a source in Fars Province. The irregular shapes of the medallions and relatively loose weave are typical Luri features. In general, Qashqa'i rugs of similar design were planned and executed with greater precision and were more tightly woven. Luri weavers allowed greater latitude for designs to work themselves out in the course of the weaving process. The Luristan piece shown below (right) has animal-head medallions of intermediate size.

Luri rugs, as well as pieces that carry the "Luri/Bakhtiyari" label, are emerging from decades of neglect to assume a significant place in the study of Iranian tribal rugs. They represent an exciting frontier for scholars and collectors whose interests and tastes lean toward authentic nomadic work.

7.28 Luri, Fars Province, 4ft 9in × 9ft 6in (145cm × 290cm); mid-nineteenth century or earlier.

7.29 Luristan, 3ft 5in × 8ft 4in (104cm × 254cm); last quarter of nineteenth century.

7.30 Luri, Fars Province, 4ft × 7ft 4in (122cm × 224cm); late nineteenth century.

The Bakhtiyaris

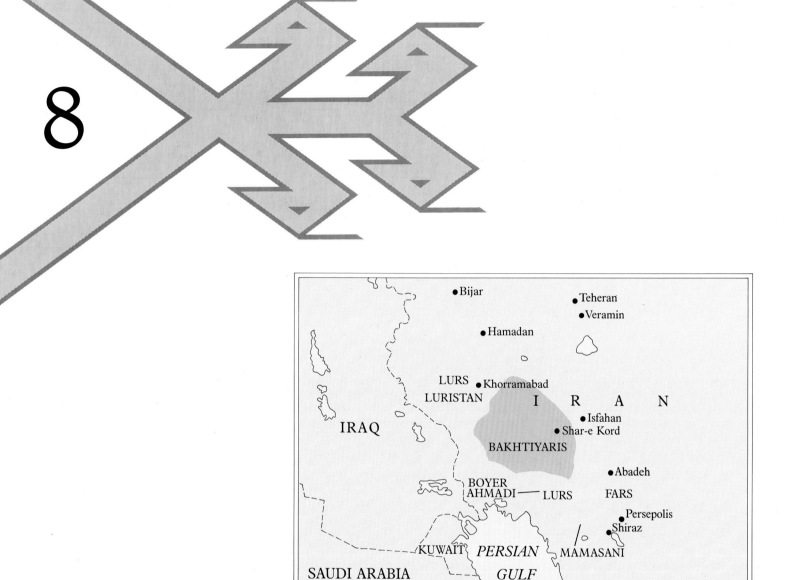

Map showing primary Bakhtiyari territories.

The roughly 500,000 members of the Bakhtiyari tribe live in areas to the east of Luristan and north of Fars Province. The majority of this population dwells in villages and towns in a district known as the Chahar Mahal, on the eastern edge of the Zagros range. An estimated 100,000 Bakhtiyaris were still migratory during the time of my visits to Iran in the early 1970s, a number which had probably not changed significantly by 1992, when this book was completed. Their migrations were strictly controlled by Iranian army officers during the final decades of the Shah's reign. By the late 1970s, some herding units traveled by a new method: four-wheel-drive trucks capable of transporting flocks off the main roads.

In past centuries, Bakhtiyaris formed their own army battalions, thereby retaining a sense of tribal identity even when serving under generals headquartered in Isfahan or Teheran. The character of compulsory military training changed in the course of the twentieth century. Young tribesmen, accustomed solely to their local cultures, were forced to mix with soldiers from all parts of the country. I met one Bakhtiyari who, resenting the army's role in

8.1 Detail from Bakhtiyari kilim, shown on page 137.

subjugating tribes, hid in remote villages for years rather than face compulsory service in the Shah's army.

The two main divisions within the Bakhtiyaris, the Chahar Lang and the Haft Lang, now have little meaning in discussions of Bakhtiyari rugs, though the Haft Lang had deeper ties with nomadism. In spite of the split between the two groups mentioned in Bakhtiyari history as early as the fourteenth century, few efforts have been made conclusively to identify weavings from either division, except for inscribed rugs which mention specific khans.

Husain Quli Khan was the first to unite these warring Bakhtiyari factions in the 1860s, forging a powerful confederacy which played a pivotal role in Persian political affairs from late in the nineteenth century until the 1920s. In *Khans and Shahs*, Gene R. Garthwaite records a mixture of legends and documented materials which summarize early Bakhtiyari history. Dr. Garthwaite's book sheds light on the complexities of political infighting among earlier generations of Bakhtiyari leaders and the role of external pressures in the unification of otherwise hostile factions. The possibility of gaining personal and family wealth was always among the motivating factors in this history.

Oil revenues from wells on tribal lands helped make Bakhtiyari khans a powerful force in Iranian society during the late nineteenth and early twentieth centuries. Their influence waned through the twentieth century after oil resources were nationalized and also due to the inability of khans to adapt tribal political methods to the realities of a modern nation-state. In the 1930s many younger khans lost some of their tribal identity. One elder Bakhtiyari leader lamented, "We . . . used to be great fellows for horses and women and hunting, but now our boys are becoming tennis champions instead."[1]

As is true of several other Iranian tribes, the confederacy's name is derived from that of its ruling family – in this case, Bakhtiar. Many members of this family occupied important government posts during the past century. Shahpour Bakhtiar, whose father was killed by Reza Shah in 1934, was elevated to the post of prime minister shortly before the Shah Reza Pahlavi was toppled in 1979. Numerous Bakhtiyari leaders fell from favor early in the Khomeini period. Some were executed on charges of inciting a *coup*. Shahpour Bakhtiar was assassinated in the summer of 1991.

Cecil Edwards, author of *The Persian Carpet*, was the first to discuss the problem of distinguishing nomadic Bakhtiyari weavings from rugs produced in Chahar Mahal villages, marketed under the Bakhtiyari name. The two types differ in construction as well as design. Chahar Mahal village rugs have only one cotton weft between each row of knots. Warps also are cotton. True Bakhtiyari rugs from nomadic sections of the tribe are double-wefted (sometimes triple-wefted), with beige or dark brown woolen warps and wefts. True Bakhtiyari weavings contain a higher proportion of traditional tribal motifs. Urban patterns have seeped into some examples. As a rule, village-made Bakhtiyari-Chahar Mahal rugs reveal more formal design arrangements. "Garden carpets" with repeating squares, and central medallion designs are common.

Our understanding of Bakhtiyari-Chahar Mahal rugs is aided by inscribed examples.[2] These inscriptions commonly identify the khan who commissioned the piece as well as the year it was woven. According to several inscriptions, aristocrats from outside the tribe also "ordered" or "commanded" the weaving of Bakhtiyari-Chahar Mahal rugs.

My own friendships within this tribe date from 1970, when I met Mahmood and Mansour Hosseini, carpet repairmen who operated studios in Isfahan and also in Shar-i-kord, the largest town in the Chahar Mahal. Their main studio in Isfahan took up one section of a historic caravanserai. They worked in the open courtyard during warm months of the year, not far from an arched entrance through which, in earlier times, loaded camels had passed.

8.2 Mahmood Hosseini, a Bakhtiyari rug repairman.

8.3 Members of the Hosseini family weaving a Chahar Mahal-Bakhtiyari pattern on their loom in Isfahan.

The Bakhtiyaris

In October of 1972, Mahmood and I traveled together through the arid plain west of Isfahan, up into the foothills of the Zagros toward Shah-i-Kord, the administrative center for the Chahar Mahal. The Hosseini home there had been built forty years earlier by Mahmood's father and included a room used solely for weaving. A large rug was always in progress during my several visits. Some of the yarns they used were vegetable-dyed; most were bright, synthetic colours. These rugs took about a year to complete and were sold to a local dealer.

During my last trip to the Chahar Mahal, prior to the revolution in 1979, Mahmood and I again went to stay with his parents, this time in the company of a well-known Isfahan rug dealer Akbar Mahani. We visited several villages in the district, including one that, by mid-afternoon, lay in the shadow of a steep mountain rising sharply from the very edge of the village. In this picturesque scene we met and conducted business with a Bakhtiyari trader dressed in traditional black trousers and cummerbund. This man's livelihood involved driving a motorcycle up into the mountains to reach nomads, with whom he exchanged salt, gold, and silver for their weavings. The great "find" of this memorable visit, and the rarest discovery of all my Asian trips, was an early Bakhtiyari kilim of remarkable design, shown on page 137.

Like most members of his tribe, Mahmood Hosseini took exception to the opinion of ethnologists that the Bakhtiyaris are, in essence, a sub-group of the Lurs. For as long as anyone can remember, "Bakhtiyari" has been a leading tribal name. During this century, their khans supported and then jolted the very foundations of the Iranian state. Therefore, any suggestion that Bakhtiyaris were a subordinate group ran counter to local sensibilities. Mahmood freely acknowledged that Kurds were a factor in some towns during earlier periods, as the name Shar-i-Kord ("City-of-Kurds") suggests. Scattered Turkic and Arab peoples also lived in the Chahar Mahal, and Armenian-owned villages still thrive in this area. These transplanted people embraced prominent features of Bakhtiyari village culture, including dress and language. Even Armenians in the Chahar Mahal adopted traditional Bakhtiyari rug designs, with some distinguishing features of their own, at times showing earlier Caucasian influences.

Several films have offered glimpses into nomadic Bakhtiyari life, including *People of the Wind* and the romantic 1920s documentary *Grass*. The latter title is shared by a book by Merian Cooper, based on her diary. With her companions, Ernest Schoedsack and Marguerite Harrison, she traveled to Iran in 1924 in order to experience the extraordinary hardships of the

8.4 Bakhtiyari families and their animals prepare to cross the Karun River during spring migration, 1920s.

8.5 Crossing the Karun. A Bakhtiyari saddlebag can be seen on the back of one of the donkeys. 1920s.

Bakhtiyari spring migration. Early in their journey, she and her companions were stretched to the limit to keep up with their hosts. Cooper recorded her impressions after crossing the Karun River:

Here's a river a half-mile wide. Its waters are swelled to a rushing torrent by the melting snows of a hundred mountain peaks. The river is icy cold. It is filled with whirlpools, cross-currents, rapids. It is tearing through mountain gorges with cliff-like jagged shores, and it is bridgeless and boatless. Here's the problem: On one side of this river are five thousand people with all their worldly goods and perhaps fifty thousand animals. There are women here, children, babies. It is spring and the herds and flocks have any number of baby animals. The people have no boats. But they must cross and cross quickly. There's little or no grazing for the animals on this side of the river. They must cross!

. . . Every tribe has in its saddle-bags quantities of goatskins. A score of skins are blown up, tied and then fastened to one side of rows of long sticks. A heavy rug is laid on top. There's your raft. There's your boat for the women and children and baby animals.

There is a place on the river where it swings through a great S. When the current comes out through that S, it strikes the western shore with terrific force. But the current is a movable force striking an immovable object. The movable force must give way. The current is thrown back from the rocks, thrown back with a swing and a jerk, and sent shooting in a long, diagonal, down-stream line, directly across to the eastern shore.

. . . The herds must be swum over. And someone must swim with them. That's the men's game. But recall again that the river torrent is ice-cold. I defy your strongest cross-channel swimmer to plunge into that stream, fight a steer by the horns and swim it across, then return and do it again and again many times in a day.[3]

This strenuous existence also had room for art, but of a kind that was grounded in day-to-day necessities. Illustration 8.5 includes a saddlebag on the back of a donkey being pulled into the Karun River. Rugs and kilims were valued as furniture, as bedding, and as insulation during the winter, as well as for the color they added to tents. All manner of bags and animal trappings had practical functions. The weaving that follows, a remarkable kilim purchased from the Bakhtiyari trader mentioned on page 134, introduces the artistic side of Bakhtiyari nomadic life.

The Bakhtiyaris

Few weavings contain such a wealth of early design forms as this damaged but remarkable Bakhtiyari kilim. Only two examples of this type have been published to date.[4]

The main border on both long sides contains thirteen panels, with only one unit repeating. Minor borders adjacent to the border panels are, in themselves, a subject worthy of study. There are "S" borders of several types, Greek keys, and other figures which are not easily described. Both the overall pattern of lateral bands and the individual design units suggest an extremely old approach to kilim design, probably with local roots. The human figures on one border panel are shown on page 58. Another border motif is now quite familiar: the animal-head medallion, shown in a detail below. Note that heads in this panel contain horns, and some include eyes. An endless knot is in the medallion's center. The appearance of animal-head medallions in a traditional Bakhtiyari flatweave shows that Bakhtiyari nomads, as well as Lurs in Bakhtiyari Province, were familiar with this pattern in an archaic form.

8.6 Detail of Bakhtiyari kilim border.

8.7 Bakhtiyari kilim, 4ft 1in × 10ft 2in (124cm × 310cm); first half of nineteenth century.

The Bakhtiyaris

This impressive piece represents one-half of a large Bakhtiyari saddlebag set. The pile "H" shape toward the middle was originally at the bottom of the piece, divided between the front, in *soumak*, and back of the bag. Saddlebags of more recent vintage but with similar field designs were plentiful in the Isfahan bazaar, fairly close to Bakhtiyari territory, throughout the 1970s, and were consistently called "Bakhtiyari" by local dealers. Nonetheless, this example could conceivably be Luri work. The "eye-dazzler" kilim portion adjacent to the flag-like square is reminiscent of some Qashqa'i and Veramin kilims. No doubt transplanted Lurs or Bakhtiyaris carried this pattern to Veramin. Qashqa'i weavers presumably adopted it from Luri-dominated groups within the confederacy.

Luri and Bakhtiyari flatweaves of this type are always noted for their unusual backs, decorated with *soumak*-brocaded panels. These backs were often exposed to view during migrations. When the bags were filled and closed, the fronts were placed down, against the animals' backs. Why only one-half of the back was decorated in this manner is a mystery. The flag-like areas in this piece include an animal-head column, amulets, and camels.

Like other pieces of this type, this bag is made up of several different weaves. Aside from *soumak* areas, there are pile portions (double or triple-wefted), plain-woven areas, and additional structures in the closure panels where loops held the bag shut.

8.8 Amulet design from the flag-like panel at the lower right of the weaving.

8.9 Bakhtiyari (or Luri), 3ft 6in × 4ft 10in (107cm × 147cm); late nineteenth century.

The Bakhtiyaris

Distinctly different types of purely nomadic Bakhtiyari weavings are shown to the right and below. The panel is from a large saddlebag. Tile-like units in the field fit into several octagons simultaneously, offering a clear example of designs assuming an infinite-repeat pattern. The borders serve as a window frame in close spatial relationship to the viewer, while the repeating field is at an undetermined distance in space.

The utilitarian weaving pictured below is called a *malband*. All Iranian tribes wove *malbands*, which were used primarily to tie loads onto pack animals but also to secure babies to frames that fit on their mothers' backs. *Malband* motifs may represent an extremely early body of designs. They illustrate a yearning on the part of nomadic women to beautify purely utilitarian woven items.

8.10 & 8.11 Bakhtiyari *malband*, 2½in × 11ft 5in (6cm × 348cm), and detail; late nineteenth or early twentieth century.

8.12 Bakhtiyari bag front; second half of nineteenth century.

The Bakhtiyaris

The rug shown below has all the features of true Bakhtiyari work: woolen warps and wefts, double-wefts, and traditional tribal motifs. Note that two minor borders contain a variation of the repeating-"S" theme. Animal-head terminals relate these borders to examples in Luri/Bakhtiyari bags. Each head has a line extending from the top, indicating a horn.

The *gabbeh* rug shown on the right may possibly be Luri work, but its pile and foundation wools have more in common with materials in nomadic Bakhtiyari rugs. The "Luri/Bakhtiyari" label is broad but sufficiently accurate. Wefts number between two and four between adjacent rows, and the handle of the piece is rather loose for a *gabbeh* with so few wefts. Its simple design scheme and strong colors make it a notable example of a thoroughly "tribal" weaving type.

8.13 Bakhtiyari, 4ft 9in × 6ft 7in (145cm × 200cm); early twentieth century.

8.14 Luri/Bakhtiyari *gabbeh*, 3ft 5in
× 13ft 8in (104cm × 413cm); late
nineteenth or early twentieth century.

The Bakhtiyaris

Woolen warps and wefts in the striking Bakhtiyari rug pictured below suggest a nomadic source, although the formal border designs imply some urban design influences. The ivory-field rug on the facing page is surely from a village in the Chahar Mahal. Like many other finely executed Bakhtiyari-Chahar Mahal rugs, this example is inscribed. The inscription translates: "By order of Sultan Mohammed Khan Moain Homayun – made by Bakhtiyari – date 1316 [1880]."

An essential aim of the art of carpet weaving is to create an appealing harmony between forms and colors – challenges that call critical skills into play. Anyone who has tried his or her hand at pile weaving discovers with humility that the achievement of even moderate success depends on considerable experience as well as innate sensitivity. The factor of time also enters into this art. Colors change slightly as pieces age, altering the color balance. Even a rug that looks relatively simple requires skills possessed by few individuals. All features of these rugs are in balance: colors, shapes, and overall proportions.

8.15 & 8.16 Bakhtiyari, 4ft 11in × 9ft 5in (150cm × 287cm), and detail; late nineteenth century.

8.17 Bakhtiyari-Chahar Mahal, 4ft 10in × 6ft 6in (147cm × 198cm); dated 1880.

The Bakhtiyaris

Designs, materials, and structural elements all point to a Bakhtiyari-Chahar Mahal source for this rather primitive "garden" rug. An examination of seventeenth- and eighteenth-century Persian workshop carpets reveals that designs of this type were originally based on Persian gardens. Simplified garden patterns became associated with the Bakhtiyari tribe within the past century due to the popularity of examples woven in the Chahar Mahal. The best examples are highly regarded in Iran as well as in the West.

Coloring in Bakhtiyari-Chahar Mahal pieces often shows more variety and depth than we find in most nomadic Bakhtiyari work. Village weavers had a substantial advantage: a group of professional dyers, masters of their craft. The light-blue, green, and orange tones seen here confirm the skill and "eye" of a village dyer. A weaver working alone, dyeing her own colors, was unlikely to achieve this level of mastery. Note the lions in the green panels, the birds in treetops, and a pair of horses in the sole yellow panel.

8.18 & 8.19 Bakhtiyari-Chahar Mahal, 3ft 9in × 6ft 7in (114cm × 201cm), and detail; late nineteenth century.

The demise of dyeing skills has been the single greatest misfortune in the steep decline of tribal weaving during the twentieth century. The Bakhtiyari-Chahar Mahal carpet shown on the right reveals the full range of a nineteenth-century dyer's art. To achieve such a lively interplay of colors against a dark-blue background called for a lavish use of dyestuffs and all the care and skill a dyer could muster.

Collectors in Asia as well as in the West now hope that a revival is possible for a craft which evolved in both nomadic and village cultures, thrived for thousands of years, and survived even into the twentieth century. Current efforts to reintroduce vegetable dyes in Iran are leading to quite positive results. Unfortunately, it is not easy to rebuild a craft that took so long to develop. In the words of a Teheran dealer, "Even money and enthusiasm cannot fully replace the work of a hundred generations." Something beyond commerce was behind the extraordinary richness and vigor of the art and craft of carpet weaving as practiced in nomadic, village, and urban surroundings. Attempts to duplicate the range, depth, and subtle shifts of color in older pieces have in the main failed.

Several older dyers in the Chahar Mahal spoke to me about the previous generation of men who had taught them their craft. As the rugs themselves corroborate, these men went to immense pains to achieve the highest results. The best were adept at a variety of colors but staked their careers on only one or two hues which no one else could duplicate. Family livelihoods depended on the formulas of these dyes; consequently, the formulas were carefully guarded. The acceptance of synthetic dyes, which require only moderate skill and much less labor, were adopted only slowly by nomadic and village Bakhtiyari weavers – later than by any other group. By the 1960s, the new varieties of synthetic dyes had finally "won." In the process, many old dye formulas were lost forever. Traditions of secrecy among master dyers worked well so long as a new generation wished to acquire this specific knowledge. In the absence of willing students, the knowledge died with the last generation who valued it.

Fortunately, the output of rugs and carpets, especially in Chahar Mahal villages, was steady and substantial during the closing decades of the last century and the early decades of the twentieth. The best of these pieces, as well as collections of superb nomadic rugs and bags, confirm the high level of sensitivity among Bakhtiyaris in the Chahar Mahal district, as well as among mountain-dwelling nomads. One of the ironies of Bakhtiyari history is that this name will be revered less for the deeds and misdeeds of its khans than for the work of unnamed weavers and dyers who attained superb results in the practice of their respective arts.

8.20 & 8.21 Bakhtiyari-Chahar Mahal, 8ft 1in × 11ft 3in (246cm × 343cm), and detail; late nineteenth century.

The Kurds

9

Map showing distribution of Kurdish populations.

Kurdish populations totaling over 15,000,000 remain scattered among five countries: Iran, Turkey, Iraq, Syria, and the former Soviet Union. Like Lurs and Bakhtiyaris, Kurds speak an Iranian language. Although the traditional center of Kurdistan is in Iranian territory, the greatest number of Kurds live in Turkey. Not even demands for a "Kurdish homeland," long a battle cry, could effectively unite this large and potentially powerful tribe under consistent central leadership. Blood feuds and the narrow viewpoints of local leaders have kept factions at each others' throats, and chiefs have shown inexhaustible appetites for discord. Yet Kurdish leaders have often demonstrated unsurpassed bravery in their age-old struggle for autonomy, a struggle that continues.

Over the centuries, segments of this great collection of tribes have fallen prey to oppression from many sources: the fourth-century-B.C. Greek invaders of Persia, Ottoman sultans, Persian shahs, Soviet dictators, and the Saddam Hussein government of Iraq. Their most recent crisis, capped by a widely publicized rebellion in 1991, followed charges of genocide against Iraq. This tragedy contains a sour irony, given the active role of Turkish Kurds during the 1915 massacre of Armenians, encouraged by elements within the central government. In the 1991 Gulf War, Saddam Hussein forced Kurds into the Iraqi front lines, where they took the brunt of

9.1 Detail of Bidjar rug shown on page 161.

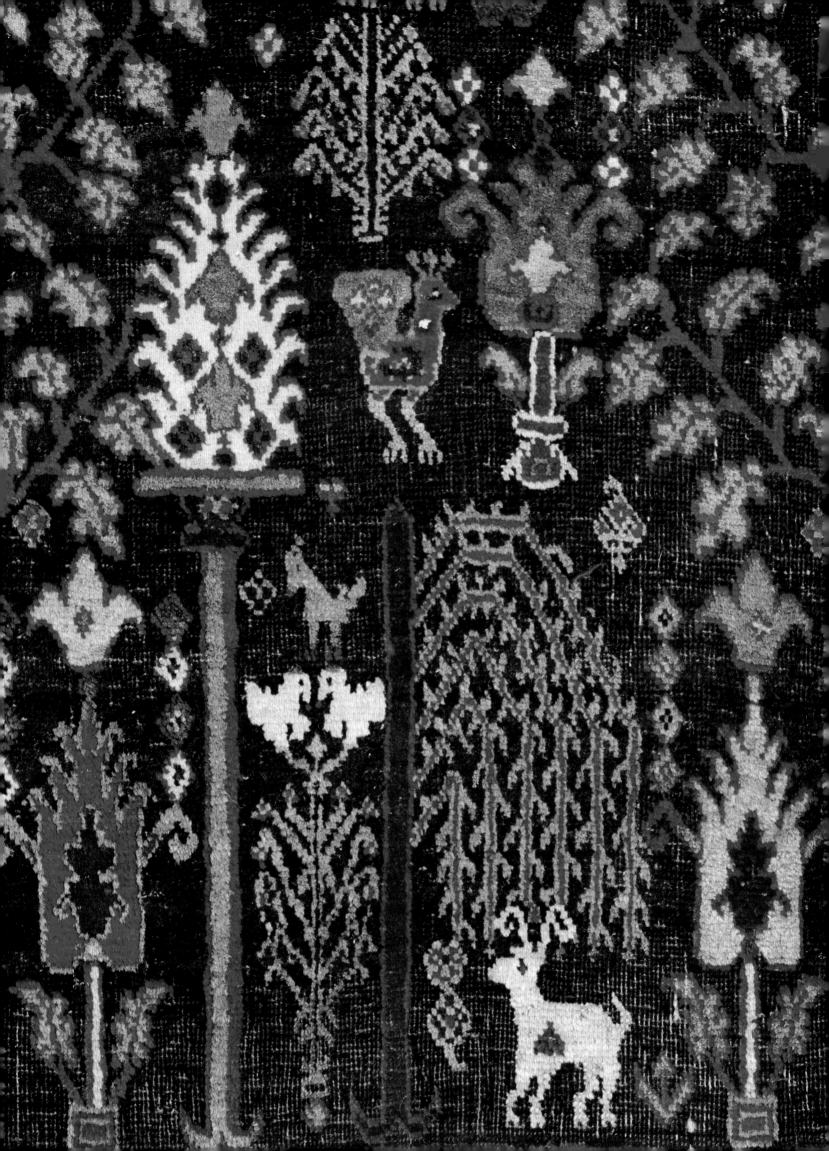

9.2 Kurdish mother and child. Like other Iranian nomads, traditionally Kurdish women have not worn veils.

9.3 Kurdish women and children in their rural encampment.

American and British bombing. The desperation of starving Kurdish villagers who escaped from Iraq following the war brought world attention to Kurdish needs and demands.

There has been considerable debate about the etymology of the name "Kurd." The founder of the Persian Sassanian dynasty, Ardeshir I, listed a king from "Kurdan" among his rivals in a third-century A.D. document.[1] More widespread use of the words "Kurd" and "Kurdistan" appear in documents of the seventh century. The pre-eminent student of Kurdish rugs, William Eagleton, summarizes ancient Kurdish roots in these terms: "Scholars who have investigated Kurdish origins have reached a variety of conclusions. They agree, however, that the Kurds, under whatever name, entered history as a mountain people occupying a part of northwest Iran from where they gradually moved south, north and west into Asia Minor and Iraq."[2]

Several Persian shahs moved Iranian Kurdish groups from their tribal heartland to northeastern Iran and also to Veramin, southeast of Tehran. The largest splinter group resides northwest of Meshed, in Khorasan Province. Kurdish work from that area is often labeled "Quchan" or "Kuchan," after a town of that name. Wilfried Stanzer's book on Kurdish weavings of Khorasan, *Kordi*, contains a rich sampling.[3]

The influence of invading groups over the past fifteen hundred years had a deeper impact on Kurds than on nomadic Lurs. The domination by Turkic overlords was more thorough, and ties with Persian urban culture were a more consistent fact of life than was the case with more isolated Lurs. Eventually, a certain amount of racial intermingling took place among all tribes in the Zagros, but especially in Kurdistan. Kurds in Turkey mixed with other people without losing their identity and are still viewed with a

9.4 Bright synthetic dyes had completely supplanted vegetable dyes by the 1950s. A Kurdish rug on the loom in 1978.

certain uneasiness by the government in Ankara. Calls for an independent Kurdistan are cheered by governments only if the rebellious Kurds live within someone else's borders.

Many tribes and innumerable clans make up the broader body of Kurdish peoples. With the exception of two pieces from the Jaff tribe, I do not attempt to specify sub-tribal origins. Eagleton remains the only writer to attribute patterns convincingly to a number of specific tribes and sub-tribes, including Iraqi and Turkish Kurds.

My primary effort here is much less ambitious, focusing once again on distinguishing rugs that contain traditional tribal designs from those based on urban patterns. The latter category includes rugs from the Kurdish towns of Bidjar and Senneh (renamed Sanandaj), where high standards continued throughout the nineteenth century. Commercial weaving workshops in Kurdistan date back at least several hundred years and probably much longer. Formal "garden" designs from Kurdish workshops have always been highly regarded by collectors of classical Persian carpets. These and other exquisite pieces paralleled workshop achievements in the Caucasus, another outlying region where urban Persian influences were strong.

In spite of the long-standing influence of professionally designed commercial patterns, Kurdish repertoires include a number of traditional tribal motifs which are independent of urban influences. Some include residual animal-head features. Close similarities to old Luri and Bakhtiyari nomadic motifs is a noteworthy feature of some of these designs. The similarities of folk patterns in rugs from Kurdistan and from the southern Caucasus are so striking that at times it is difficult to know if a certain rug should be labeled Kurdish or Kazak. The term Kurd-Kazak is sometimes heard. When applied accurately, it conveys a connection between Kurdish work in the southern Caucasus and Iran. Parallel comments can be made about many Kurdish rugs from Anatolia, which are often identified as Kurdish. In spite of the Turkish government's long-standing reluctance to recognize their substantial Kurdish constituency, dealers in Turkey commonly label Kurdish work correctly. However, the possibility that Kurds influenced an extremely broad range of traditional rug and kilim patterns in Anatolia is rarely, if ever, acknowledged. The diffusion of Kurdish people into both the Caucasus and Anatolia could well date to the first millenium B.C.

The resilience of the Kurdish people depends partly on the physical strength of its men and women, the theme of many local legends. The following narrative appeared in *Woman's Share in Primitive Culture* by Otis Mason, who made slow headway while traveling in rugged portions of Kurdistan late in the nineteenth century.

Soon we came to a place where the road was washed away, and we were obliged to go around. We saw a woman there with a loaded donkey which could not pass with its load. The woman took the load on her back and carried it over and led the donkey over. She also carried a load of her own weighing at least one hundred pounds, and she had a spindle in her hands. Thus she went spinning and singing over the rugged way which I had passed with tears . . . .

In 1978, I traveled in the comfort of a jeep to several Kurdish villages as part of a plan to renew the use of vegetable-dyed yarns among village weavers east of Hamadan. The photograph shown as Illustration 9.4 resulted from this visit. It provides the most graphic evidence of the need for such a project: a new Kurdish rug on the loom. Committees attempting to upgrade Kurdish dyeing and weaving in this locale included a team from the university in

9.5 A Kurdish nomadic couple. Folded weavings serve as saddles.

9.6 A weaver's home in Iranian Kurdistan.

9.7 A Kurdish villager in prayer, late nineteenth century.

Hamadan and a skilled dyer of yarns, Abbas Sahahi. Several government ministries favored this project which also enjoyed the support of former Empress Farah. Political events following 1978 derailed this enterprise, but a new, better-organized attempt is possible, given the current informed leadership in Iran. Without the help of government funding and central direction, weavers are unlikely to return to vegetable dyes for the simple reason that they prefer strong synthetic colors. Towns around Bidjar could be an ideal starting point for a project of this nature, since their rugs are widely known, and a revival of old patterns as well as traditional dyes would be well received in international markets.

Several Kurdish towns are situated on the top of hills (*tel*s) that grew up through the ages from the accumulated rubble of preceding villages, each built on the same site. To probe early Kurdish history, the inhabitants need only dig under the floors of their own homes. People living in these long-established Kurdish villages surrounded by fellow-Kurds, and eating their meals while sitting on Kurdish rugs, naturally feel that their spot is the center of the world and that in spite of all adversities, Kurdish culture will exist forever.

The Kurds

The piece shown below is an excellent example of a classic Kurdish tribal pattern from the Jaff tribe. A relationship between these repeating lozenges and Luri/Bakhtiyari animal-head medallions is apparent. Kurdish village and nomadic weavers deleted eyes and horns from these motifs, whereas some Lurs and Bakhtiyaris retained them.

The coloring of the bag front encompasses an unusually broad range of hues. Half-medallions at either side of the field, composed of concentric stripes, help frame the infinite-repeat pattern. Kurdish bag fronts of this design type were made in substantial numbers; rug sizes are less common. Note how effectively the ivory border frames the infinite-repeat field in the rug shown on the facing page.

9.8 Jaff Kurd bag front, 2ft 10in × 2ft 1in (86cm × 64cm); late nineteenth century.

9.9 Jaff Kurd, 4ft × 6ft 1in (122cm × 185cm); late nineteenth century.

The Kurds

The piece shown below is related to the two plates on the previous spread in its reliance on repeating shapes. Here, each shape is outlined by a contrasting color. The barber-pole border works as a framing device by introducing a repeating rhythmic element, contrasting with the field pattern. This barberpole border is aligned symmetrically on both sides so that the red and white stripes point in opposite directions. The weaver effectively tucked changes of direction into two corners of the border.

The handsome rug shown on the opposite page is less tribal in feeling than previous examples. The use of cotton warps suggests a village source. Both cotton and wool have been used for warps in Kurdish rugs since the final decades of the nineteenth century.

9.10 & 9.11 Kurd, 4ft 4in × 7ft 9in (132cm × 236cm), and detail; second half of nineteenth century.

9.12 Kurd, 4ft 1in × 5ft 7in (124cm × 170cm); late nineteenth century.

Bidjar has long been noted for the hard-wearing quality of its rugs; and many nineteenth-century examples have survived. The irregularities in the borders of the piece pictured on the right relate to its purpose and essential nature. It is a *wagireh*, or sample rug, intended to familiarize weavers with new designs. Numbers of surviving *wagireh* record the great variety of designs produced in and near Bidjar.

This piece includes many details that do not immediately catch the eye. Pairs of sheep or goats nibbling at willow trees are obvious in the upper field, but birds in each tree are nearly concealed. Human figures appear in pairs, with the heads of the men turned in a way that suggests that they are speaking to their companions.

Given the strong urban and commerical ingredients in Bidjar work, it can be debated whether these are truly Kurdish rugs. However, Bidjar is well inside Kurdish territory, and the great majority of weavers there were Kurds. The use of the symmetric knot establishes another link with traditional Kurdish tribal weaving.

The saddle cover pictured below is also from the Bidjar area. The lion figures are related to the formalized lions of urban weaving rather than to traditional nomadic versions.

9.13 Bidjar saddle cover, 3ft × 3ft 6in (91cm × 106cm); second half of nineteenth century.

161

9.14 Bidjar, 4ft 9in × 6ft 7in (145cm × 201cm); second half of nineteenth century.

The pendants extending from the central medallion in this large Bidjar carpet (opposite) terminate in bird heads which include eyes, a form related to the traditional Kurdish weaving shown below. This connection raises the question of how a figure associated with tribal weavings became part of a formal design.

The interchange of tribal and urban motifs throughout the centuries, although a two-way street, did not bear equal traffic in both directions. During periods of disarray or decline in cities, tribal design traditions remained relatively stable, particularly among several nomadic Iranian groups. However, periods of artistic renewal in cities brought forth fresh generations of exquisitely planned urban rugs and carpets. These may have included some tribal elements from time to time, but in general, professional carpet designers invented their own designs, based on current artistic forms in miniature painting, manuscript illuminations, and, to a lesser extent, architecture. As the high accomplishments of urban designers became more widely known, a heightened demand for rugs naturally focused on rugs in these styles. Rug merchants may have contributed to these trends, both as owners of workshops and in their roles as wholesalers and retailers. Until recent years, virtually all rug dealers in Iran favored delicately patterned rugs with high knot counts. Their tastes both influenced and reflected their clients' preferences.

As we noted in Chapter 6, village weavers, eager to participate in the growing rug markets, tended to copy designs that sold well. At the same time, much older, traditional motifs survived in outlying villages and among nomads. In larger towns such as Bidjar, fragments of older folk legacies tended to resurface and become part of hybrid urban/tribal patterns. This may explain the appearance of bird heads in such a formal design scheme.

9.15 Kurdish kilim pillow cover; late nineteenth century.

9.16 Bidjar, 7ft 1in × 12ft 10in (216cm × 391cm); second half of nineteenth century.

The Kurds

The Kurdish town of Senneh also produced workshop rugs of extremely high quality. Finely executed Senneh kilims are as famous as their pile-weave rugs. The piece shown on the facing page is one of the finest examples to appear on the market in recent decades.

The designer of the elaborately patterned Senneh rug shown below applied uncommon skill in arranging complex vegetal forms, mixed with several types of bird. This piece contains silk "rainbow warps," so-named because the color of the dyed silk warps varies across the width of the piece.

9.17 Senneh, 4ft 7in × 6ft 7in (140cm × 201cm); late nineteenth century.

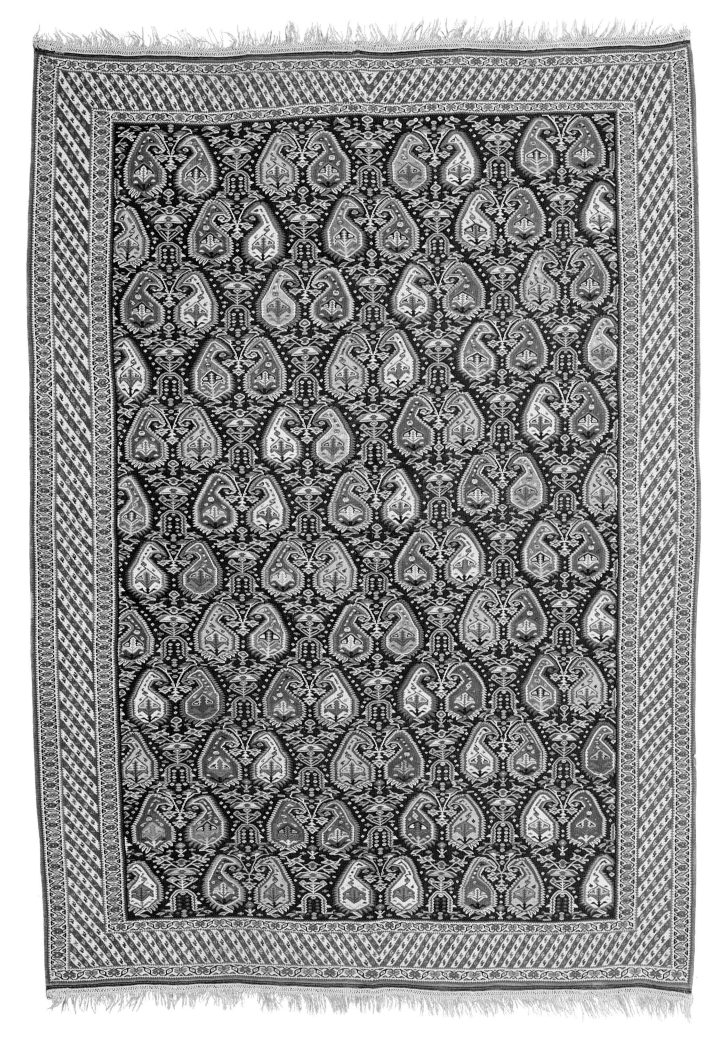

9.18 Senneh kilim, 3ft 7in × 5ft 10in (109cm × 178cm); second half of nineteenth century.

The Kurds

The substantial output of Kurdish weavings from the Quchan area in north-eastern Iran is represented by these two examples. Clues that identify the Quchan attribution are subtle, depending on coloring and technical features, as well as designs. The rug shown below has flatwoven end panels which are characteristic of a common type of Quchan Kurdish *soumak* work. Minor borders appear to be borrowed from northeast Persian Baluch weavings. Wefts are dyed an intense red, brighter than found in Kurdish rugs from Kurdistan, which feature both undyed brown and dyed red wefts. The repeating field designs are shared by virtually all tribal groups. They may be purely geometric ornaments that grew out of earlier versions of animal-head shapes.

The Quchan Kurdish kilim shown opposite must have been made by a mature weaver possessing the greatest technical expertise and aesthetic judgment. The spacing of motifs and sensitive color choices hardly suggest a beginner's effort.

Because of the large numbers of Kurdish rugs formerly available on the world's rug markets, weavings of all Kurdish regions have only recently assumed greater interest in the eyes of collectors. Choice examples are rapidly joining the ranks of other sought-after tribal weavings.

9.19 Quchan Kurd, 4ft 8in × 7ft 1in (142cm × 216cm); second half of nineteenth century.

9.20 & 9.21 Quchan Kurd kilim, 3ft 4in × 5ft 11in (102cm × 180cm), and detail; late nineteenth century.

The Qashqa'i Confederacy

10

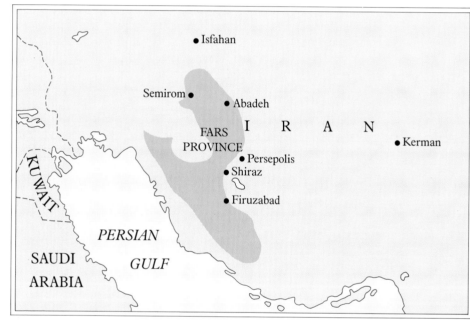

Qashqa'i territories in Fars Province, Iran.

The name of this confederacy is based on that of its ruling family. It is rarely correctly pronounced in the West. It has three syllables (Ghash-ga-ee), with emphasis on the final long "e" sound. Informally, members of the Qashqa'i family call themselves "Janikhani" or, alternatively, "the sons of Jani Khan," referring to the founder of the Qashqa'i Confederacy in the late 1700s. Descendants of Jani Khan remained actively at the head of the confederacy until the death of Nassr Khan in 1984. Writing in 1992, it is unclear whether there can be an effective Qashqa'i *khan* again.

Large numbers of rugs carrying the Qashqa'i label attest to the prominent role of weaving in the society of this once-powerful confederacy. For at least two hundred years, a steady stream of commercial Qashqa'i rugs, many with urban-influenced designs, have been a part of this tradition. However, substantial numbers of kilims, animal trappings, *gabbeh* rugs, and other pile rugs have been woven for domestic use, as wedding gifts, or as parts of dowries. The prominence of this tribal group has long been expressed through the medium of its weaving traditions.

10.1 Detail of Qashqa'i (Shekarlu) rug shown on page 175.

In 1991 the Qashqa'i numbered about 400,000, including both nomadic and settled members. Their roots can be traced in part to Turkic groups that moved into western Asia from the steppe region east of the Caspian Sea beginning in the ninth century. Substantial Indo-European admixtures among the Qashqa'i have softened Mongolian facial features which are conspicuous among Turkoman or Uzbek tribespeople. Specific tribes within the confederacy reached southern Iran by different routes and at different times from the fourteenth through the seventeenth centuries, mixing with various Indo-European and other nomadic and village peoples along the way. Evidence of Turkic origins survives in the Turkic dialect spoken by the great majority of Qashqa'i. However, some members speak Luri. Tribal schools initiated during the 1960s made many Qashqa'i children literate in Persian.

A careful examination of traditional tribal motifs in Qashqa'i rugs and kilims indicates that older folk designs entered from two primary sources. The more important influences came from neighboring native Iranians, some of whom were absorbed into the confederacy after some Qashqa'i people arrived in southern Iran. Many rug and kilim patterns are closely linked to local native Iranian traditions. A few designs support the conviction of members of the ruling family that their forbears lived in northwestern Iran or the Caucasus for several centuries before moving to southern Iran. This could well explain the similarity of finely executed Qashqa'i kilims to those produced in Shirvan, in the Caucasus – both dominated by horizontal bands of geometric patterns. Lurs in northern Fars did not weave such designs. Corresponding Qashqa'i and Caucasian peacock motifs were discussed briefly on page 42. There is some question whether any designs can be traced directly to the influence of Turkomans or other Turkic steppe peoples. (Some scholars arrive at an opposing conclusion on this point.)

One of the main challenges facing anyone who approaches Qashqa'i designs – as with the designs of many other tribes – is that of distinguishing traditional folk motifs from those inspired by urban rugs. Several types that fall into the traditional category have already been mentioned: older *gabbehs*, some kilims, varieties of tasseled animal trappings, *malband* (animal bands), and *jajim* (extremely thin flatweaves that lack borders on two sides). I saw all of these in use in villages and nomadic camps during the 1970s. During the early years of that decade, most of those offered for sale in the Bazaar Vakil in Shiraz had signs of indigenous use. By the late 1970s, all classes of tribal weavings were being produced for the flourishing tourist trade.

The impact of weaving workshops in Qashqa'i towns and villages has

10.2 Spinning is a constant activity in tribal homes. The Qashqa'i kilim in the background was woven entirely of undyed yarns, spun by women in a family who had settled on the outskirts of Shiraz.

been long-lasting and profound. Dealers and collectors have begun to understand the significance of this influence, which has had several effects on Qashqa'i work. High knot counts and consistently high wool quality became the rule, as we would expect in rugs competing with refined workshop production. The commercial success enjoyed by Qashqa'i weavers in workshop, village, and nomadic surroundings led to a weaving renaissance in southern Iran during the nineteenth century (perhaps starting in the eighteenth), laying the groundwork for similar developments within the neighboring Khamseh Confederacy. Attention to fineness of weave carried over into Qashqa'i flatweaves and saddlebags, both of which have enjoyed favorable markets in the West. The number of finely-woven Qashqa'i saddlebags (*khorjeen*) in the West since the early 1900s suggests that many were woven for export.

Few tribal groups in Asia matched Qashqa'i villagers and nomads in their responsiveness to new design ideas or their capacity for experimentation. As happened in Kurdistan, dealers played an essential role in the commercial side of Qashqa'i weaving practices, if only because they encouraged finely woven pieces with more curvilinear patterns. I knew dealers in the Bazaar Vakil whose travels included a circuit of Qashqa'i villages, where they bought new rugs and encouraged the weaving of certain designs. Workshop pieces from the town of Firuzabad were always on view in the bazaar, and competent weavers could readily copy them. Nor are carpets the only source of ideas: a western visitor in the mid-1970s saw a Qashqa'i woman copying a motif from an imported floor tile.[1] In this connection, Lois Beck, author of two important volumes, *The Qashqa'i of Iran* and *Nomad: a Year in the Life of a Qashqa'i Tribesman in Iran*, related to me the following incident:

While conducting anthropological research among the Qashqa'i in the 1970s, I carried a notebook which I had been bought in Yugoslavia. Its cover featured an Albanian gileem [kilim] design. One day I visited a Qashqa'i woman who was well-regarded as a weaver. We talked about a variety of subjects in a friendly way and I didn't take notes. However, at one point she said to me, "You'll want to write down what I'm going to tell you." I took out my notebook, wrote down her comments, and then put the notebook back in my bag. The notebook cover was exposed for a matter of seconds, and there was no indication that the woman paid any special attention to it. Much later, I visited a female cousin of this woman, another weaver. She had just finished a rug which had a peculiar and somewhat familiar design. I looked and then looked again. It was based on the motif on my notebook cover! When I asked her where she learned it she said that her cousin (the weaver who had momentarily seen my notebook) had made a rug based on the same design. It was an attractive pattern and so she wanted to try her hand at it.

Lois Beck told me that in 1977 she saw a Qashqa'i rug that copied a map of Iran that appeared in a children's school book. She spoke with Mohammad Bahmanbegi, who was instrumental in founding the tribal weaving school in Shiraz. When asked what designs were produced at the school, he said that they mostly used Kashkuli patterns and also designs from a sub-tribe called "Bolu." Since the early nineteenth century or earlier, several Kashkuli-controlled workshops in Firuzabad produced a steady stream of consistent styles, including mille-fleurs examples discussed on pages 92–94. By the early 1970s, the current generation of this design type employed cotton warps, a feature identifying recent examples. Earlier versions had wool or silk warps.

The sale of rugs made in workshops was organized by the workshop owners. Individual weavers or their husbands were free to take rugs directly into the bazaars in Shiraz or elsewhere to sell. A tribesman wearing a Qashqa'i hat and carrying a rug over his shoulder was a familiar sight in the bazaar. I saw numerous Qashqa'i women exercising their formidable bargaining skills while purchasing cloth, spices, or jewelry but rarely observed one in the process of selling her rug in the bazaar, a task regarded as men's work.

As we have noted, weaving was an important business for tens of thousands of Qashqa'i women and a substantial contribution to family economies. We would have to look to several Turkoman tribes, including the Tekkes and Salors, for a parallel situation. More than any other tribal weavers, Qashqa'i and Turkoman women endeavored to satisfy the market's preference for high knot counts and symmetrical patterns. The use of silk heightened the saleability of some examples. During this process, old traditional motifs either fell by the wayside or were dramatically stylized. Some Qashqa'i village rugs do not include a single traditional tribal motif. On the other hand, several nomadic Qashqa'i tribes located close to Luri districts continued to produce rugs with few urban influences.

Predictably, the commercial success of Qashqa'i rugs led to the application of the name "Qashqa'i" (or "Kashkai") to products from neighboring tribes. For decades, many finely woven or attractive rugs from southern Iran were automatically given this label by European and American dealers. Today, the growing body of literature on the rugs of southern Iran has reversed this old habit, along with the loose application of "Shiraz" to local weavings. Only a small percentage of Qashqa'i rugs were woven in Shiraz proper.[2]

The Qashqa'i provide a useful testing ground for the theory that Turkic groups brought rug designs and weaving techniques when they started entering western Asia during the ninth century.[3] If this were true, we could expect groups in Iran that contain numerous Turkic-speaking members to hold closely to old design legacies. If Turkic motif traditions were important identity-markers or carried other significant overtones it would seem likely that these tribes would have sustained their own design legacies with a measure of steadfastness. Correspondingly, they would have resisted native Iranian motifs that were external to Turkic heritage. However, as we have seen, both urban designs and those from native Iranian traditions were readily absorbed and adapted. *"Herati"* and other Qashqa'i designs that resemble patterns found in Central Asian Turkic rugs often prove to be tribalized urban forms that share a common urban origin.

Thanks to having purchased rugs in Shiraz for a number of years, I became acquainted with dealers there who were able to furnish more precise tribal and sub-tribal labels than are known in the West. Several Qashqa'i tribal names are interesting in themselves. The Farsimadan were predominantly a Turkic group; their name means "those-who-do-not-know-Farsi [Persian]." The Shishboluki tribal name combines the words for "six" and "district." The precise meaning of this combination in the group's history is unknown. Kashkuli Bozorg are the large or greater (*bozorg*) Kashkuli; Kashkuli Kuchek, the smaller. Darrehshuri means "salty valley." The Amaleh tribe has long been made up of retainers, servants, and others closely linked to the leading *il khan*'s family. Amaleh literally means "workers." One hapless sub-tribe bears the name Gallehzan ("robbers of flocks").

Some gypsies have traditionally lived among the Qashqa'i. They have adopted Qashqa'i dress, the Shiite Muslim faith, and other local customs and support themselves as musicians, tinkers, and makers of metal objects, including beating combs for weavers.

Most Qashqa'i weavers dyed their own colors. Although aniline reds and oranges are fairly common in late-nineteenth-century rugs from Kashkuli workshops, nomadic examples tended to be free of any synthetic colors until the 1950s. The Shishboluki tribe, especially, held to their traditions in this regard. During the 1950s the new synthetic "chrome" dyes became popular with weavers, who were still adjusting to them during my visits in

10.3 Qashqa'i kilim weaving, Fars Province, 1977.

10.4 Two young Qashqa'i weavers in their tent.

10.5 Larger Qashqa'i rugs are group projects calling on the skills of both older and younger weavers.

the 1970s. One weaver commented, "The old dyes are too expensive. Besides, the new ones make such happy colors." As a foreigner and outsider, who was I to tell tribal weavers what colors were attractive? But the market itself can make the point. At the time of writing, all-vegetable-dyed Qashqa'i rugs and kilims are selling at a premium in Shiraz. New efforts sponsored by the sculptor and author Parviz Tanavoli and the Zollanvari family, rug merchants centered in Shiraz, show that weavers are now willing to return to traditional dyes.

Political setbacks among the Qashqa'i since the 1950s may or may not prove to be permanent. One observer of Qashqa'i political developments quoted a Persian proverb: "The camel is dead," meaning, "It's finished." This may be true; paramount leaders have not been able to move freely in Fars from 1982 through the remainder of that decade, and into the early 1990s. However, some Janikhani families remain keenly interested in political affairs.

So far as Qashqa'i rugs are concerned, it is important to note that many Qashqa'i still live as shepherds and thus have access to wool of high quality. Rugs that fully warrant the name "Qashqa'i" may join the thousands of older weavings that merit our admiration and that stand above the shifting political fortunes of Iran's important tribal federations.

It remains to be seen whether the world's rug collectors will continue to favor floral, curvilinear Qashqa'i rugs over more traditional examples. In my opinion, this long-standing preference overlooks the most vigorous Qashqa'i work. The respective artistic strengths of both urban-inspired and traditional designs can be seen and appreciated in sharper relief as knowledge about tribal rugs increases. The sampling that follows favors atypical examples, most of which originated among Qashqa'i nomads.[4]

The Qashqa'i Confederacy

The style of ivory border seen in both these examples helps identify them as "Shekarlu," a weaving group first defined by dealers in Shiraz who were familiar with Qashqa'i products of the last century. "Shekarlu" no longer appears on lists of Qashqa'i sub-tribes. However, my emphasis on traditional tribal motifs makes Shekarlu rugs, which contain many of these, a logical point of departure for this section. Both pieces contain a variety of motifs suggesting extremely old tribal sources. Prominent designs in the piece shown on the right include lions, peacocks, animal-head medallions, and animal-head trees. Small human figures and two-headed animals are less prominent.

Warps in Shekarlu rugs are invariably ivory; wefts are dyed red-orange. Knotting densities vary significantly from piece to piece but are usually relatively low, less than ninety per square inch. In their motifs and weaves, they are among the most "tribal" of Qashqa'i rugs.

10.6 & 10.7 Qashqa'i (Shekarlu), 5ft × 8ft 3in (152cm × 251cm), and detail; last quarter of nineteenth century.

10.8 Qashqa'i (Shekarlu), 4ft 6in × 7ft 9in (137cm × 236cm); last quarter of nineteenth century.

Dramatically stylized peacocks in this rare Qashqa'i *gabbeh* include an especially interesting detail: animal heads sprouting from the birds' tails. This distinctive feature could be linked to styles of early zoomorphic art in which extra heads were attached somewhat randomly to animal or bird figures. (See detail below.) In any event, it is an extremely old rug design. Similar details can be seen in fourteenth- and fifteenth-century village rugs from Anatolia. Stylized creatures in the rug shown on page 273 have some hints of this feature.

The animal in the central panel must be a horse, given the saddle. Its human head may have resulted from a playful moment on the part of the weaver but could have communicated a specific meaning. Such questions in connection with one-of-a-kind rugs from the nineteenth century and earlier are extremely difficult to resolve.

This particular *gabbeh* is especially dense and heavy with only three or four weft threads between each row of knots. Pile length is relatively short – less than half-an-inch. Parviz Tanavoli, who has studied *gabbehs* intensively, concludes that most examples with such features were woven in the twentieth century.[5] However the rich texture and high quality of the wool in this piece, as well as its archaic motifs, strongly suggest a nineteenth-century origin.

The rug is tentatively attributed to the Shishboluki, a major tribe within the confederacy. Certain shades of yellow in the piece suggest this origin, and diagonal lines connecting shapes in the upper field are probably a carry-over from more formal Shishboluki rugs.

10.9 & 10.10 Qashqa'i (Shishboluki?), 5ft × 7ft 4in (152cm × 224cm), and detail; last quarter of nineteenth century.

The Qashqa'i Confederacy

Qashqa'i weavers have adapted traditional south Persian *gabbeh* and kilim designs to achieve a new, distinctive effect. The *gabbeh* shown below has the same dense construction as the previous example, with only three or four wefts between adjacent rows of knots; however, most Qashqa'i and Luri *gabbehs* have between four and twelve weft threads between rows of knots. This construction feature substantially reduced weaving time, as well as the weight of the fabric. One Qashqa'i tribesman to whom I spoke emphasized the factor of reduced weight and, therefore, portability in explaining the popularity of *gabbeh* rugs in all strata of Qashqa'i society.

Kilims of the type shown on the facing page were woven as hammock-like cradles. The best examples were subjected to minimal use and were probably woven by professional weavers hired by élite families. Small white threads in the outer right-hand border mark successive days of work. To my knowledge, organized workshops did not make this type of kilim, which nomads also produced in coarser weaves. Long tassels are a common feature of woven cradles. The weaver's careful planning in this case is revealed in small white squares at each corner of the field and in many other balanced details.

The unusual elegance of both of these weavings places them in a special class: pieces with obvious tribal roots, made outside workshops, for members of the tribe's élite. They also provide evidence of the extensive overlapping of kilim and *gabbeh* patterns.

10.11 & 10.12 Qashqa'i *gabbeh*, 4ft 1in × 8ft 8in (124cm × 264cm), and detail; early twentieth century.

10.13 Qashqa'i kilim cradle, 4ft 1in × 4ft 11in (124cm × 150cm); early twentieth century.

10.14 Detail, Qashqa'i horse cover; late nineteenth century.

The weaving of horse covers for prosperous members of the tribe continued among the Qashqa'i through at least the 1950s. However, one single development threatened to end this form of weaving: the arrival of the jeep in rural Iran. Morteza Ghashghai, the son of a Qashqa'i khan, told me of the day during the Second World War when a British Army colonel arrived at his family home in Abadeh in a jeep: *This was something new. My older brother and I exchanged glances as we looked at the vehicle. Neither of us had to express our thoughts aloud. Here was something much better than automobiles, which were suitable only for decent roads. A jeep could go anywhere, even up into the mountains.*

Aspects of Qashqa'i culture were permanently altered by this single invention. Jeeps and other four-wheel-drive vehicles began to replace the horse. With this development, the age-old need for horse covers and other trappings diminished.

The detail opposite is from another piece of this type. As in the complete piece pictured below, designs were achieved by extra weft-wrapped (*soumak*) threads. Some animal motifs in both examples suggest ancestral ties with the Caucasus.

10.15 Qashqa'i horse cover, 3ft 6in × 5ft (107cm × 152cm); late nineteenth century.

The Qashqa'i Confederacy

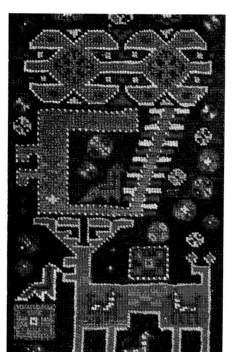

Deer and stylized peacock forms in the rug shown below are clearly related to the two previous pieces. Designs in the central vertical column with the ivory background include animal forms with three heads. This is to my knowledge the sole published example of this unusual form.

The motifs in the rug shown on the right have a strong tribal feeling. It may be nomadic work. The Qashqa'i label is tentative, given the fact that many of the same motifs appear in Luri rugs and bags. The factors of high quality, knotting density of 144 knots per square inch, and slightly depressed warps all support the Qashqa'i attribution.

10.16 & 10.17 Qashqa'i, 6ft 4in × 9ft 5in (193cm × 287cm), and detail; late nineteenth century.

10.18 Qashqa'i, 3ft 6in × 5ft 9in (105cm × 175cm); late nineteenth century.

Carefully designed kilims of the quality shown below may not be nomadic work. More sophisticated Quashq'i rugs represent workshop and village-centered cottage-industry weaving.

The diagonal motifs in the kilim are based on "S" forms, turned on their sides. By experimenting with a variety of colors and by emphasizing different lines and shapes, the weaver explored a number of possibilities based on a single design unit. The innermost border in this piece is found in many Bakhtiyari kilims. Only a weaver of exceptional creativity and technical mastery could make a piece such as this.

A careful study of the borders in the rug pictured opposite suggest that the weaver was not working from a cartoon, but had to struggle with the resolution of corners. She must have been working on her own loom, without direct supervision. Checkerboard ends are in pile. The ivory fringe is a common feature of Qashqa'i work.

10.19 Qashqa'i kilim, 4ft 11in × 6ft 3in (150cm × 190cm); late nineteenth century (E. Herrmann).

10.20 Qashqa'i rug, 3ft 10in × 4ft 11in (117cm × 190cm); late nineteenth century.

A number of Qashqa'i saddlebags in public and private collections are refined commercial weavings, rather than truly indigenous objects. By contrast, the pieces shown here and the horse cover shown on page 181 epitomize work that Qashqa'i nomads produced for themselves. These were easy to locate during my first trips to Shiraz and were never expensive. However, the best examples have become increasingly difficult to come by and are now avidly collected in Iran as well as in the West.

Jajim are thin flatweaves, used as covers and ground cloths. Their striped designs relate them to *malbands*. Two *malbands* are shown. The pile example (top) is especially rare. It shows no signs of daily use and may have been woven as a dowry object or perhaps a gift. The flat-woven *malband* (middle) was made by a card-weaving method and is finely patterned. The horse trapping (bottom) is a superb example of the same flat-woven technique.

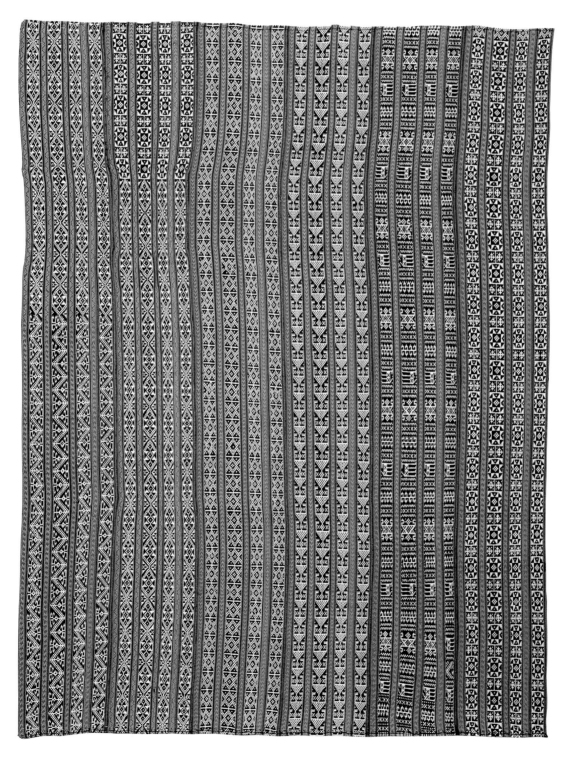

10.21 Qashqa'i *jajim*, 5ft 10in × 7ft 6in (180cm × 228cm); nineteenth century.

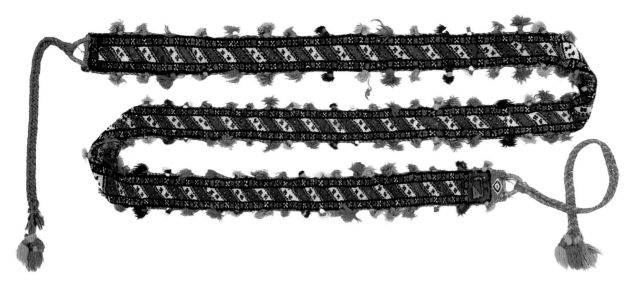

10.22 Qashqa'i pile *malband*; first quarter of twentieth century.

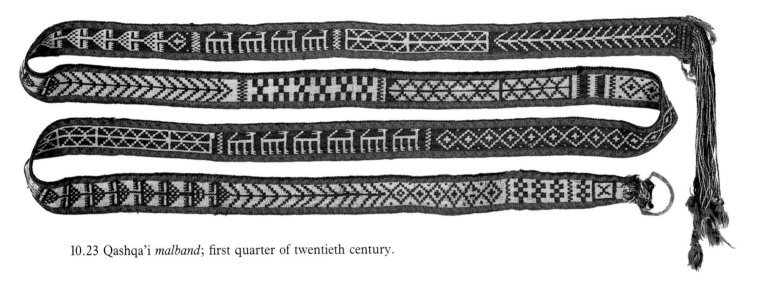

10.23 Qashqa'i *malband*; first quarter of twentieth century.

10.24 Qashqa'i horse trapping, 2in × 2ft 1in (5cm × 64cm); early twentieth century.

The Qashqa'i Confederacy

The piece shown here depicts a scene taken from a bas-relief at Persepolis. Work on this magnificent ceremonial city was begun in the sixth century B.C. and was still in progress when Alexander of Macedonia (356–323 B.C.) burned and looted it in 330 B.C. in the course of his Persian campaign. The remains of this site cannot help but impress those who visit it with the grandeur of early Persian civilization and the tragedy of its destruction.

This rug is a striking example of Qashqa'i workshop production, probably from a town controlled by Kashkuli khans. It successfully evokes the grandeur of Iran's ancient royal and religious traditions, in which *Ahuramazda*, the winged deity, reigns above the king, who, in turn, is held aloft by representatives of the nations who support him.

The impact of urban-style Qashqa'i weavings was discussed in the introduction to this chapter and in Chapter 6. Formal Qashqa'i pieces offer a mixture of tribal and urban patterns and demonstrate the improvisational talents of Qashqa'i weavers. In spite of their formality, these rugs reveal a tribal spirit that distinguishes them from perfectly symmetrical urban models. Whether one's tastes lean toward indigenous tribal motifs or toward refined pieces comparable to urban rugs, the large numbers of distinctive weavings produced by the Qashqa'i tribe include fine examples of both.

10.25 Bas-relief detail, Persepolis.

10.26 Qashqa'i (Kashkuli), 4ft 11in × 7ft 2in (150cm × 218cm); second half of nineteenth century.

The Khamseh Confederacy

11

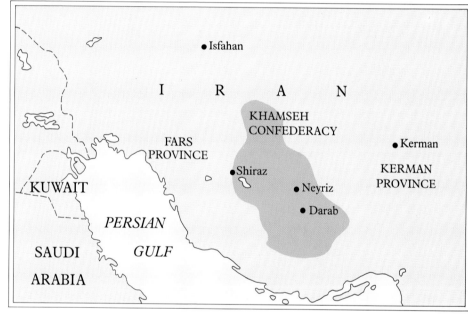

Map showing the territories of the Khamseh Confederacy.

The name "Khamseh" is derived from the Arabic word for "five," "*khams*," and means "the confederacy of five."

Tribes of the Khamseh Confederacy lived to the southeast of Qashqa'i territories in southern Iran. Their weavings include some of the most fascinating traditional tribal rug patterns, such as the "bird rugs" – of which this chapter offers some outstanding examples. Other patterns of both tribal and urban derivation make this group highly prized.

Early Khamseh Confederacy history involves the intrigues and interference by foreign governments which characterized south Persian political life during the nineteenth century. Over this period Qashqa'i khans resisted the Shah's influence in the region and fought his most active allies, the British. The Ghavams, a prominent commercial family in Shiraz, joined forces with the Shah and the British in a joint effort to challenge Qashqa'i power. Their primary strategy in this effort was the formation of a new tribal confederacy made up of five ethnically unrelated tribes. These tribes were: Arab, who were mostly of Arab ancestry, but with some Lurs; Baharlu and

11.1 Detail of Khamseh Confederacy rug shown on page 207.

Ainalu, both Turkic in background, as the "lu" ending would imply; Basseri (whom we shall examine in some detail); and Nafar, a small Turkic group, absorbed into the Basseri during the twentieth century. Because of the central role of the Arab tribe in the confederacy, other people in southern Iran tended to call the entire group "Arab," distinguishing them from Qashqa'i tribes, called "Turk" or "Tork."

Most of the Khamseh rugs that I showed in *Tribal Rugs of Southern Persia* were ascribed to precise groups within the confederacy, such as "Arab-Khamseh." I now prefer the more general "Khamseh" designation for the great majority of rugs from this group, although a few designs can be ascribed to specific component tribes. Some educated guesses can be made, based on information available in and near Shiraz. Cecil Edwards (*The Persian Carpet*) was the first authority to indicate the distinctive features of Khamseh work. He listed the five tribes and attributed specific designs to them. Some of Edwards' information has been supplanted by fresh material, building on his contributions to the study of south Persian rugs.[1] In registering corrections of my own and other people's work, I wish to emphasize the complexity of ethnic mixtures in southern Iran, especially in Khamseh territories. Labeling most examples simply "Khamseh" sufficiently distinguishes them from Qashqa'i work to the west and Afshar products to the east.

Forcing Arab, Turkic, Luri, and other native Iranian nomads into a single political unit was bound to fail in the long run. There was no cultural "glue" to bind them together. Beyond obtaining a supply of weapons, forming a confederacy gave very little to rank-and-file tribesmen that they did not already have. If anything, it piled even more burdens on people who were already preoccupied with their subsistence lifestyle. In the long run, several tribes were weakened as confederation forestalled these tribes merging with the neighboring Qashqa'i.

Few groups equal the Khamseh Confederacy in the great variety of motifs they produced and the insights a detailed examination of their weavings can provide. I find special interest in native Iranian patterns in Khamseh rugs, especially in "bird rugs." A related Luri example shown in Chapter 7 suggests that this pattern was shared with Lurs in and near Luristan. It may

11.2 Members of the Khamseh Confederacy Basseri tribe and their flock, during the autumn migration.

11.3 Basseri tents are pitched in patterns determined by tradition.

very well have come into Khamseh tribes through Luri or other native Iranian peoples.

Rugs of the Khamseh Confederacy include a rare instance in which a Persian pattern can be traced reliably to Central Asia. Pomegranate patterns, seen as repeating border motifs and as field designs (see page 210), probably originated in Yarkand, Khotan, or nearby towns in Chinese Central Asia, far from Khamseh territories. It is possible to suggest a chronology in which Turkic peoples carried pomegranate designs with them during their migrations from the east, possibly as early as the twelfth or thirteenth century, and brought them to southern Persia. Their descendants sustained these forms through succeeding centuries.

A thumbnail sketch of this region's tribal history may help to clarify the extremely complicated ethnological picture. Before the fourth millennium B.C., a small indigenous population lived in small settlements and possibly as nomads. The racial background of this original population is unknown. Indo-European groups began arriving possibly as early as the fourth millennium but certainly during the third and second millennia. Nomadism was undoubtedly practiced in southern Iran at this time. Tribal populations were presumably a mixture of "Indo-Iranians" (a major division within broader Indo-European peoples) and earlier indigenous stock. The Lurs and Leks represent such mixtures. Six centuries into the Christian era, Arab immigrants spread Islam throughout Iran and added a fresh ethnic ingredient. The custom of pile weaving was surely more deeply planted in Iran than in Arabia at the time of the Arab invasion, and it is doubtful that Arabs brought a significant body of rug designs with them.

The permanent settling of Turkic tribes in southern Iran was augmented by later Turkic immigrations, some of which occurred from staging-sites in the Caucasus and northwestern Iran, rather than directly from central Asian Turkic homelands. In any case, ethnic intrusions from several directions (Arabic and Turkic) are a fundamental aspect of the history of this region during the last two thousand years. The fact that several Khamseh sub-tribes continued to speak Luri well into the twentieth century implies that ethnic groups within the Khamseh Confederacy remained segregated to some extent. However, ethnic distinctions have assumed less importance as modern central governments subdued and restricted nomads throughout Iran. According to Fredrik Barth, who lived for seven months among the Basseri tribe in the 1950s, members of the ethnically mixed Basseri had an overriding common goal which transcended language, ethnic background, or earlier tribal affiliations: the wish to continue living as pastoral nomads.[2]

The survival of traditional political structures among the Basseri allows us a detailed look at this aspect of nomadic life. These structures allowed a total population of about 16,000 tribespeople, absorbed in day-to-day subsistence, to act as a unified, harmonious unit. The smallest political division among them was fittingly called "the tent." A single family occupied a tent, and five or six tents formed the next organizational level, the herding unit. This grouping was dictated by an aspect of nomadic economy which forced all but the wealthiest families to join with other families. A lone shepherd could oversee roughly four hundred animals at one time – far more than all but the most affluent families could afford. The solution was to combine smaller flocks from several families into a single large herd. The milking of animals, setting up and breaking camp, and many other activities proceeded more efficiently under this system.

Numerous herding units fused during migrations to form a "camp." For political and other purposes, each camp was led by a "whitebeard" (*riz safid*) or a "headman" (*kadkhuda*), appointed by the man who directed the tribe as a whole, the khan. The posts of *riz safid* and *kadkhuda* tended to be hereditary, and arranged marriages bonded families into consistent camp alliances. Larger units, called *oulad* and *tireh*, comprised a number of camps. (Qashqa'i tribes included a yet-larger unit, the *tayefeh*. Qashqa'i political structures differed in the names applied to certain subdivisions, but shared basic features with the Basseri.)

Khamseh Confederacy tribes were led by their khans. (Less important leaders were sometimes called *kalantar*.) Barth notes that *the position of the chief is one of great power and privilege. His tent must be large and his manner imperial; pettiness of any kind is inappropriate to him. His hospitality should be boundless – whereas the tribesmen tend to be parsimonious – and he should provide spectacular gifts of weapons, and stallions from his large herd of horses, to his more prominent subjects.*[3] The khan's primary responsibilities were to represent the tribe in dealings with the government, with landowners or other settled people, and to oversee tribal migrations. He also served as a court of last resort for disputes within the tribe. Barth notes that *"the chief's 'court' hearings are singularly lacking in formality. Any direction by the chief is an order, any definite statement is a decision, whether expressed as an aside in a conversation, or while washing his hands or taking his meal. Ceremony and pomp are only emphasized in 'foreign' relations* vis à vis *non-Basseri visitors, particularly other chiefs and prominent men of the sedentary society."*[4]

Chiefs spent most of their time in towns and cities, where they maintained fine homes. The Ghavan family, which performed the functions of an *il khan*, lived in one of Shiraz's most imposing residences. When the head of the Ghavan family or even someone of the rank of Hassan Ali Zarghami, the Basseri khan, visited nomads, they experienced a regal style of nomadism, quite different from the daily lives of their people. The size of a chief's tent had a bearing on the weaving of rugs, as it could house very large ones.

Fredrik Barth admired Basseri rugs; he reports that most pile weavings were used within the tribe and rarely were sold. This practice had changed by the time of my first visits to southern Iran in the early 1970s. New Basseri saddlebags, woven of synthetic-dyed yarns, were readily available in the Bazaar Vakil in Shiraz, undoubtedly woven to sell rather than for domestic use. As anyone visiting Shiraz at the time could readily confirm, there were ample quantities of old saddlebags for nomads to acquire for next to nothing

11.4 Basseri girls making cheese balls,
which will be preserved by drying.

from friends or relatives who had forsaken nomadism.

The official disbanding of the Khamseh Confederacy in 1956 resulted in
the appointment of an army colonel as administrative head of the Basseri
tribe. Whenever possible, however, Basseri tribespeople continued to deal
directly with their khan, Hassan Ali Zarghami, for whom they expressed
considerable respect. The colonel, nominally the head of the tribe, referred
some decisions to Chief Zarghami, and the tribe adapted to the new restrictions. Yet a fundamental change had occurred.

Having been jailed by the Shah several times, Zarghami had every
reason to hope for the eventual downfall of the Pahlavi government. But the
coming of this event in 1979 did not bring all of the anticipated benefits for
the Basseri tribe or for Zarghami personally. Used to speaking his mind with
few restraints and going his own way, he was unable to adapt to the realities
of the new Islamic order. Hassan Ali Zarghami died in 1982.

At the time of writing, conditions have stabilized in Iran, and the
government is in a position to be magnanimous toward remaining nomads
and their village-dwelling relatives. The last generation of effective khans has
left the scene, and nomadic tribes no longer pose any conceivable threat. We
can hope that weaving enterprises similar to those instituted in the DOBAG
project in Turkey (see page 23) will be developed among Iranian villagers
and nomads, including the remnants of Khamseh Confederacy tribes.

Formerly misidentified as "Qashqa'i" or sold under the generic label
"Shiraz," Khamseh rugs have now acquired a reputation of their own. A significant percentage of Khamseh rugs contain tribal motifs of the most traditional form, and some contain truly ancient motifs, including two-headed

animals, animal-trees, and stylized birds.

As we have observed, Khamseh and Luri "bird rugs" belong to a unique family of weavings which appear to be based on local tribal patterns, independent of any urban influences within the last millennium or more, and also independent of influences from invading tribes. As suggested in Chapter 4, they may represent a style of tribal art with mythological roots extending quite far into Iran's past. Efforts to interpret the original meaning and purpose of these bird forms may not be fruitless but are apt to be speculative. We have not yet constructed a solid foundation from which to study such subjects in detail. It is enough for the present to appreciate motifs such as this as a special and important body of evidence that folk populations in Asia held these motifs in sufficient esteem to repeat them in ever-new generations of objects.

Dealers in the Bazaar Vakil in Shiraz called this the *murgh* motif; "murgh" means either "chicken" or "bird" in Farsi. Many western dealers, favoring the first of the alternative translations, call these "chicken rugs." The sacred *si-murgh* ("thirty birds"), spoken of in the twelfth-century Persian masterpiece *The Conference of the Birds*, reflects the "bird" connotation. If the meaning of these motifs does relate to chickens, it is not as common barnyard fowl but in a more symbolic sense. Among Yezidis, images of roosters were sometimes substituted for peacocks.[5] Birds were a favorite symbol in both nomadic and urban art in ancient periods, not only in Iran but in all parts of Asia.

The three-medallion design shown here is a classic one found in many south Persian rugs. The relaxed and improvisational approach to the motifs strongly suggests a nomadic source. I have not attempted to ascribe this piece to a specific Khamseh tribe. What is important is the sheer attractiveness of the weaving itself and the remarkable design legacy it represents.

11.5 & 11.6 Khamseh Confederacy, 4ft 7in × 6ft 1in (140cm × 185cm), and detail; second half of nineteenth century.

The Khamseh Confederacy

More formal approaches to the bird pattern are exemplified by these two pieces. The three-medallion convention was disregarded in the infinite-repeat piece shown on the facing page. Many two-headed animal figures appear in the piece pictured below. Animals in the rug pictured opposite sprout small *boteh*-like motifs above their heads. These *boteh* are traditional tribal ornaments, free of urban influence. Their original meaning or purpose is obscure.

The question of whether pieces with such consistent patterns were made in a nomadic or a village environment is also unresolved. Nomad weavers were certainly capable of quite precise work, on a par with that of town weavers. However, resolute consistency in motifs in a tribal rug such as the piece pictured on page 199 is more in tune with town or village practices than with those prevailing in nomadic camps.

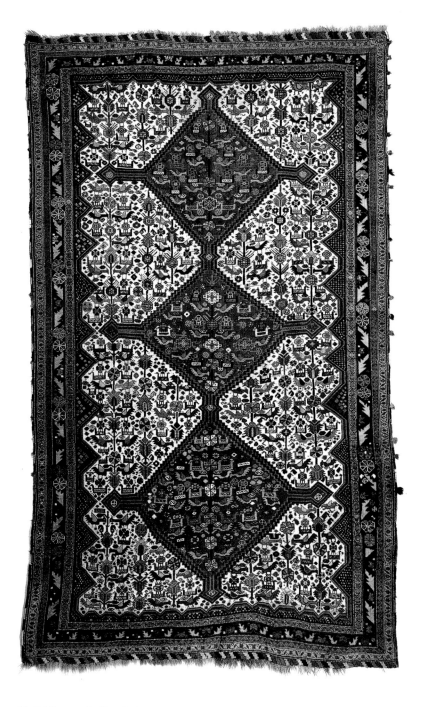

11.7 Khamseh Confederacy, 5ft 2in × 8ft 7in (157cm × 262cm); second half of nineteenth century.

11.8 Khamseh Confederacy, 4ft 1in × 6ft 3in (124cm × 190cm); second half of nineteenth century.

The Khamseh Confederacy

The weaver of the piece shown on the right achieved a harmonious secondary pattern within an infinite-repeat design. Strong diagonals have emerged by altering the direction of the birds and also through control of colors in the birds' bodies and wings. Wider borders in many Khamseh rugs suggest an urban influence, but the main border in this piece is a purely tribal one, shared by some Afshar rugs.

Another distinguished bird rug appears below, again in the classic three-medallion arrangement. Additional borders at both ends are a common feature of numerous rugs from southern Iran.

11.9 Khamseh Confederacy, 5ft 6in × 9ft (168cm × 274cm); mid-nineteenth century.

11.10 Khamseh Confederacy, 4ft 4in × 7ft 2in (127cm × 218cm); late nineteenth century.

The Khamseh Confederacy

Most Persian tribal rugs featuring lions originated among the Qashqa'i, Luri, or Bakhtiyari tribes. The unique example shown on the facing page is from a Khamseh group. The combination of birds and lions in the field and the careful placement of forms make it one of the rarest of Khamseh weavings. The major border is indigenous to southern Iran, but the minor borders were borrowed from Senneh weavings.

The four birds in the center of the rug are closely related to birds in the bag front below. The outer border in this bag front is related to a border discussed on page 110 in Chapter 7.

11.11 Khamseh Confederacy bag front, 2ft × 1ft 8in (64cm × 51cm); second half of nineteenth century.

11.12 Khamseh Confederacy, 4ft 1in × 6ft (124cm × 183cm); second half of nineteenth century.

Repeating stripes, often described in rug literature as "cane patterns", provide an effective background in some rugs. The example shown on the opposite page incorporates a surprising adaptation: cane patterns within the medallions. This adjustment accentuates a sense of spatial depth. Bands of *abrash* in the field heighten the impression that the smaller field motifs are floating in space.

The piece shown below is equally unusual. The careful selection and placement of colors have produced a remarkably balanced piece, suggesting the work of an experienced weaver.

11.13 Khamseh Confederacy, 4ft 1in × 6ft 2in (124cm × 188cm); last quarter of nineteenth century.

11.14 Khamseh Confederacy, 4ft 11in × 9ft 4in (150cm × 284cm); late nineteenth century.

The majority of rugs produced by any tribal group repeat and adapt familiar traditional designs. Rugs containing several original motifs, not seen in other weavings, are therefore of special interest. They illustrate improvisation skills on the part of an artist-weaver and suggest a desire to create a unique work of art, perhaps for a special occasion.

Near the bottom of this piece, above the lowest pair of trees, is a human form with outstretched arms. Pairs of smaller human figures are placed on the extreme right and left sides, just outside the ivory field panel. The curious manner in which motifs are scattered throughout the field is another indication that the rug had some special purpose.

The clusters of three *boteh*, joined together, are unfamiliar. Two five-sided forms in the lower field resemble primitive buildings with three shapes on top. Pointing devices at the bottom of these forms direct attention to an animal. The large birds with tree-like tails are also unusual.

11.15 & 11.16 Khamseh Confederacy, 4ft × 7ft 1in (104cm × 216cm), and detail; late nineteenth century.

The Khamseh Confederacy

This rug provides further evidence of the improvisational talents of Khamseh weavers. We see a number of familiar motifs, including animal-head trees, camels, lions, sideways "S" shapes, and animal-head medallions. The weaver added something of her own to these patterns: clusters of rectangular panels. The style of the major border is relatively common in Khamseh pile work (see page 205).

Technical factors help us to distinguish Khamseh from Qashqa'i rugs. Brown warp threads, seen here as fringe, typify Khamseh pieces; Qashqa'i warps are ivory colored, as a rule. Khamseh pile weavings are less stiff in handle than most Qashqa'i pieces, except for Shekarlu/Qashqa'i rugs, which are floppy. Knot counts are often lower in Khamseh work than in Qashqa'i pieces. Both symmetrical (Turkish) and asymmetrical (Persian) knots are found in Khamseh rugs. One technical detail that frequently differentiates Khamseh and Qashqa'i work is the factor of "depressed" versus regular knotting. As in urban rugs, Qashqa'i knots are usually depressed, revealing only one ridge on the back for each knot in rare cases of ninety per cent depression and two ridges of distinctly unequal size when depressed less than ninety per cent. A minor degree of depression is present in some Khamseh work. In many cases there is none.

This distinguishing technical feature applies to this piece. The presence of regular (as opposed to depressed) knotting, as well as a relatively loose weave, helps to confirm a Khamseh Confederacy source. The primary border pattern with its highly stylized animal figures also serves as an identifying feature.

11.17 & 11.18 Khamseh Confederacy, 3ft 4in × 6ft 8in (99cm × 203cm), and detail; late nineteenth century.

Repeating pomegranate motifs in the major border and field of the piece shown below indicate a likely relationship between Khamseh pomegranate designs and motifs in rugs from eastern Turkestan. If this analysis is correct, the precursors of these forms may have been more closely related to early urban rug designs in northwestern Chinese provinces than to nomadic traditions. Turkic nomads may have learned the pattern while living near Yarkand or another Central Asian town and then carried it to southern Persia.

The Khamseh rug on the right confirms the impact of more recent urban influences within this tribe. The so-called "mother-and-daughter *boteh*," in which a smaller *boteh* appears within a large one, is descended from Kashmiri shawl patterns. Similar designs were woven in several European textile centers, including the Scottish town of Paisley. The popularity of this pattern among customers in Britain and continental Europe contributed to a thriving export market for Persian rugs with the *boteh* design, and also for tribal interpretations of it.

Khamseh rugs include many other patterns which merit our careful study. Future writing on tribal rugs seems certain to grant more generous space to this important family of tribes.

11.19 Khamseh Confederacy, 5ft 3in × 10ft 7in
(160cm × 323cm); mid-nineteenth century.

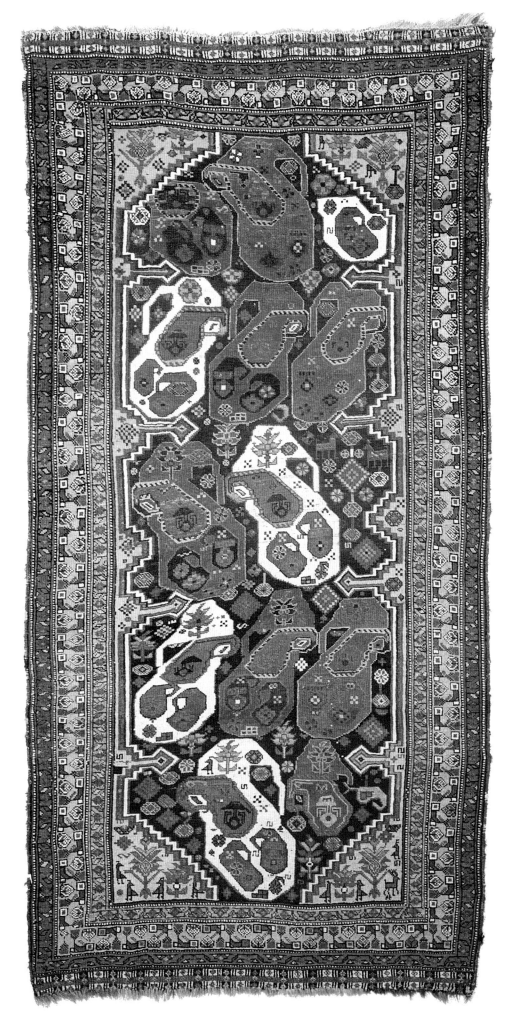

11.20 Khamseh Confederacy, 3ft × 5ft 10in (91cm × 178cm); late nineteenth century.

The Afshars

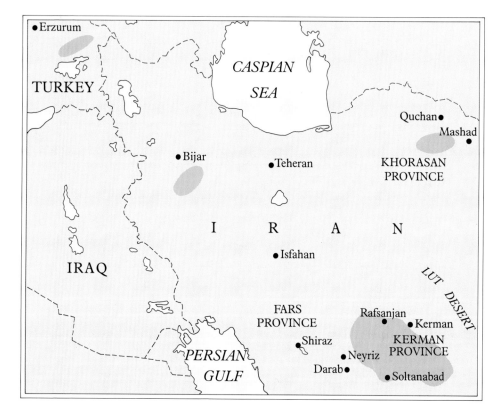

Map showing primary Afshar territories.

Afshars live primarily in southern Iran, east of Khamseh Confederacy territories. They are now largely sedentary; only a few thousand live as nomads. Parviz Tanavoli, one of the few modern writers with first-hand experience in this area, reports that contemporary migrating Afshars live in the depths of poverty. Conditions are somewhat less desperate in the dozen or so Afshar villages that remain, where a traditional Turkic dialect is still spoken. Most descendants of this tribe have mixed extensively with Persian people in hundreds of villages which dot the spacious territory south of the city of Kerman.

The original contingent of Afshars was moved to this region in the sixteenth century by Shah Tahmasp, the second monarch of the Safavid dynasty (1502–1736). No other dynasty of Persian history left such a wealth of achievements in art, painting, metalwork and weaving as did the Safavid.

12.1 Detail of Afshar rug shown on page 225.

The Afshars

12.2 An Afshar village in the autumn. Animal dung is stacked for use as fuel through the winter.

The first of the line, Shah Ismail, had been installed as a ruler partly with the help of Afshars and other Turkic-speaking tribes in northwestern Persia. This accomplishment behind them, these Turkic groups fell to quarreling among themselves, with competing chiefs vying for local power. Shah Ismail had been able to hold these conflicts in check by persuasion and personal authority. Predictably, the old dissensions erupted with fresh fervor after Ismail's death. Ismail's heir, Tahmasp, solved the problem by identifying the most recalcitrant group, the Afshars, and forcing a large number of them to move from the troubled area to the southern part of the country. Subsequent shahs moved other Afshar groups to the same region. As a consequence, a large body of weavings from southern Iran bear the label "Afshar." As Parviz Tanavoli and others have noted,[1] clusters of Afshars continued living elsewhere in Iran and in eastern Turkey. A few of their descendants can be found near Mashad, as well as in the region near Bidjar, and in other areas.

Native Iranian nomads, including Lurs, had long resided in Kerman Province,[2] a region encompassing both lowlands and mountains, suitable for seasonally migratory shepherds. Aside from their traditional Turkic dialect, the Afshars' customs offered few hints of their origins. Like Qashqa'i tribes, they absorbed some long-established Iranian peoples, a process suggested by several designs showing clear ties with Luri patterns. They were also absorbed by native groups and became indistinguishable from them. The list of tribes that lived in this area is very long.[3] Tanavoli told me that some residents of Afshar ancestry he had met in one village know only a few Turkic words and preserve only vestiges of their prior Afshar identity. A century ago, when many Afshar rugs were woven, the situation was undoubtedly different. One surviving rug motif points to an earlier era of Afshar history, when they were a Turkoman group. Examples are shown on pages 216 and 217.

Whereas other south Persian tribes borrowed carpet designs from various distant urban workshops, Afshars were strongly influenced by those of a relatively nearby center, Kerman. The rugs shown on pages 222 and 223 exemplify the tribalization of Kerman motifs – in this case a vase form. Related patterns appeared in Kerman carpets for several centuries.

In his book *The Persian Carpet*, Cecil Edwards recorded a nomadic Afshar population of 40,000 in the early 1940s. Annual rug production at that time totaled 25,000 pieces. These figures suggest that, on average, each woman in the tribe wove more than one rug each year. As Edwards noted, this is an impossibly high figure, given that large numbers of women did not weave at all. He found the answer to this enigma in numerous villages populated by ethnic Persians, rather than Afshars, in which men as well as women wove, producing rugs resembling true Afshar work in both design and structure.[4]

12.3 Among nomads, the weaving of rugs, bags and tenting material is accomplished entirely by women. This Afshar woman used a basic horizontal loom to make a highly practical fabric.

Corroboration of Edwards' observation comes from Anthony Smith, author of *Blind White Fish in Persia*,[5] which recorded Smith's experiences in the Afshar district while studying man-made underground irrigation streams. His description of village workshop methods accords with those in Kerman, Kashan, and other cities.

Behind the carpet sit those who are making it, usually women and children but sometimes men. . . . The women make the knots amazingly quickly, the children take a little longer. The pattern is called by someone sitting in between the carpets who sings it to them in a strange, chanting voice. His words are repeated by one of the four who are following him; four because the two sides of the carpet are symmetrical and there are two carpets. During this chanting only the knots which mark the end of a colour are filled in, the remainder being completed when he has ceased. . . . A weaver can make 8,000 knots in one day.[6]

12.4 Although horizontal looms are the rule among Afshar nomads, upright looms are common in villages where Afshar-like weavings are produced. Here a group of girls work on a room-sized piece.

The task of identifying true nomadic Afshar work is complicated by the fact that related designs were woven in Persian-controlled villages as well as in those controlled by Afshars and by other tribal groups. Consequently, the accuracy and appropriateness of the Afshar label is sometimes debated.[7] As is true of the term "Kazak," universal recognition militates in favor of keeping it. However, also like "Kazak," "Afshar" needs to be viewed as a generic label, subject to future revision as detailed information accumulates about specific patterns and who wove them. Gradually, exact town names may become associated with particular styles. Throughout the 1980s, I spoke many times with an Iranian dealer in New York's wholesale market who gave the impression of knowing town or village names for every Afshar piece that he had in stock. I was unable to confirm his data independently but assume that such levels of detailed information still survive in Sirjan, Rafsanjan, and other towns where rugs with the Afshar label are marketed.[8]

Nomadic Afshar pieces include salt bags, saddlebags, horse covers, *soumak* rugs, and an assortment of small tribal woven objects. Pieces for domestic use sometimes reveal urban influences but with qualities of verve and individuality that would never appear in items made in an urban workshop. Woolen warps and wefts predominated in Afshar work until cotton was adopted in the 1930s. Wool warps are almost invariably ivory in color, though minor admixtures of darker wool or goat hair are occasionally found. Foundation and pile wools tend to be soft, and the spin is not as tight as in Qashqa'i rugs. Wefts are commonly dyed red, sometimes with a decidedly orange tinge which distinguishes them from Khamseh work.[9] Another helpful identifying feature relates to size. Formats of approximately 4 by 5 feet were used so frequently that one can often correctly guess "Afshar" simply by seeing these familiar proportions.

Written material about Afshar rugs is modest but growing. Few tribes reveal such imaginative diversity of patterns, ranging from traditional medallions with Turkoman overtones to Kerman-inspired vase patterns. The various streams of influences in Afshar work account for the periodic discovery of yet another unidentified pattern, often tied to design sources far removed from the tribe's nomadic origins.

The Afshars

Tribal rug designs can occasionally provide important clues to a tribe's history and earlier relationships to other groups. To unlock this material requires a careful examination of many motifs from a given tribe. Historically, the Afshars were a Turkoman tribe which became separated from other Turkoman groups. The six-sided shapes that fill the field of the Afshar *soumak* pictured below share similarities with guls from the Chodor Turkoman tribe. Chodor guls are always spaced more openly, but at the tops and bottoms of many Chodor guls are pairs of highly stylized birds in precisely the same position occupied by birds in these repeating six-sided Afshar forms. At present, however, we are unable to determine whether related nineteenth-century Chodor guls changed more than these Afshar forms, or vice versa.

Early Iranian tribal influences may account for the repeating animal-head medallions in the piece shown on the right. Secondary designs within the medallions closely resemble motifs frequently seen in Luri work. The presence of Lurs in Kerman Province was reported by the American anthropologist Henry Field.

12.5 & 12.6 Afshar soumak, *5ft 3in × 6ft 4in (160cm × 193cm), and detail; late nineteenth century.*

12.7 Afshar, 5ft × 8ft 9in (152cm × 267cm); late nineteenth century.

The Afshars

It is difficult to know whether the few "bird rugs" from this tribe represent the influence of neighboring Khamseh Confederacy weavers or of long-standing local Luri traditions. The rug shown on the facing page contains two-headed animals, unusual trees, and riders standing on horses. The horses have feedbags in place, as well as saddles, and under them, blankets or horse covers. The piece shown below has more in common with Khamseh examples, without completely mimicking any known pattern. Both rugs reflect native Iranian tribal influences, rather than motifs drawn from the Afshars' Turkic roots. The presence of characteristic ivory warps and red-orange wefts confirms that they were made in the Afshar region.

12.8 Afshar, 4ft 1in × 5ft 8in (124cm × 173cm); late nineteenth century.

12.9 Afshar, 6ft 2in × 11ft (188cm × 335cm); last quarter of nineteenth century.

The Afshars

The Afshar bag shown below contains an extremely old motif related to the "phoenix and dragon" allegory, popular from Europe to China. Sometime in the past, probably in the eighteenth or early nineteenth century, the single bird image was revised to form a mirror-image, and the dragon component was dropped from most rugs. Variations of the motif seen on the right are sometimes used in an infinite repeat design.

The origin of this motif is obscure; I have heard no explanation suggesting how it came to be adopted by Afshar weavers. It could have been carried with displaced Afshars when they moved to southern Iran in the sixteenth century. During earlier centuries, phoenix and dragon symbols appeared in rugs from China, Anatolia, and Persia.

12.10 Afshar saddlebag, 1ft × 1ft 9in (30cm × 53cm); late nineteenth century.

12.11 Afshar rug, 4ft 1in × 5ft 10in (180cm × 129cm); late nineteenth century.

The Afshars

The pieces shown below and on the right represent an important category of Afshar weavings: those that copy urban patterns, particularly from the nearby city of Kerman. It is apparent that Kerman vase designs took hold in the Afshar district and gradually became tribalized. These two rugs represent early and late stages of this process. The piece shown below is so urban in appearance that the name "Afshar" can be applied only with qualifications. It was probably made in a workshop. This conclusion is not based solely on the complexity and delicacy of the forms, for nomadic weavers were also capable of extreme refinement in their work. It is, rather, the overall structure of the design, including the use of portions of the central medallion as corner spandrels, that indicates its urban provenance.

The drawing of vases in the blue-field example opposite remains rather formal, though these are not entirely identical from one end of the piece to the other. The central medallion, corner spandrels, and major border pattern are all more relaxed. Field motifs include purely tribal details.

12.12 Afshar area, 5ft 5in × 5ft 10in (165cm × 177cm); nineteenth century (E. Herrmann).

12.13 Afshar area, 4ft 11in × 6ft 4in (150cm × 193cm); late nineteenth century.

The Afshars

Repeating vases in the rug pictured below strongly suggest an urban-inspired pattern; however, many improvised elements hint that this was a cottage-industry product created by a single weaver, rather than a thoroughly planned workshop rug. The style of the main border is rather common in Afshar work and is unique to this tribe. The warps in this piece are machine-spun cotton. Although cotton was not widely used in the Afshar area until the 1930s, its availability throughout Asia since the 1860s made it possible for village weavers in many areas to abandon the use of woolen warps. Rugs with wool warps and wefts are favored by collectors, as these factors help mark the age and authenticity of a given piece. The disadvantage of woolen foundations is that they contribute to ripples and other irregularities in the weave.

I am unable to state whether the field pattern in the piece shown on the facing page is a traditional one or was acquired from an outside source. Warps are wool, and the piece could represent either nomadic or village work. Multicolored edge wrappings in blocks of distinct colors are a common feature of both Afshar and Khamseh Confederacy rugs.

12.14 Afshar area, 4ft 2in × 5ft 8in (127cm × 178cm); late nineteenth century.

12.15 Afshar, 3ft 11in × 4ft 10in (119cm × 147cm); late nineteenth century.

The Baluch and Related Tribes

13

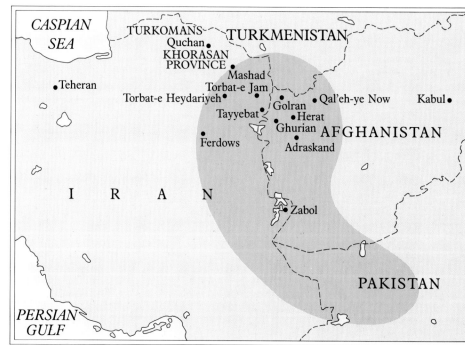

Map of the regions within which Baluchi villagers and nomads live and migrate.

The Baluch tribes are unevenly distributed among three nations: Iran, Afghanistan, and Pakistan. Few pile rugs come from Baluchistan proper, which is situated mostly in Pakistan territory, where flatweaves predominate. Early chronicles place Baluch peoples farther to the west, in Iran, south of the Caspian, and later in Kerman Province. Baluchis who wove pile rugs during recent centuries lived primarily in western Afghanistan and across the Iranian border in Khorasan Province, the largest administrative sector in northeastern Iran. Large numbers of Baluch and Baluch-style rugs are still made in Afghanistan, mainly in nomadic camps. Most examples from the Iranian side originate in villages.

Dealers and collectors have come to realize that many rugs commonly

13.1 Detail of Iranian Baluch rug shown on page 247.

called "Baluch" are, in a strict sense, incorrectly labeled. A number of examples come from neighboring peoples, including the Timuri and Aimaq tribes. However, the search for precise names, even when successful, does not always promote a clear comprehension of this subject. An interest in design origins prompts me to take a simpler approach to Baluch and Baluch-inspired rugs, focusing on motifs rather than on the names of villages and sub-tribes. We again find that some motifs are entirely tribal in their roots, while others are derived from urban patterns. Of particular interest is evidence that centuries of improvisation have not eradicated close ties between old Baluch forms and those of other native Iranian tribes. This is to be expected, given the early history of the Baluch in Iran. Colonel Jeff Boucher has included a succinct history of the Baluch in *Baluchi Woven Treasures*.[1]

According to some writers, Baluch weavers depended heavily on Turkoman or other Turkic traditions for their oldest tribal motifs. Partly for this reason, Baluch and Turkoman weavings were sometimes discussed jointly. This proposed relationship, whether stated or implied, was an adjunct of the "Turkic origins" theory. Such a viewpoint relegated Baluch rugs to the status of a derivative group. The possibility that Turkic weavers learned extremely old motifs from Indo-Iranian tribes was not considered[2] – nor were similarities between traditional Baluch forms and other native Iranian work. The fact that a few recent Baluch designs are indeed copies of relatively recent Turkoman patterns may have confused matters. These copies, usually featuring Tekke or Salor-style guls, are readily recognized and need not be a complicating factor. The patterns were adopted by Baluch and Kurdish weavers in northeastern Iran after widespread market recognition made pile rugs resembling Tekke- and Salor-style rugs saleable.

Siawosch Azadi's *Carpets in the Baluch Tradition* recorded elements of their history, including a reference to the Persian poet Ferdowsi, published in the eleventh century.[3] According to a legend adapted by Ferdowsi, the Baluch tribe was in Iran as early as the sixth century. Other historical and legendary references, as well as the Indo-Iranian dialect spoken by Baluch people, place them entirely in Iran during earlier phases of their history.

While it is true that a few Baluch designs leaned heavily on Turkoman models, a greater number of older Baluch patterns reveal relationships with motifs found in the work of other Iranian tribes, particularly the Lurs, Bakhtiyaris, and Kurds. For example, animal-head shapes in some Baluch rugs and kilims have blocks of colors containing eyes (page 236), just as many Luri and Bakhtiyari weavings do. There are other shared motifs, including animal-head trees and repeating "S" borders (page 234) common in Baluch rugs. Such ties with native Iranian weavings from the Zagros are not surprising given the Iranian origins of the Baluch, who continue to speak an Indo-Iranian language. Also, like other native Iranian tribes, they tend to live in tents, rather than in felt-covered yurts. Barring overwhelming influences from neighboring cultures, it is not surprising that such a group sustained traditional motifs from their Iranian homeland.

The fact that Baluch design repertoires connect this tribe, with its Iranian heritage has value in any effort to clarify and test broader theories of design origins. By comparing motifs from a variety of Iranian tribes with those of Turkic-speaking tribes, it becomes apparent that an old assumption in rug studies – that is, the primacy of Turkic motif traditions – was incorrect. The Baluch are particularly significant in this regard. Even when they lived close to Turkomans, they produced weaves that sustained many motifs related to native Iranian patterns, as well as other patterns which are purely "Baluch."

The analysis of Baluch motifs and their relationship to forms employed by other native Iranian tribes has its limits. It does not apply to at least three types of Baluch motifs: those borrowed from urban rugs; those that copy

13.2 Early twentieth-century Baluch chiefs pose for a Western photographer.

13.3 A Baluchi nomadic encampment.

Turkoman guls and other readily-marketable Turkoman patterns; and those that developed locally in past centuries and have a uniquely Baluch flavor. Examples of all of these appear in this chapter.

Baluch and Baluch-style rugs are among the easiest to identify. Colors tend to be dark, making them difficult to reproduce accurately in print. The best examples often have elaborate and lengthy kilim ends. Multiple edge-wrappings (selvedges) of densely-spun goat hair are common. Examples convincingly dated earlier than the mid-nineteenth century are rare, probably because their soft wool and loose knotting made them relatively fragile. Another factor was the sheer quantity of Baluch rugs on the market, which caused purchasers to regard them less highly and to treat them carelessly. With few exceptions, those in good condition were woven in the late nineteenth or the twentieth century.

Many Baluch rugs from eastern Iran reveal obvious urban influences, especially *Herati* and *mina-khani* patterns, found in both rugs and saddlebags. Baluch prayer rugs include an Islamic element, the prayer-arch.[4] "Head-and-shoulder"-style *mihrabs* are seen more frequently in Baluch rugs than in work from any other tribe.[5]

I am uncertain whether families of nomads I encountered in the course of my first trip to Afghanistan in 1973 were true Baluch or from another group with similar customs. In one camp I found a Baluch-style rug being woven; in another, a woman was hand-spinning cotton from a drop spindle. (See illustration 13.5.) Considering that machine-spun cotton has been universally available since the 1870s, to discover someone hand-spinning cotton in the 1970s was something of an anachronism.

Rug weaving remains a vital source of income for many thousands of Baluch living in nomadic camps, towns, and villages. Few tribes continue

13.4 A Baluchi mother and child.

13.5 A nomadic weaver spinning cotton in 1973. In line with Afghan standards of modesty, a photograph was permitted only on condition that the woman's face not be included.

subsistence nomadism to the extent still found in western Afghanistan. Important benefits could result if the United Nations or another international organization were to fund a project to reintroduce vegetable-dyed yarns to weavers in this area, including Baluch, Timuri, and Aimaq districts, whose rugs have lost their appeal in contemporary markets because of their synthetic dyes. It is not too late to reverse this process of decline. Beginning such a project in Afghanistan would be a logical step, given the need to rebuild the economy after the devastating war. Apart from current problems with synthetic dyes, qualities of authenticity, or "tribalness," have survived in the current work of nomadic and village weavers in this region.

The Baluch and Related Tribes

Early Baluch weavers presumably learned the peacock pattern centuries ago when the tribe lived close to other native Iranian groups. Central Asian tribes do not weave this design, but Kurds and other Iranian tribes do. Removed by migration from the bulk of native Iranian tribal traditions, the Baluchis gradually developed a unique version of the peacock pattern. It is found in both rugs and nomadic bags.

Motifs carried from one geographical region to another can sometimes augment our knowledge of earlier tribal movements in the same way that language studies do. We have already observed the viewpoint that some folk images served the functions of writing for pre-literate societies. This principle, although generally sound, requires considerable care in its application. Many simple designs, such as crosses, zigzags, and other forms based on horizontal, vertical, and diagonal lines, may look alike from one region to another, yet have no historical ties.

The ceaseless movement of peoples and their cross-influences had a myriad influences on weaving and rug designs and are therefore a vital aspect of our study. Yet easy generalizations are all but impossible. Precise and clearly articulated motifs such as repeating peacocks offer a secure point of departure – one that relates the oldest Baluch design forms to native Iranian traditions.

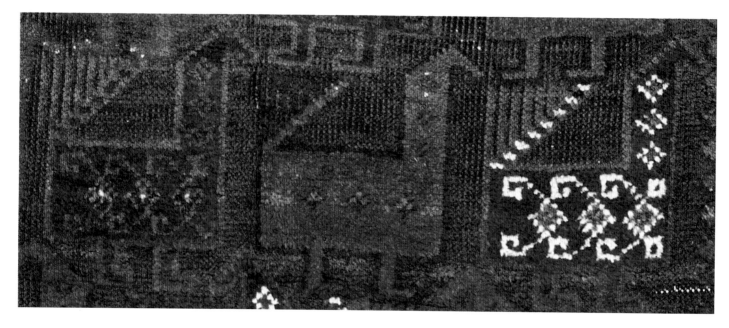

13.6 & 13.7 Baluch, 3ft 11in × 6ft 6in (122cm × 193cm), and detail; early twentieth century.

Both of these Baluch pile textiles feature the confronting-bird theme, a pattern that was probably known to Baluch weavers for a long period. One possible etymology of the name "Baluch" points to "cockscomb" or "cock," suggesting a totem-like meaning for either the Baluch bird motif or possibly the peacock design.

Note the complex animal-head trees in the main borders of both the saddle cover and the rug. "S" figures appear in end borders on the opposite page. Silk threads were used to good effect in flatwoven portions of both the rug and the saddle piece. Many Baluch weavers incorporated bright bits of silk into their work, including salt bags and trappings.

13.8 Iranian Baluch saddle cover, 2ft 5in × 2ft 7in (76cm × 80cm); early twentieth century (E. Herrmann).

13.9 Iranian Baluch, 2ft 4in × 4ft 5in (73cm × 135cm); early twentieth century.

The Baluch and Related Tribes

13.10 Highly stylized animal figures in four corners of the Baluchi medallion, below.

13.11 More naturalistic animals are shown on the edge of the field.

Some Baluch weavings contain eight-sided shapes which initially give the impression of being totally abstract. On closer examination, these forms reveal their uniquely Baluch character. The bag front pictured below is of particular interest since it appears to contain both explicit and stylized animal figures. Illustration 13.10 depicts a figure which appears in each corner of the central octagon. Although the stylization is extreme, a bird or animal appears to be suggested. Illustration 13.13 features another animal motif, one which is grouped around the periphery of the octagon. Again, the stylization is extreme. Illustration 13.11 pictures explicit animal figures that are also found in the weaving.

The rug shown on the facing page features eight-sided forms which convey the impression of sharing close ties with Turkoman guls. On closer examination, this assumption seems unfounded. The repeating asymmetrical motifs that make up the octagon have parts that suggest a head and a tail. Whether this pattern represents a local adaptation made in recent centuries or a zoomorphic motif with a much longer history cannot be known. Repeating animal-head shapes with blocks of knots suggesting eyes extend from a vertical pattern between the pairs of octagons.

13.12 Baluch bag front, 2ft × 2ft 2in (61cm × 66cm); early twentieth century.

13.13 Geometric components in motifs in the bag front are composed of extremely stylized bird or animal figures.

13.14 Greatly stylized forms, when repeated, make up medallion shapes in the Baluch rug, right.

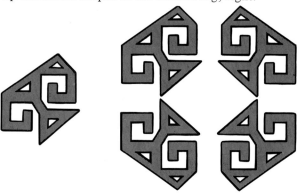

13.15 Baluch, 3ft 3in × 5ft 8in (99cm × 173cm); late nineteenth century.

The Baluch and Related Tribes

The primary motifs in the piece shown opposite were formerly considered direct descendants of eight-sided Turkoman guls. The illustrations below offer an alternative possibility. Drawings suggest a hypothetical chain of modifications that could have led from animal-head-based designs to the eight-sided Baluch shapes. A second Baluch rug with more complex versions of the same pattern is also shown below.

The formation of some Turkoman guls, including Tekke guls, may represent a combination of tribalized urban forms and old tribal ornaments, such as these traditional Baluch motifs.

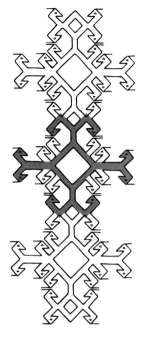

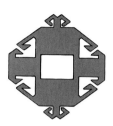

13.16 Baluchi motifs with animal heads.

13.17 Baluch area, 2ft 9in × 4ft 3in (84cm × 130cm); late nineteenth century.

13.18 Baluch area, late nineteenth century.

The Baluch and Related Tribes

Repeating animal-head medallions are centered in tile-like patterns in the Baluch cushion cover shown below. Tall animal-head trees flank the central field panel. On close examination, the meander border proves to be made up of "S" shapes. All of these details suggest affinities with native Iranian work.

The piece pictured opposite is from the Mushwani tribe, a sub-tribe in western Afghanistan. Coloring in many twentieth-century Mushwani rugs is quite dark, without lighter tones. This older example reflects a more colorful era of Mushwani products. The field motifs invariably feature concentric medallions with rounded projecting shapes. The relationship of these medallions to animal-head medallions in Kurdish rugs from northeastern Iran infers contacts between the Mushwani and Kurds.

13.19 & 13.20 Baluch *balisht* (cushion cover), 1ft 11in × 3ft 7in (58cm × 109cm), and detail; late nineteenth century.

13.21 Baluch (Mushwani), 3ft 6in × 6ft 3in (107cm × 190cm); late nineteenth century.

The Baluch and Related Tribes

These two pieces represent work of the Timuri tribe, whose ethnological roots are something of a mystery. They are not Baluch *per se*, but live near Baluch tribes, with whom they share a number of motifs. The kilim pictured below contains several stylized ancestral tribal forms, including motifs based on animal heads, swastikas, and "S" shapes. Few Timuri weavings compete aesthetically with these examples, which remain firmly in the Baluch tradition.

13.22 & 23 Timuri, 4ft 8in × 9ft 6in (143cm × 290cm), and detail; second half of nineteenth century.

13.24 Timuri, 5ft 3in × 8ft 6in (160cm × 259cm); second half of nineteenth century.

The Baluch and Related Tribes

This classic Baluch prayer rug is among the most attractive examples of its type. The hands on either side of the rectangular prayer arch (*mihrab*) suggest the prayer ritual itself. During the ritual, a Muslim places his hands on the prayer rug during phases of the prescribed sequence. For some Muslims, hand images pictured in paintings, brass work, and tapestries represent a design called *panj-tan*, symbolizing five key figures in the early history of the Shiite faith. Although most Baluch are of the Sunni branch of Islam, the picturing of hands in a prayer rug surely carries an Islamic reference.

Foreign travelers in Afghanistan are often fascinated by the sight of men engaged in their prayers, which can be practiced either on a piece of cloth or on a rug. A prayer rug *per se* is not obligatory but certainly desirable. During a visit in 1974, I returned from Mazar-i-Sharif to Kabul late one day with my driver. The car I had rented was packed with weavings, perhaps one-sixth of which were prayer rugs. Pieces over one hundred years old were still to be found in northern Afghanistan at that time. I expected the driver to take an armful of rugs and begin helping me, but he took only one piece and disappeared. Five minutes later, sweating from moving rugs, I went to look for him. He was off to one side in the hotel lobby, saying his evening prayers on the prayer rug he had chosen.

The repeating field motifs in this piece suggest highly stylized leaves of a style peculiar to Baluch rugs. It may be related to an old border pattern, as suggested by Illustration 13.25.

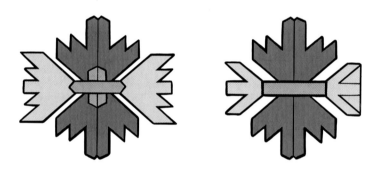

13.25 Transitional drawings suggest a possible origin of common Baluch leaf designs.

13.26 Baluch, 3ft 3in × 5ft 3in (97cm × 162cm); second half of nineteenth century.

As previously indicated, I personally favor the oldest tribal designs, which represent ties with an earlier phase of tribal history. However, outstanding examples confirm the contribution that urban patterns made to Baluch repertoires. The piece shown on the opposite page exemplifies this connection.[3]

The rug shown below is one of the finest examples of Baluch weavings inspired by Turkoman patterns.

We can look forward to continuing re-evaluations of the place and importance of Baluch work in the spectrum of tribal rugs. This group may well belong among the handful of tribes whose work is relatively ancient in inspiration. Baluch, as well as that labeled "in the Baluch tradition," forms one of the richest veins of under-appreciated tribal wearing.

13.27 Iranian Baluch, 4ft 5in × 8ft 7in (135cm × 262cm); late nineteenth century (E. Herrmann).

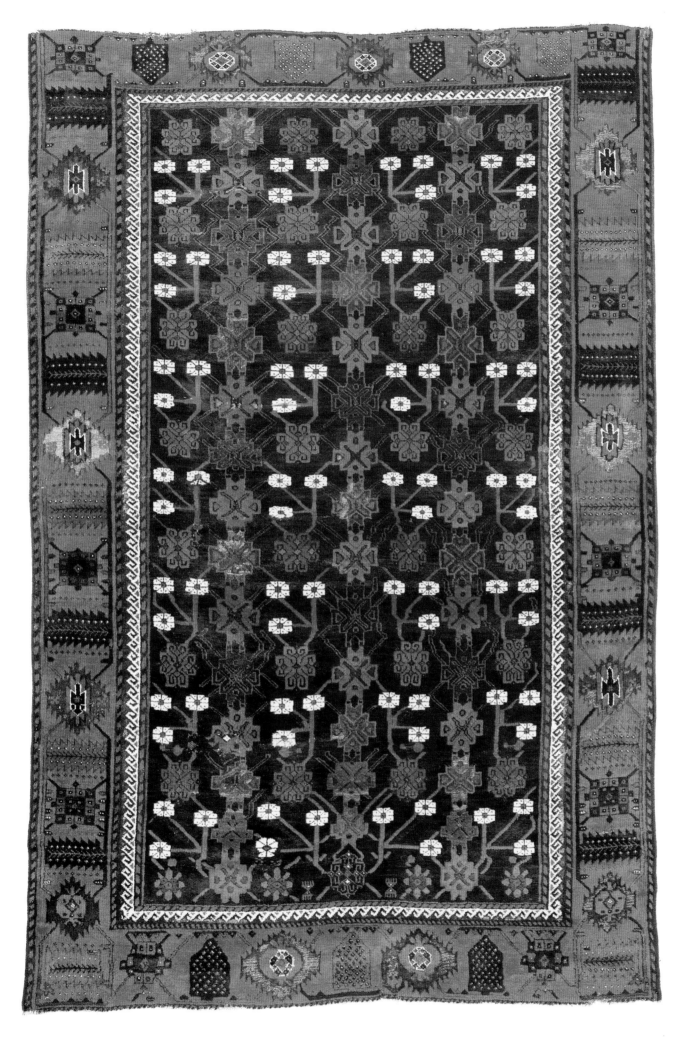

13.28 Iranian Baluch, 5ft 4in × 7ft 10in (162cm × 240cm); nineteenth century (E. Herrmann).

The Shahsavan Confederacy

14

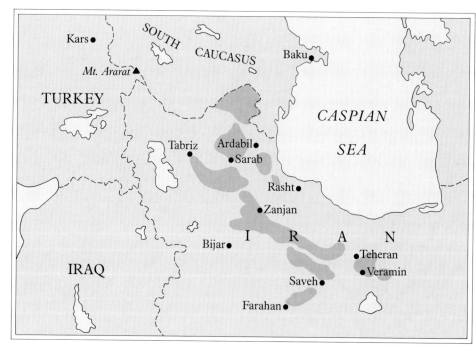

Map of Shahsavan territories.

The Shahsavan tribes live primarily south and west of the Caspian Sea, both in and near the northwestern Iranian province of Azerbaijan. Like the Qash-qa'i, the Shahsavan are a confederation of ethnically mixed tribes, rather than a homogeneous people. Constituent members of the confederacy have traditionally identified themselves by their specific tribal names but acknowledge a common Shahsavan heritage. Although this confederation is Turkish-speaking, intermarriage with native Iranian and Anatolian people has influenced the physical appearance of individuals in this group. Kurds lived in northwestern Iran and the southern Caucasus, and some Kurdish factions were absorbed by the Shahsavan.[1] The decision to adopt Turkish as the official Shahsavan language corresponded to both political needs and common usage in northwestern Iran. Even Kurds, long a major population in the area

14.1 Detail of Shahsavan flatweave shown on page 257.

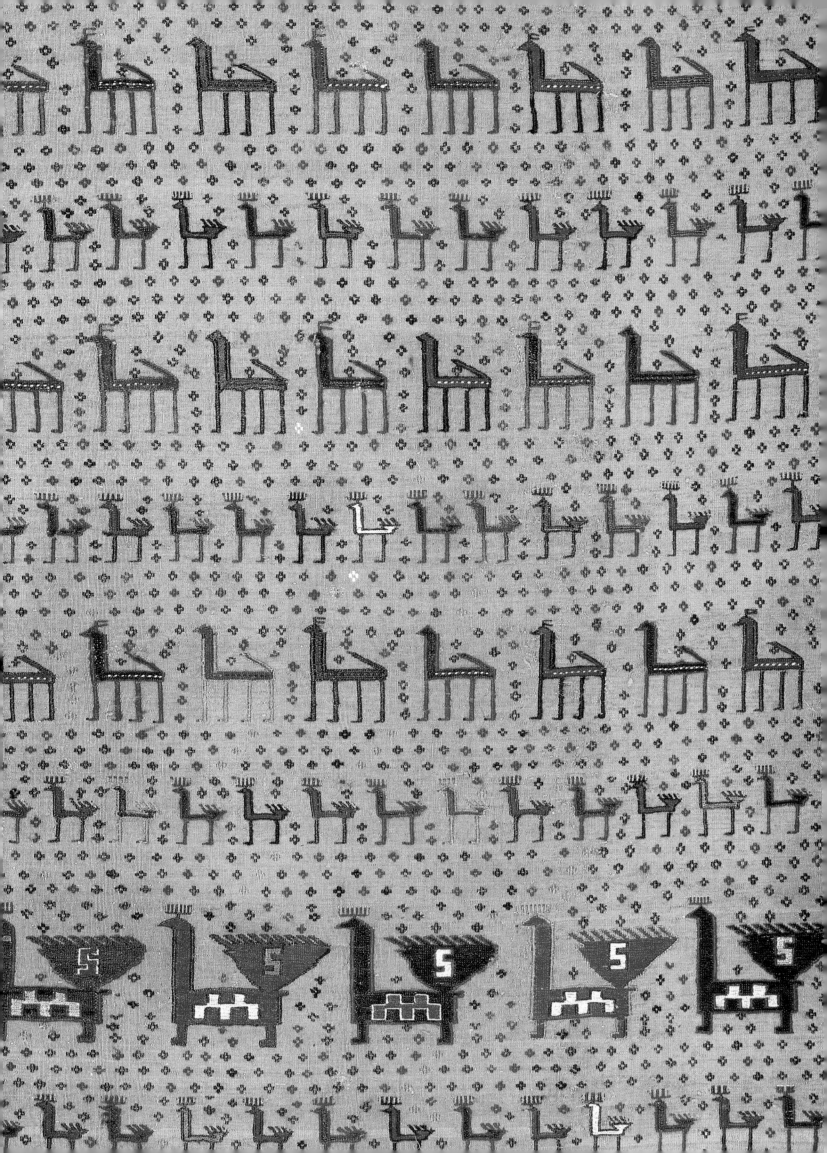

north of Tabriz, spoke Turkish by the time the Safavid dynasty was founded.

As was true of the Afshars, Persian dynastic struggles played a major role in Shahsavan history, even accounting for their name. "Shahsavan" means "those who love the Shah." Shah Abbas (1589–1629) made use of an old rallying cry of Safavid monarchs, "Shahi Savani!" to inspire the formation of a new army loyal only to him. Before this action the Persian nation was at the mercy of an independent army, loyal solely to itself. Contemporary histories report that ten thousand men responded to Shah Abbas' call on the first day. This devoted and effective force restored stability and drove Uzbeks and other unfriendly groups out of Persia.

Some of the tribespeople who responded to the "Shahi Savani" cry remained as a more-or-less cohesive tribal body in northwestern Iran and were officially granted the name "Shahsavan" by Shah Abbas. They settled on extensive land grants south of the Caucasus Mountains, and adopted a style of nomadism that had been prevalent in this region since the arrival of the first Turkic peoples, if not earlier. Their yurt dwellings, called *alachiq*, are based on a wooden framework, which is covered by large pieces of felt. Most Iranian nomads make use of black goat-hair tents, but the cooler weather of northern Iran makes the *alachiq* a more practical dwelling. Kilims commonly adorn the floors, and decorative woven bands stabilize the wooden substructure. Accounts by Herodotus and other early travelers indicate that dwellings of a similar type have been in use since the first millenium B.C.

The fact that some tribes within the confederacy had already lived in this locale before the Shahsavan were formed is of some importance in seeking the origin of Shahsavan woven designs. Their richly varied geometric patterns reveal no urban design influences. Consequently, the question arises: are Shahsavan designs related primarily to Turkoman motifs from the

14.2 Although always decorative, the great majority of Shahsavan textiles are practical objects, used on horses, camels and donkeys.

14.3 A Shahsavan weaver at work on a vertical loom.

steppes or to west Asian traditions shared by Iranian and Anatolian weavers? The latter include Kurds, whose presence in neighboring areas in Iran, Turkey, and the Caucasus may have contributed significantly to design histories in those areas. Further work is needed to clarify this subject, but strong correspondences with Kurdish motifs suggest that native Kurdish elements may have had a major impact on later Shahsavan repertoires. Similarities with traditional Caucasian designs is also a factor. Several Shahsavan patterns are so similar to folk weavings from the southern Caucasus that dealers formerly lumped many Shahsavan flatweaves, particularly *soumaks*, under the name "Caucasian."[2]

I saw many examples of Shahsavan *soumak* work for sale in Ardebil during several visits, beginning in 1970. At the time, most dealers there catered to western tastes and terminologies by calling them "Kaffcaus" (Caucasian). The name "Shahsavan" was all but unknown in the West. Walking through the bazaar of Ardebil, I wondered at the time how so many "Caucasian" weavings could be smuggled through such a tightly guarded Soviet border. Barbed-wire fences on land and boat patrols on the Caspian Sea reduced unauthorized travel from the Soviet side to a bare minimum. If any smuggling occurred in this region, the quantity must have been insignificant. An unexpected answer to the mystery of all these "Caucasian" weavings for sale came during the late 1970s and throughout the 1980s, first in commentary by Jenny Housego in an exhibition catalogue entitled *Yörük*, and later in *HALI* articles. These so-called "Caucasian" pieces, we learned, were made in Iran by northwest Persian nomads, the Shahsavan.

At present, there are still few fixed standards for describing characteristic features of Shahsavan knotted rugs.[3] The numerous *soumak* weavings are more completely documented. Bedding bags (*mafrash*) constitute one of

4.4 Shahsavan *alachiq* (yurts) are supported by a wooden sub-structure. This nomadic family was preparing to attach felt pieces to cover their winter home.

the most plentiful types of Shahsavan weavings, and many excellent examples were still on the market during the early 1990s. These cloth boxes, roughly resembling the Luri/Bakhtiyari example shown on page 112, were used to hold clothing, blankets, and kilims. The remarkable variety of motifs decorating *mafrash* suggests a highly developed design sense on the part of Shahsavan weavers. According to Tanavoli, some motifs could be traced to specific sub-tribes until recent decades, when commercial influences led to stylistic mixtures.

Tanavoli's comments on the history of this tribe reveal more than the usual burden of calamities and atrocities at the hands of central governments. A critical turning point came in the early nineteenth century, when important pastures in the Caucasus, long under Persian control, were lost to czarist Russia. Attempts to reassert Shahsavan rights in the Caucasus led to extraordinary retaliations, culminating in a Russian policy of extermination. The Qajar Persian dynasty failed to intervene on the Shahsavan tribe's behalf. Commenting on this era of Shahsavan history, Tanavoli describes one of the most painful moments in nineteenth-century Iranian tribal history.

During the tribe's autumnal migration to its winter quarters, the Russians intercepted them. They stripped them of their belongings and redistributed all their wordly goods in the presence of an official representative of the Iranian government. In addition to their animals, their tents, their felts, and even their clothing were confiscated. The precise date of this event is unknown to the Shahsavan alive today, but many a proverb has been composed about the period, and that year is recorded as a milestone in their history. All events were said to have occurred either before or after "the year of distribution."[4]

In spite of this setback, the Shahsavan gradually recovered, rebuilding their flocks and accumulating collections of woven goods. During the late 1930s, they were greeted by the same disaster that awaited all of Iran's nomads: Reza Shah's forced-settlement period. Losses of human and animal life were severe. After Reza Shah abdicated in 1941, most Shahsavan returned to their migratory life. Today, several groups migrate seasonally, living in villages most of the year and taking up nomadic life during the summer, with their felt-covered *alachiq* and their weavings.

Unfortunately, favorable tribal rug markets during the 1970s and 1980s led members of this tribe to sell their collections of superb indigenous nomadic weavings. Many fine examples appeared in the markets of Tabriz, Teheran, and London in the late 1980s. Since then, contemporary copies of old Shahsavan pieces, woven from naturally dyed threads removed from old flatweaves, have appeared. Distinguishing these contemporary copies from authentic Shahsavan articles will add to the challenges awaiting future students of this important confederacy of tribes.

The Shahsavan Confederacy

As we have noted, Shahsavan designs appear unrelated to commercial urban rug styles. All Shahsavan motifs can therefore be viewed as purely tribal patterns. Although neighboring Azerbaijan villagers in Shahsavan territories were employed in workshops, there is no evidence that this practice reached local tribespeople until quite recently.

Prior to the publication of writings by Jenny Housego and Parviz Tanavoli, the piece shown below would have been labeled "Caucasian." We are now on secure ground in applying the Shahsavan label to this bag front, and to the brocaded horse cover shown on the facing page. Both pieces include two-headed animals, but of different styles. These motifs were probably a part of local design repertoires well before formation of the Shahsavan Confederacy in the seventeenth century.

14.5 Shahsavan bag front, 1ft 8in × 1ft 8in (50cm × 50cm); late nineteenth century.

14.6 Shahsavan horse cover, 5ft 2in × 6ft (158cm × 183cm); early twentieth century.

The Shahsavan Confederacy

The popular theme of animal motifs is prominent in these Shahsavan flat-weaves. Note the entire border of animals in the bag front below. In the piece shown at right, peacocks with "S" shapes in their tails serve as an effective counterpoint to small repeating animals.

A set of field motifs in the bag front is expanded in Illustration 14.8, below a form taken from a Luri rug shown on page 128. These drawings provide additional evidence of the manner in which animal-head patterns become radically stylized, acquiring a geometric appearance.

14.7 Shahsavan bag front, 2ft × 1ft 10in (61cm × 56cm); fourth quarter of nineteenth century.

14.8 The Luri motif, top, appears to be the forerunner of more stylized Shahsavan forms, below.

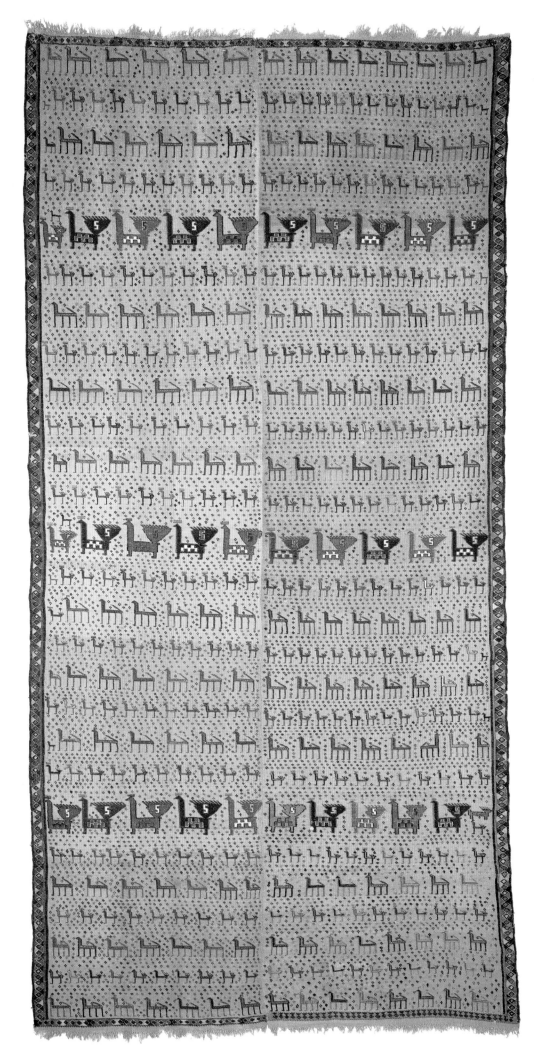

14.9 Shahsavan flatweave, 6ft 1in × 12ft 4in (185cm × 375cm); nineteenth century (E. Herrmann).

The small *soumak* weaving shown below is noteworthy for an uncommon feature: every motif in the piece could be multiplied to form infinitely repeating patterns. This is most apparent in the three field panels, all of which function as tiny windows through which we see patterns that repeat in every direction. Interlocking positive and negative designs in the upper and lower panels contribute to this effect. Such complicated interplays of geometric shapes are one of the primary contributions of tribal and village women to Asian art.

Field designs in the pile rug shown opposite display a simple yet fascinating infinite-repeat arrangement based on a common border pattern. The "bird-head" basis of this pattern has long been recognized.

Structural features of Shahsavan pile weavings differ little from many south Caucasian rugs. Knots are of the symmetrical type. There are two shoots of wool weft, usually dyed pinkish to red, but sometimes (as in this case) undyed. Wool is often quite soft, giving a flexible handle.

14.10 Shahsavan bag, 1ft 7in × 2ft (48cm × 61cm); second half of nineteenth century.

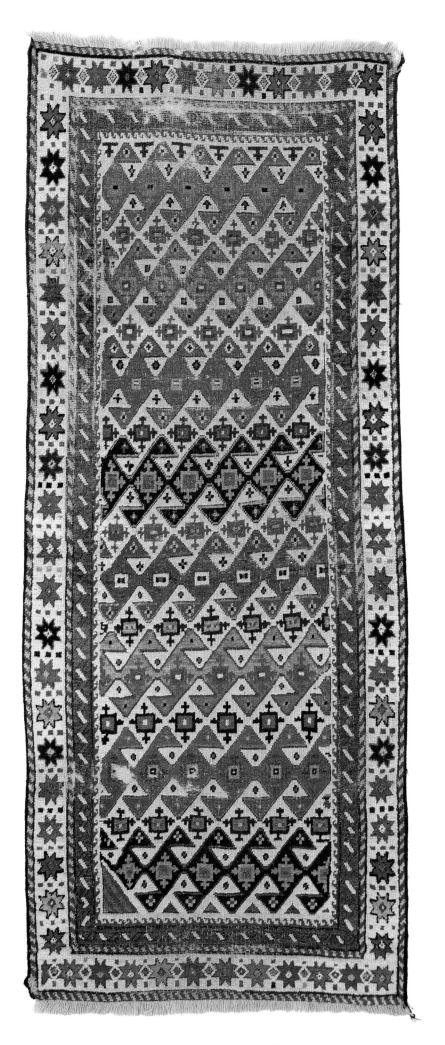

14.11 Shahsavan, 2ft 1in × 7ft 1in (64cm × 216cm); nineteenth century.

Several Persian tribes produced popular textiles known as *jajim*, thin flat-weaves decorated with vertical stripes. As noted in Chapter 10, *jajim* patterns often closely resemble motifs found in *malbands*. The unusual rug shown on the right is a knotted pile piece in a *jajim* design. The Shahsavan attribution is advanced tentatively in this case, but seems likely.

A bag front shown below exemplifies Shahsavan pile work of this type. Extra-weft-wrapped *mafrash* are among the most common functional Shahsavan weavings found on the market. The example shown in Illustration 14.13 suggests affinities with Kurdish patterns.

14.12 Shahsavan bag front, 1ft 7in × 1ft 7in (48cm × 48cm); late nineteenth century.

14.13 Shahsavan *mafrash*, 1ft 8in × 3ft 3in × 1ft 6in (51cm × 99cm × 46cm).

14.14 Shahsavan (?); late nineteenth century.

The pile bag front pictured below can also be attributed to the Shahsavan. The wool in this piece is quite soft, and the handle is more relaxed than in pile weaves from the southern Caucasus. White threads are cotton. As is true within all tribal confederacies, weaving habits varied from one Shahsavan sub-tribe to another, accounting for differences in motifs as well as slight variations in materials and structures.

The rug shown opposite is tentatively attributed to the Shahsavan. Human figures, a human face (center), and animal-head-based shapes all contribute to a most unusual pattern.

The mixing of various tribal bloodlines within the Shahsavan Confederacy makes the tracing of design within this group especially challenging. Many details remain to be resolved in this area of study – one that made enormous strides during the 1980s.

14.15 Shahsavan bag front, 1ft 4in × 1ft 3in (41cm × 38cm); late nineteenth century.

14.16 Shahsavan (?), 6ft × 8ft 10in (183cm × 269cm); late nineteenth century.

Anatolia

Anatolia (Turkey)

The term "Anatolian" has become the preferred label for traditional weavings from the region now known as "Asia Minor." Although the label "Turkish" is perfectly acceptable, "Anatolia" ("land of the East", from the Greek word meaning sunrise) carries nuances of something much older than the founding of the modern Turkish state. Since the early 1980s, debate on the subject of design origins has involved four main schools of thought. One, the Turkic-origins view, states that designs came to Anatolia, the Caucasus and Iran with Turkic tribes who migrated westward from Central Asia. A second viewpoint saw the oldest designs originating in Anatolia and moving eastward. Other students of this subject pointed to possible Chinese origins, carried to western Asia by Turkic-speaking groups. The fourth – and to my mind the most plausible – explanation, emphasizes Iranian tribal origins.

Many nomadic and village women in Anatolia wove patterns that have features in common with the traditional rugs and kilims of Iranian tribes in the Zagros, northwestern Iran, and the Caucasus, but with many inventive adaptations. A connection with motifs found in these neighboring areas is not surprising, given the lack of any significant natural barriers to impede the movement of peoples, especially from the southeast. Substantial numbers of Kurds, whose ancestors were called by other names, have lived in both Iran and Anatolia for the past fifteen hundred years and probably much longer. It

15.1 Detail of Anatolian rug shown on page 273.

is likely, in my opinion, that ancestral Kurds carried early tribal designs from the region within present-day Iran into both Anatolia and the Caucasus. This suggestion does not depreciate the contributions of tribal and village weavers in these latter regions or rule out the possibility that some motifs may have originated there. Indisputably, women in both areas devised adaptations which took root in their immediate locales. Efforts to determine what influences set these processes in motion, and when, have aroused controversy among rug scholars and helped to focus attention on basic questions of design origins. A key point of debate is whether a substantial body of traditional designs already existed in Anatolia before the arrival of Turkic-speaking groups from the steppes, and, if so, how they came to be there. Some advocates of this theory have attempted to trace a large body of motifs back to neolithic times. This is the essence of the "Goddess of Anatolia" thesis, which has been strongly challenged by a number of critics.[1] The theory rests on the proposal that kilim designs from recent centuries are direct carry-overs from eight-thousand-year-old wall paintings depicting goddesses. However problematical key aspects of the "goddess" theory may be, it has helped broaden the discussion, allowing earlier assumptions to be reviewed and questioned.

The subject of Anatolian motifs is complicated by the complex ethnic mix of the region.[2] Beyond ethnological considerations, centuries of commercial weaving enterprises and profound Islamic influences account for scores, if not hundreds of patterns. However complex the panorama of Anatolian rug production has been, the viewpoint is widely accepted that designs many centuries old survived in a number of village and nomadic weavings. These motif traditions were so pervasive that they tended to invade formal design schemes adapted from carpets produced in commercial workshops.

It seems likely that several factors led to the gradual alteration of some types of motif. One factor was the commercial rug-weaving industry – itself

15.2 A weaver near Pamukkale in 1967. In the background a kilim dust cover protects sacks of belongings.

composed of several levels. One level consisted of groups of professional carpet designers, hired to produce original work according to contemporary aesthetic principles. It should be stressed that their task was not to revise or improve local folk motifs but to develop fresh variations of more formal, precisely controlled patterns. Their efforts to balance forms and colors called acute sensitivities into play – ones that transcend common considerations of marketability and profit. Some of these designers produced carpets of great subtlety and refinement. Other designers, in more commercially oriented workshops, developed attractive, if less inspired, carpet patterns. A step below this level were more casually organized enterprises including cottage-industry weavers who produced rough copies of marketable designs.

It was at this stage of the process that a second factor came into play: an older stream of folk designs. Market acceptance of urban designs that had been stylized in cottage-industry settings opened the door for village weavers to do what came naturally: mix even more folk elements into their patterns. These elements included geometric border schemes, eight-pointed stars, animals, animal heads, fragments of animal-head columns, "S" shapes, cross-based designs, and many others. Individuals who contributed to these modifying processes were probably not conscious of their role in altering forms that they had inherited from *both* design streams – that is, from urban carpet designs and from tribal and village traditions.

Elements in the famous "Dragon and Phoenix" rug, shown on page 55, could well relate to this process. Dozens of head-like forms project from both the phoenix and the dragon figures. Heads of birds and animals appear around several sides of the two octagons which constitute the field. These adaptations were well established in a number of Anatolian weavings of the fifteenth century.

Although many Anatolian rugs suggest a combination of urban and folk motifs, most nineteenth-century Anatolian kilims and some pile rugs contain no urban influences whatsoever. It appears that traditional design vocabularies, often featuring parts of animals, were already firmly established in Anatolia before the arrival of Islam in the seventh century. Older motif repertoires, like old folk beliefs, legends, and related cultural inheritances, survived among nomads and also in more remote villages through cycles of upheavals which reshaped many aspects of Anatolian life.

Efforts to unravel the origin of the oldest Anatolian rug and kilim motifs have, until now, neglected a parallel study of Iranian tribal designs. A substantial cultural bridge existed between Anatolia and Iran well before Turkic-speaking and Arab elements entered the region. A vital component of this bridge, as we have noted, was their shared Kurdish population. If Kurds did not literally carry early Iranian rug and kilim designs into Anatolia, they may have acted as a link between the two areas, a kind of membrane through which motifs and other aspects of culture were transmitted.

The complexity of Turkey's ethnic mixture has led many writers to resort to oversimplifications in order to avoid entrapment in a labyrinth of obscure details. The three names used most frequently in referring to populations who maintained nomadic or semi-nomadic lifestyles in Turkey are "Yürük," "Turkoman," and "Kurd." Closer study shows that none of the terms is used consistently.

"Yürük" is derived from the word *yurumek*, meaning "to walk." At times it has been applied as a generic label for all nomads, at other times to specific groups who call themselves "Yürük," and on still other occasions to nomadic or semi-nomadic peoples who do not fall readily into the other main groups, "Turkoman" and "Kurd." Like a number of terms in rug literature, use of the "Yürük" label is a matter of tradition rather than of precise knowledge. In reality, "Yürük" cannot be viewed as either an ethnic or political label, but one that has been applied by town-dwellers to various nomadic portions of the Anatolian population, and by nomads themselves, without consistent clues as to just who these people were.

"Turkoman" or "Turkmen" is a more precise label. However, problems arise in attempting to apply it in a consistent way. Some groups who call themselves "Turkmen" are descended at least in part from Turkoman tribes who entered the area around the eleventh century when the Seljuks began to dominate the region. People who took on the name "Turkmen" were primarily rural cousins of Turkic-speaking elements who formed the new ruling class in cities, where they became called "Seljuks." Mixing with local populations had a profound effect on Turkomans in Anatolia and Iran, especially in towns and cities, but in rural areas as well. An additional confusing factor is that some Turkic-speaking groups whose descendants also refer to themselves as "Turkmen" entered Anatolia from Bulgaria and other areas during the last century, when the Ottoman empire was contracting in size and power. These people could have adopted a safe local name ("Turkmen") in order to obscure their origins. Today we have few ways of ascertaining which group we are dealing with when in a camp of nomads calling themselves "Turkmen." Complicating matters yet further is the fact that people who call themselves "Turkmen" do not have the appearance of Turkomans of the steppes, northern Afghanistan, and northern Iran. They look and dress much like neighboring groups who call themselves "Yürük," or even "Kurd." Weavers among them produce patterns that have much more in common with traditional village and nomadic work of this region than with Turkoman designs in Central Asia.

A basic problem is that tribal labels became politicized in Turkey, just

15.3 A village spinner.

15.4 Preparing yarns prior to warping a loom.

15.5 A village woman associated with the DOBAG project weaves local yarns colored with vegetable dyes.

as they did in southern Iran. ("Qashqa'i" and "Khamseh" are political labels more than ethnic ones.) Hints of this factor can be found in remarks in Turkish textbooks of the 1920s and '30s that claim Alexander of Macedonia to be a Turk and in the official statements that a formerly substantial Armenian population, many of whose members were massacred, never existed. Armenians are not the only people who lived in Anatolia for untold centuries only to disappear from official accounts; newspapers in Turkey have rarely referred to Kurds during most of the twentieth century. This enormous population was called "mountain Turks." Certainly, the perennial tendency to rewrite history according to the prevailing political orthodoxy has exerted strong direct and indirect pressures on those studying rugs from this region.[3] These difficulties have even had a bearing on the names that nomads apply to themselves, or have applied to them by their neighbors.

If "Yürük" and "Turkoman" are not precise tribal labels, what of the third nomadic group in Anatolia, the Kurds? "Kurd" (or, according to local usage, "Kirt") is certainly a more reliable label, if only because few individuals or groups would go out of their way to wrap themselves in such an unpopular identity – one that set them at odds with dominant elements in Turkish society. Some people called "Yürük" presumably have Kurdish blood in their ancestry, and "Turkicised Kurds" have been identified.[4]

In part because of the complexity and awkwardness of many of these questions, most writers emphasize village and regional names, rather than tribal labels. Again, I prefer to concentrate on motifs rather than on highly specific tribal or village nomenclature. Because many traditional Anatolian weavings shed light on important questions in the sphere of tribal design origins, the brief sampling that follows emphasizes an older stream of folk designs. A small sampling of pieces will convey the essential picture.[5]

The survival of outstanding Anatolian rugs from the fourteenth century onward, as well as oil paintings of that era that include images of rugs, offers us glimpses into an important phase of Anatolian weaving – one that suggests ties to earlier zoomorphic-style themes. Two frequently reproduced Anatolian rugs are shown on these pages. Both are commonly dated to the fifteenth or sixteenth centuries but later dates have also been proposed.[6] Explicit and stylized animal-head devices connect them with design styles that were diffused over a wide geographical area.

15.6 Central Anatolia, 5ft 1in × 7ft (154cm × 227cm); fifteenth century.

15.7 "The Marby Rug", Anatolia, 3ft 7in × 4ft 9in (109cm × 145cm); fifteenth or sixteenth century.

The Metropolitan Museum in New York acquired this remarkable rug in 1990. The proposal of a fourteenth-century date arosed little debate. Animal figures in the rug bear no precise parallels with animals in other rugs but are related to a broad body of animal motifs in Anatolian and Iranian weavings.

Several drawings below show that design components extending from the animals' tails are closely related to portions of Luri/Bakhtiyari animal-head columns. This could be a helpful observation, given the early date of the rug. These details suggest that fragments of the animal-head column had already been removed from their original form and were adapted by Anatolian weavers by no later than the fourteenth century. Precise chronologies and dates are impossible to formulate, but it appears likely that still earlier Anatolian weavings included more complete renderings of the animal-head column. The question of how the complete patterns survived among nomadic weavers in the Luri/Bakhtiyari group remains unsolved, but evidence suggests that these patterns, or portions of them, were already known in Anatolia during the early centuries of the second millennium A.D.

Several head forms which embellish major design components have lines extending from their tops, representing horns.

15.8 Head motifs with horns are closely linked to portions of Luri/Bakhtiyari animal-head columns.

15.9 Outer border "S" motifs include dots suggesting eyes.

15.10 Anatolia, 4ft 1in × 5ft (124cm × 152cm); fourteenth century.

"S" and animal-head shapes play a prominent role in the motifs in the rare eastern Anatolian rug shown at right, from the village of Sarkisla, in a Kurdish-dominated region of east-central Anatolia. The border pattern was derived from repeating "S" borders, common in Zagros nomadic bags but also used by Anatolian and Caucasian village weavers. The frog-like shapes within the repeating medallions were presumably a local adaptation. (Symmetrical geometric forms at times bear coincidental resemblances to insects, crabs, and other creatures.)

Diagonal lines of reciprocal animal heads serve as outlines for the repeating lozenges. Although they are concealed by shifting color blocks, similar shapes can be found within concentric medallions in the Konya-area rug, shown below.

15.11 Konya area, 5ft 3in × 7ft 1in (159cm × 215cm); eighteenth or early nineteenth century.

15.12 East-central Anatolia, 4ft 5in × 5ft 8in (135cm × 173cm); nineteenth century.

Anatolia

Reed screens were woven by numerous groups in order to protect the fronts of tents or yurts from wind and dust. The segment of a reed screen shown opposite has a bearing on several lines of inquiry in design-origin studies. The two medallions are ringed with animal-head shapes, much like many rug and kilim medallions. The coarse and unrefined nature of reed screens necessitates large and relatively simple patterns. In this case, the similarities to rug and kilim patterns are quite striking.

Interest in reed-screen designs developed on the heels of observations offered by Josephine Powell during the fifth International Conference on Oriental Carpets, Vienna, in 1986. Among the regions with a claim to having developed or contributed to the oldest reed-screen patterns are Central Asia, Anatolia, and Iran. Parallel development in several areas is clearly possible. Until recently, Kurds in both Iran and Anatolia have been neglected in this study.

Early Kurdish influences may be a factor in the adoption of quite similar patterns in innumerable Anatolian villages. Like hundreds of other designs, the detail from a kilim from the Fethiye region, shown below, bears clear parallels to the reed-screen patterns shown on the right-hand page. Few comparisons shed such compelling light on the potential importance of Kurdish migrations in the development of shared design vocabularies in western Asia.

15.13 Detail, Anatolian kilim, Fethiye region.

15.14 Segment of a
Kurdish (?) reed screen,
4ft × 25ft 4in (122cm ×
772cm); nineteenth
century.

Anatolia

The rug shown here holds a special place in the "east-to-west" or "west-to-east" controversy. Archaic motifs within the repeating hexagons in the field of this piece have been used to support both the Turkic-origins and the Anatolian-origins theories. The former viewpoint sees these motifs as heraldic Turkic emblems. The latter sees them as "goddess" or "birth symbol" forms. A less cumbersome possibility, the Iranian-origins theory again focuses on the Kurdish populations of Anatolia and Iran. As mentioned on page 154, scholars specializing in the early history of this area are in agreement that Kurds, or their ancestors in the Zagros, gradually moved northward, an expansion encountering no major geographic barriers. According to the Iranian-origins thesis, Kurds carried motifs with them. Thereafter, non-Kurdish women gradually acquired and mastered Kurdish motifs from the newcomers. Over many centuries, village and nomadic weavers in both Anatolia and the Caucasus improvised new variations from old Kurdish patterns, thereby creating complex networks of motifs that varied from village to village. Nearly all of the motifs of this type include animal-head shapes, although details such as eyes and horns were usually dropped. Inevitably, motifs became increasingly abstract.

If this point of view is correct, Turkomans and other Turkic peoples may well have learned some of their basic designs from the west – Anatolia, the Caucasus and Iran. Although local weavers adapted some designs to suggest rather abstract human figures, similarities between Anatolian motifs and "goddess" images are coincidental.

Illustration 15.15 shows the possible stages of the transmutation of forms which had their origin in animal-head columns. The actual processes, of course, must have been significantly more complex. The series begins with an animal-head column segment from a Zagros weaving from Iran, a configuration that has more variations than any other in the vast repertoire of tribal or village motifs.

15.15 Repeating medallions in the rug, right, may have evolved from kindred forms in archaic animal-head columns.

15.16 Kurdish (?) 4ft 1in × 4ft 7in (125cm × 140cm); eighteenth century.

Like many other kilims from Anatolia, these pieces were woven in two strips, which were then joined together, accounting for the mismatched effect in several medallions. Since kilims were rarely made for external commercial markets, such irregularities presumably mattered little to village weavers.

Anatolian weavers developed so many variations of traditional patterns that unfamiliar examples are still being discovered. Some represent village work. Others were made in Kurdish or Turkoman nomadic camps. Nowhere in Asia were so many possibilities explored and so many different paths taken, many of which are linked to common sources. Quite apart from their appeal for the scholar, these rugs have an enduring fascination in their own right, simply as works of art.

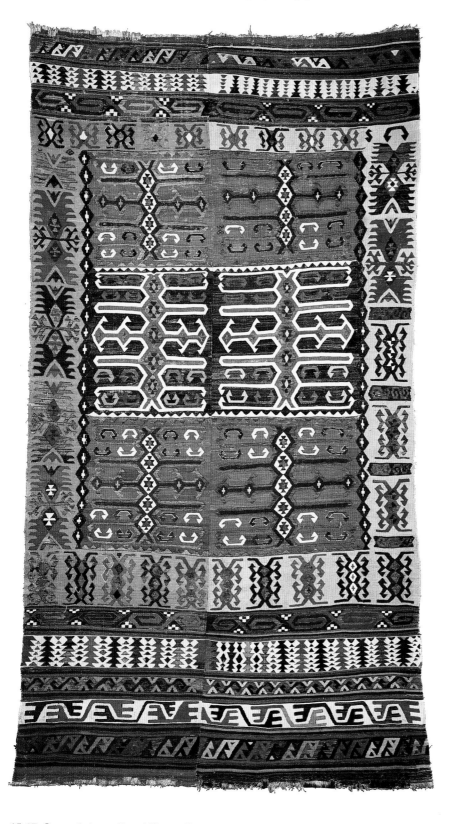

15.17 Central Anatolian kilim, 5ft 11in × 10ft 3in (180cm × 313cm); nineteenth century.

15.18 Western Anatolian kilim, 4ft 5in × 10ft 6in (135cm × 320cm); nineteenth century.

The Caucasus

Map of principal regions and cities in the Caucasus.

The southern edge of the Caucasus region adjoins Anatolia near Mount Ararat and shares a lengthy border with Iran. Mountains and secluded valleys have provided an isolated habitat for a great variety of ethnic groups since ancient times. Some of these peoples are of such obscure origins that philologists and ethnologists have no clues to their relationships with other ethnic families. Over eighty languages were spoken in the Caucasus during the nineteenth century and half that number still persist today. Intense ethnic conflicts characterize this region at present, just as they did a century ago; the independent republics of Armenia and Azerbaijan are still torn by rivalries.

Given the strength of racial, religious, and clannish divisions, we might logically expect various peoples in the Caucasus to weave dramatically different patterns. In general, this is not the case. There are clear regional differences, but rugs made by Armenians, Azeri Turks (Azerbaijanis), Kurds, and others share many design forms. Local patterns often resulted from rear-

16.1 Detail from Shirvan rug shown on page 290.

ranging common elements, as well as from the gradual adaptation of workshop patterns, imparting to them a more folk-art flavor.

One fundamental problem in approaching Caucasian rugs is the separation of stylized workshop patterns from designs with authentically ancient roots. Both became deeply established in village traditions. Second- and third-generation alterations to commercial patterns frequently mixed with older tribal forms in a manner that almost concealed the workshop-derived elements.

My approach in the following small sampling of Caucasian rugs is similar to that in previous chapters: the emphasis is on rugs with traditional folk designs. The result is far from a general survey, but offers evidence of a common foundation supporting the most conservative veins of weaving in this region, a foundation sharing much with the tribal and village traditions discussed in previous chapters. I have given limited attention to patterns which arose in commercial workshops because the subject has already been well documented by Charles Grant Ellis, Kurt Erdmann, Serare Yetkin, and other authors in this field. Traces of workshop influences will be pointed out in several rugs.

Most designs shown in this chapter represent the oldest forms used continuously in the Caucasus. To refer to this lineage as 'older' calls for some clarification. Collectors and scholars specializing in 'dragon' and 'vase' carpets from the sixteenth, seventeenth and eighteenth centuries consider these classic types as the older vein of Caucasian work. From their viewpoint, most rugs shown in this chapter are 'late' examples. Thinking chronologically, this orientation is correct – a seventeenth- or eighteenth-century dragon carpet is certainly older than nineteenth-century Caucasian Kurd or Armenian Kazak examples. However, there is now recognition that design elements in many

16.2 View from a village high in the Caucasus mountains.

nineteenth-century village rugs predate the classical period by hundreds of years. Seen in this light, numerous village designs from the late nineteenth-century are older than sixteenth-century workshop patterns. Indeed, some village products of the nineteenth-century were untouched by workshop influences.

Historical evidence dating their ancestors' arrival is scant, but Kurds and Kurdish culture have been long established in the southern Caucasus. Scholars are unable conclusively to determine their tribal name in ancient times, but it is tenable to propose that ancestors of Caucasian Kurds brought a body of rug and kilim designs into the region when they first migrated northward from Iran. This suggestion gains credence when older Caucasian folk motifs are compared with Kurdish designs in Iran. Numerous rugs from the southern Caucasus differ relatively little in construction and structure from traditional Kurdish weavings. These similarities fade as we move further north in the Caucasus.

Inevitably, rug weaving in this region has undergone major changes in the course of the twentieth-century. The 1917 revolution set the stage for Soviet collectivization policies which hastened the end of folk weaving as it had been practised for so long. Rigid 'five-year-plan' rugs replaced more relaxed patterns. At present, the design and weaving of rugs continue as commercially-oriented crafts in several Caucasian republics, but with results hardly comparable with those formerly achieved by village women without guidance or interference. Except for a few ingenious copies, efforts to reproduce the beauty and feeling of antique examples have fallen far short of the mark. We can hope that future decades will somehow encourage the renewal of weaving as a more spontaneous local craft. However severe ethnic divisions in this area may be, a conference of weavers composed of Kurds, Armenian Christians and Azerbaijan Moslems could lead to the realization that these seemingly inrreconcilable lineages have many designs in common.

The Caucasus

This rug from the Moghan district, north of the Iranian boundary, offers an excellent point of departure, since it contains medallions which connect with stylized animal-head themes found in the major border and, by extension, with patterns in many thousands of rugs. Heads with long necks extend from medallions along a vertical axis in the center of the piece.

Like many Caucasian village weavings, the weave of this piece is loose and the wefts are lightly packed, making a supple fabric. Maximum visual impact has been achieved with a minimum of knots. High knot-counts are extremely rare in the southern Caucasus.

Historical documentation on the location of the weaving workshops that produced classical Caucasian carpets is scanty. Larger population centers were presumably favored, leaving villagers and nomads free to continue weaving an older stream of designs such as that we see here.

16.3 & 16.4 Moghan, 4ft 1in × 6ft 9in (124cm × 206cm), and detail; nineteenth century.

The Caucasus

Field work by Jon Thompson has led to a revised attribution for a group of kilims from the Daghestan region. Formerly called "Avar," they appear to be the work of a Turkic-speaking group, the Kumyk. Drawings are hardly needed to establish a connection between primary motifs in the example shown on the right and animal-head variations from Iran.

Primary designs in the rug shown below are descended from formal workshop patterns. However, a merging of workshop and older folk patterns is evident in the long necks which sprout from the large geometric forms. This particular piece is one of several historically important rugs from the viewpoint of the market. Its record-breaking sale in 1988 brought the rug market a small step closer to other international art markets.

16.5 "Star" Kazak, 5ft 9in × 7ft 2in (175cm × 218cm); first half of nineteenth century.

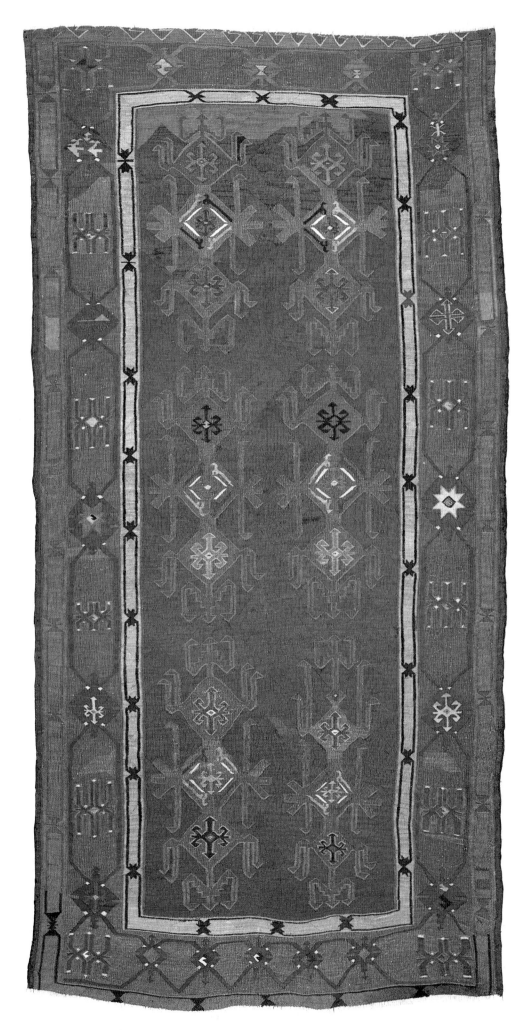

16.6 Daghestan (Kumyk?) kilim, 4ft 5in × 9ft 2in (136cm × 280cm); nineteenth century.

The Shirvan district is located in the southeastern Caucasus, adjacent to the Caspian Sea. Rugs from this locale are among the most finely knotted examples from the entire region. Effective outlining of forms and crisp, precise drawing characterize Shirvan work. Major border motifs and animal designs in the piece pictured on the right represent an ancient lineage. The *boteh* may have descended from workshop patterns. Note that of the eight vertical columns in the field, seven have a different background color.

The piece below also contains some forms shared by Persian tribal and village weavings, as well as extremely stylized workshop patterns.

16.7 Shirvan, 3ft 10in × 6ft 11in (117cm × 211cm); late nineteenth century.

16.8 Shirvan, 3ft 4in × 6ft 1in (103cm × 186cm); second half of nineteenth century.

A high level of productivity characterized Caucasian village weaving during the nineteenth century. The making of rugs was a cottage industry which supported many village economies. Armenian dealers shipped large quantities of pieces to rug markets in Europe and elsewhere. The best of these objects must have struck the eyes of their first owners as strongly as they ours today. Some numbers were protected from severe floor use, surviving through the twentieth century in nearly original condition.

It is uncertain whether the complete patterns seen in these two rugs were produced earlier than the mid nineteenth century, but both examples contain a number of archaic forms within a merging of urban and traditional design components.

16.9 Kuba, 3ft 3in × 3ft 8in (99cm × 112cm), 1860.

16.10 Chajri, Eastern Caucasus, 4ft 5in × 9ft 4in (135cm × 280cm); nineteenth century.

The Caucasus

This remarkable piece also exemplifies the successful blending of folk motifs with workshop influences. Such superb patterns were not woven in great numbers. One reason for this was the significant role of individual weavers working in their own homes. If a gifted woman discovered a new and highly pleasing adaptation, the number of examples produced might be limited to her own work. A lifetime of effort was measured in several dozen rugs.

The speed with which designs were changing during the nineteenth century was another factor. In an artistic environment of this nature the tendency for weavers to adapt new designs and experiment with forms was strong. Such an era, relatively close to our own time, provides a valuable opportunity to study not only the objects that were produced, but also the processes of cultural change that they reflect. Ebbs and flows in urban weaving production and the periodic resurgence of folk forms represent cycles that have been repeated many times in the history of weaving in Asia.

However, nothing comparable to the decline to extinction witnessed during the course of the twentieth century occurred previously.

16.11 & 16.12 Kazak, 3ft 3in × 4ft 9in (99cm × 145cm), and detail; mid-nineteenth century.

Turkomans and other Turkic-speaking Peoples of Central Asia

17

Territories occupied primarily by Turkomans and other Turkic-speaking groups.

Turkic peoples have dominated most of the region from the Caspian Sea to northwestern China since the early centuries of the Christian era. The consolidation of large Turko-Mongolian tribal confederations on the fringes of northern China may well have been an indirect consequence of the building of the Great Wall, during the third century B.C. Before that period, small tribal groups had been relatively free to raid and trade in northern China in order to satisfy their appetite for luxury goods. Barring the path of these smaller groups led to a logical escalation: the formation of large confederations outside the Great Wall with military potential commensurate with the new obstacle. As a consequence, the forerunners of Turkic-speaking tribes gathered, marshalled strength, and gained control over large areas.[1] Although political control over these territories has passed into other hands, including the Russian and Chinese governments, descendants of these once-

17.1 Detail from a Salor wedding trapping shown on page 302.

powerful nomads numbering many millions still live throughout Central Asia.

From the viewpoint of rug scholars, Turkomans are the most important group within this large ethnic cluster, at least in terms of quantity. Turkoman weavers are famous for a wide assortment of weaving types, including main carpets, smaller rugs, bags of various kinds, long tent bands, nuptial trappings, and other objects intended only for family use. The Turkoman tribal family planed an important role in carpet making as a business enterprise for several centuries, if not longer, and geared its output for regional markets as well as distribution in Russia, in other parts of Asia, and throughout Europe. During much of the nineteenth century, their geographical placement near major trade centers made it relatively easy for traders from Russia, Persia, and elsewhere to exploit Turkomans, both as a source of inexpensive labor and as a market for western inventions and trinkets.[2] Several tribes lived close to the Central Asian Railway. The great majority of Turkomans were gradually influenced by commerce that hinged on western developments in commercial transportation. More remote Asian tribes (epitomized by sections of Lurs in Iran but also including scattered elements within Turkoman, Uzbek, and other Turkic groups in Central Asia) were less inclined to bend local weaving traditions to commercial pressures. Among Turkomans, only the Chodor tribe appears to have been relatively untouched by urban influences.

Descendants of various Turkoman sub-groups make up the majority of the population of the Turkmen Autonomous Republic.[3] Numbers of Tukomans have also resided for many centuries in northern Afghanistan and northeastern Iran. The remains of several tribes presently living in northern Iran arrived there in waves during the late nineteenth century and again in the 1920s and 1930s, when thousands of families escaped Stalin's collectivization policies. Both Turkomans and other Turkic-speaking groups, including Uzbeks, seized the opportunity to move across the Afghan border during that period, and were welcomed. I met a number of such people in Afghanistan. Some women in these households continued to weave. Others did not. One Turkoman aristocrat I met in Mazar-i-Sharif was offended when I asked if his mother was a weaver. Without saying it in so many words, he let me know that such an activity was beneath his family's social stature. They prized weavings but left the activity of making them to women of a lower social rank.

Apart from Turkomans in Afghanistan and several former Soviet republics, groups calling themselves "Turkoman" also reside in scattered villages in Turkey, and in small clusters elsewhere. Most Turkish nomads and

17.2 Turkoman girls in a workshop in town of Aktsha, close to the Russian border. They have copied motifs from a contemporary rug from their area.

17.3 An Afghan village dyer rests during the early afternoon siesta.

17.4 A leading family of carpet merchants in Mazar-i-Sharif, Afghanistan, near the Uzbekistan-Afghan border, 1973. The door surround (*kapunuk*) overhead was a relatively new weaving, but inside their shop were substantial stores of antique pieces. By 1976, antiques were a rarity in Mazar-i-Sharif and Kabul.

villagers who identify themselves as Turkomans share the Mediterranean complexions, hair coloring, and facial structures of their Anatolian neighbors. This is not the case of Kazakh and other Turkic-speaking refugees from the Afghan-Soviet war who were given homes in Turkey as a humanitarian gesture. From the ethnological viewpoint, they represent a truly Turkic group.

The name "Turkoman" is largely a western adaptation. Some authors prefer "Turkmen," which approximates the pronunciation heard in most parts of Asia.[4] In recent years, rugs from major Turkoman tribes have come to be sold under their specific tribal labels. These include "Salor," "Tekke," "Saryk," "Yomud" (Yomut), "Ersari," "Chodor," "Arabatchi," and others. All of these groups contained many sub-tribes, some of whose names are encountered in rug literature, though not consistently. From the 1930s through most of the 1970s, a common theme in writings focusing on Turkoman rugs and Turkoman peoples was their assumed role as carriers of the earliest rug designs. As remarks above suggest, the "Turkic origins" theory has lost support in recent years. Even before it was directly questioned, authors who were active in Turkoman studies turned to other aspects of the subject. These included detailed factual data touching on tribal names, the study of certain weaving types, such as *asmalyks*, and also specific structural peculiarities.

Like other tribes, the Turkomans varied in their attachment to a purely pastoral nomadic existence. Tribal leaders mixed in urban societies and were exposed to urban commercial trends.[5] Nomadism declined among Turkomans following Russia's acquisition of the region in 1881, with a further reduction in the 1920s and 1930s. Through the 1970s, some Turkomans on both sides of the Afghan-Soviet border continued to live in yurts during summer months. Major restructuring within the Soviet Union which began in late 1991 may lead to revitalization of some tribal identities, but it is difficult to envisage practical steps that could effectively reverse changes wrought in the past.

The photograph of Turkoman girls (Illustration 17.2) was taken in the village of Aktsha, the first town west of Balkh on the main road in northern Afghanistan. These shy and industrious girls were absorbed in copying a contemporary version of an old pattern. A local rug merchant owned the workshop in which they labored.

The weaving of goods to supply foreign markets has long been an important enterprise among most Turkoman tribes, particularly the Tekkes and Salors, the politically dominant tribes during the nineteenth century. First-hand reports confirm the role of weaving as a commercial endeavor throughout the nineteenth century, a practice that surely originated much earlier. In *Narrative of a Journey into Khorasan*, J. B. Fraser commented, *The manufactures of the Turkomans consist chiefly of carpets, which they weave of very beautiful fabric.*[6] Edmond O'Donovan noted the mixture of family and commercial motives for weaving in *The Merv Oasis: Each girl generally manufactures two extra fine carpets, to form part of her dowry when she marries. When this has been done, she devotes herself to producing goods for the markets at Meshed and Bokhara.*[7] According to Babadjan Basalely, whose father was in the carpet business in Merv until 1916, there were no workshops in Merv proper. He told me that carpets that were gathered in Merv for export were woven in tribal camps. In other population centers, such as Bukhara, cottage industry output was augmented by rugs produced in organized workshops.

By the second or third quarter of the nineteenth century, if not earlier, the market for Turkoman rugs of various sizes had led to the production of many bag fronts and other objects which had previously served entirely utilitarian purposes. Throughout the 1970s, dealers and collectors tended to call items of these types that had survived in good repair "dowry objects." However, the remarkable number of items which had been in the West for many decades, including substantial numbers in nearly mint condition, gradually led writers in the West to question the provenance of these weavings and to challenge their authenticity as domestic tribal objects.[8]

Because of the large number of Turkoman rugs, bags, and bag fronts on the market, serious collectors of Turkoman weavings have focused their attention on a select group of examples considered the *crème de la crème*. These include five-sided *asmalyks*, used in wedding processions. Finely woven pieces bearing the "Salor" and "S-group"[9] labels achieved top-of-the-market status in the 1970s and 1980s. Earlier questions about commercial motives supporting the manufacture of Tekke rugs and bag fronts may gradually spread to "Salor" and "S-group" pieces, as well. Are these nomadic weavings, or are they, in the manner of finely woven Qashqa'i rugs and saddlebags, products of disciplined workshops? The absence of *abrash* in the majority of "S-group" examples and the use of knots depressed ninety degrees suggest the possibility of supervised workshop production.[10]

Connections between classic Salor patterns and Persian art of the Timurid dynasty (c. 1336–1530) have been discussed by several writers.[11] Yet the search for traditional designs free of foreign influence, at least in recent centuries, is rewarding. Many archaic motifs appear to be the result of much earlier cross-cultural influences. These include two-headed animals, "S" forms, linked-"S" borders, animal-head trees, and numerous variations of animal-head medallions. The latter at times include horns or topknots. The question of how these widely shared patterns came to Central Asia is still debated. The striking similarities between many Turkoman designs and motifs found among the Baluch and other Iranian tribes has been discussed in Chapter 13.[12]

There can be no question that some motifs were created by Turkoman nomads themselves. Like any migratory peoples, yurt-dwelling Turkomans needed an assortment of bags and other trappings. Some bags and bag fronts that passed through markets in the West must have been made for use within tribes. Tent bands were a purely nomadic weaving form, used to decorate and help support tribal yurts. Functional weavings such as *ok bash* (pole covers) were always indigenous objects. As late as the early 1990s, some Turkoman families still used *asmalyks* and other special pieces during wedding ceremonies.

Rug making continues to provide income for thousands of Turkoman

17.5 A Kirgiz nomad family attaching decorative bands around the framework of their yurt.

women in the various countries where these people now reside. Unfortunately, few of these weavers have ever seen outstanding examples from the last century. As rug books and periodicals circulate more widely, the day may come when remaining Turkoman weavers will, like us, look at pictures of splendid antique pieces and marvel at evidence that rug making as a commercial and family-centered art once thrived in Central Asia. If so, workshop efforts to reconstruct portions of this broken legacy, using vegetable-dyed yarns, may be successful.

UZBEKS, KIRGHIZ, AND OTHER TRIBES OF CENTRAL ASIA

Turkic tribes in Central Asia who are distinct from Turkomans include the Uzbeks, Kirghiz, Karakalpaks, and Kazakhs. A few Arabic groups live in Central Asia, and Indo-Iranian tribes with deep historical roots in the region are also important. The majority of nomads in Afghanistan speak Persian.

A few antique weavings from these various groups were available during my first visits to Afghanistan in 1973 and 1974. Many were smuggled into Afghanistan's free market from Uzbekistan and neighboring Soviet republics, then under the strictest Soviet control. A driver who took me to Mazar-i-Sharif and other points in northern Afghanistan had formerly driven a fuel truck back and forth across the Soviet-Afghan frontier and was therefore qualified to explain the system. A continuous flow of truck traffic between the two countries, and also between China and Afghanistan, facilitated smuggling, both with and without the cooperation of border guards. A scattering of antique Turkoman, Uzbeki, Kazakh and Karakalpak rugs and felts were displayed openly in Kabul, but less openly in Mazar-i-Sharif, close to the Soviet border. Prices were low on the Soviet side, since they were dictated by a central bureau, rather than by the forces of supply and demand. The advantage of low prices meant nothing to individual buyers, who were not allowed to buy in any case. Old pieces were sold in blind lots, and only to those firms who simultaneously bought bales of new rugs. Barring extra-legal transactions, it was impossible to purchase single antique pieces. If an individual did buy something in a casual, person-to-person exchange, it was apt to be confiscated upon leaving the country. The development of freer market systems in the Central Asian republics will presumably make smuggling out of Uzbekistan and neighboring areas unnecessary and unprofitable.

For several centuries, the Uzbek population has incorporated a broad range of cultural levels, including merchant families in large towns and cities. Their workshops designed and produced both pile and flatwoven articles of high quality. Uzbeks who lived in more isolated areas wove rugs of a less refined appearance containing traditional tribal motifs.

The Kirghiz, Karakalpak, and Kazakh people, all of whom are related ethnically but have long existed as distinct Turkic-speaking tribes, are little known by most rug collectors. Weavings from each tribe have been reliably identified by Russian, European, and American scholars. If rarity alone determined price, then Kirghiz and Karakalpak rugs would lead the market. The best examples of these weavings will continue to evoke intense interest on the part of a small band of connoisseurs.

17.6 Kirgiz woman inside a yurt. Baggage and textiles are stacked behind her.

Among the world's most refined tribal workshop weavings are carpets and smaller pieces from the Salor Turkoman tribe. The exact circumstances in which earlier examples were made are undocumented, but may have always involved a mixture of indigenous traditions and commercial influences. Components of Salor major guls of the type seen on the opposite page include animal or bird heads related to Illustration 17.8, from an Ersari Turkoman rug. In Chapter 6 I suggested that tribally affiliated weavers added zoomorphic themes to design elements that were foreign to earlier native traditions.

The exquisite wedding trapping shown below contains large blocks of silk in the two primary medallions. Field designs in Salor weavings of this type are a composite of influences from several sources. These include fifteenth-century Persian carpet patterns of the Timurid period. The pointed *mihrab*-like shapes (called *"kejeba"*) are a clear case of urban art influencing tribal weavings.[13] Such design components challenge the notion that these pieces were woven purely for nomadic use.

17.7 Salor wedding trapping, 7ft 4in × 2ft 6in (224cm × 76cm); first half of nineteenth century.

17.8 Animal-head detail in a nineteenth-century Ersari carpet.

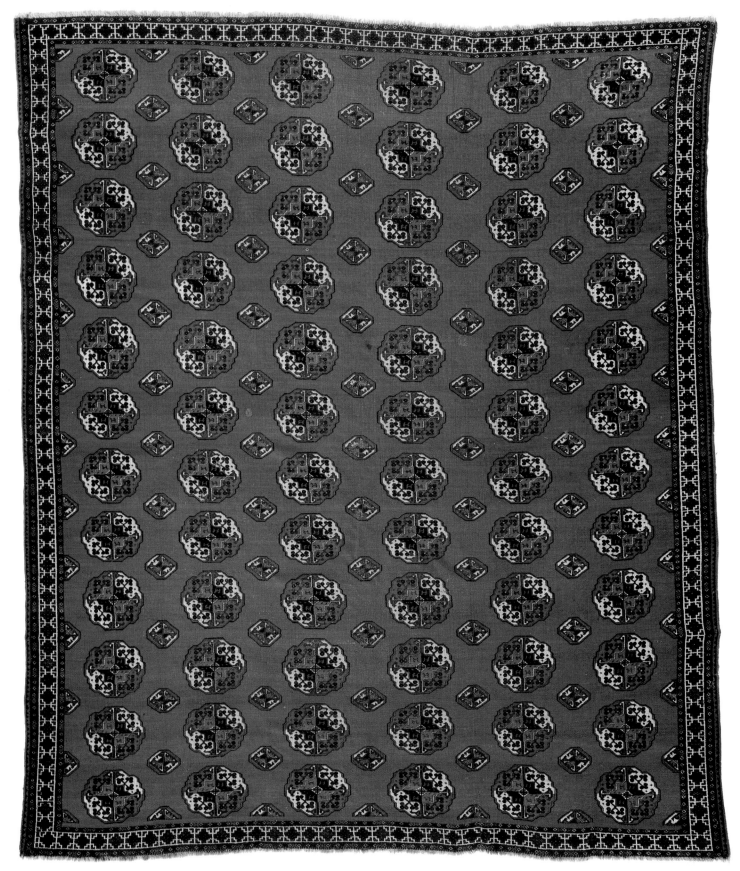

17.9 Salor, 8ft 11in × 10ft 6in (272cm × 320cm); first half of nineteenth century.

The origin of infinite-repeat patterns marked by intersecting lines, common to Tekke rugs of this type, has aroused the interest of several writers. Some authors point to repeating medallions in Persian rugs of the Timurid period (fourteenth to sixteenth centuries) as a likely inspiration for such infinitely repeating field arrangements. Others see the influence of Chinese textiles with repeating roundels.[14]

In Chapter 6, while discussing the evolution of the Tekke gul, I suggested that a large central medallion was gradually compressed and tribalized (see page 100). However, this would not account for the repeating formation in which these guls invariably appear. Answers to this riddle remain hypothetical, but it is possible that Turkoman weavers, having been exposed to either Chinese or Persian textile patterns based on an infinite-repeat scheme, adopted this approach in their own rugs. It is also possible that spontaneous experimentation occurred among either village or nomadic weavers. In either case, small secondary guls of a more tribal flavor became part of these patterns.

Tracing individual motifs and designs which represent several lines of influence is difficult because prototypes were presumably limited to relatively few examples. The fewer the number of pieces produced, the smaller are prospects that key examples survived. We are forced to speculate that many stages of trial and error occurred before these patterns evolved into commercially popular arrangements. We do know from extant examples that the Tekke pattern changed slowly after the late eighteenth century. Tribalization of the Tekke guls may have proceeded more slowly after market popularity exerted a stabilizing influence.

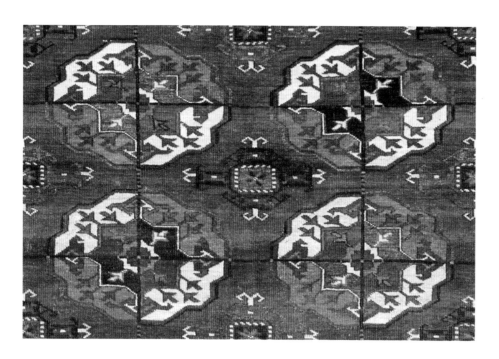

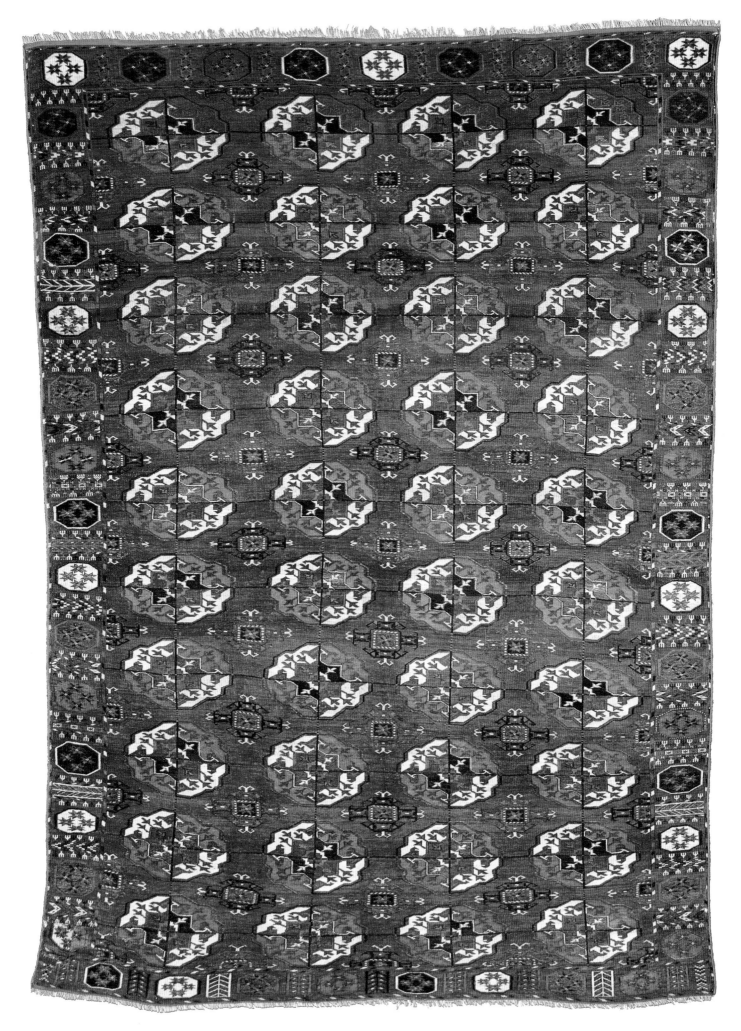

17.10 & 11 Tekke, 6ft 1in × 8ft 6in (186cm × 260cm), and detail; nineteenth century.

The Tekke *asmalyk* shown below features two-headed animal motifs. The connection between two-headed animals in Turkoman rugs and ancient Luristan bronzes was first noted by Robert Pinner in *Turkoman Studies I*.[15] The absence of motifs of this kind in the art of Turkic-speaking peoples suggests that it was acquired from contacts with Iranian groups. The timing and exact sources of such contacts may be difficult to trace, but the outlines of several possibilities can be postulated. One involves Iranian groups that are well known to us from recent histories, including the Baluch, who lived within and on the periphery of Central Asia. Tribes who migrated eastward many centuries earlier may also have carried these forms. It is known that Turkomans absorbed Iranian peoples who had once dominated the steppes. Motifs that originated in Iran may also have been carried by means of trade.

Asmalyks were made in pairs in order to cover both sides of the lead camel in a wedding procession. We rarely find an unbroken set more than eighty years old. The piece shown above on the opposite page features a Turkoman variation of the animal-head tree motif. The lower piece includes human figures.

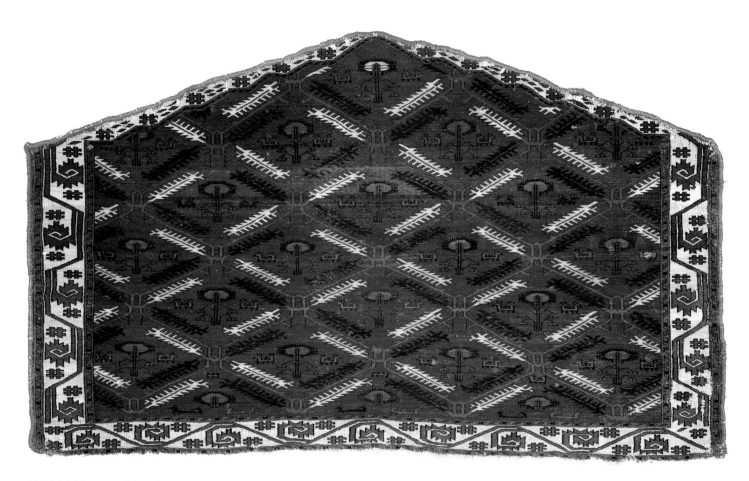

17.12 Tekke *asmalyk*, 4ft 11in × 2ft 10in (150cm × 87cm); first half of nineteenth century.

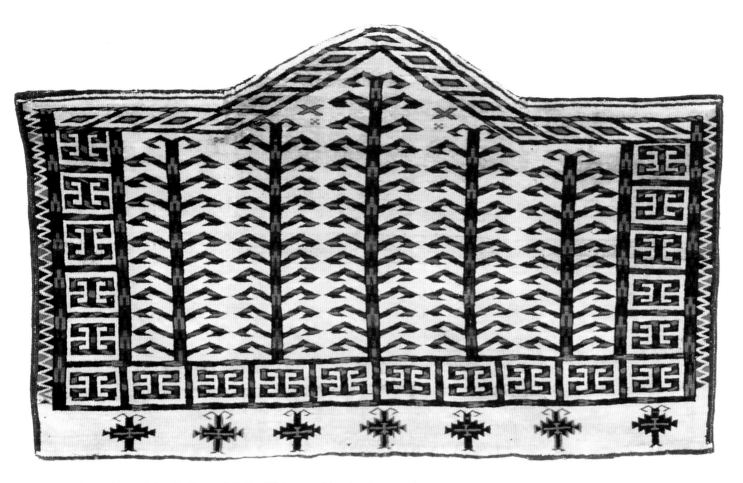

17.13 Yomud *asmalyk*, 4ft 1in × 2ft 6in (124cm × 81cm); nineteenth century.

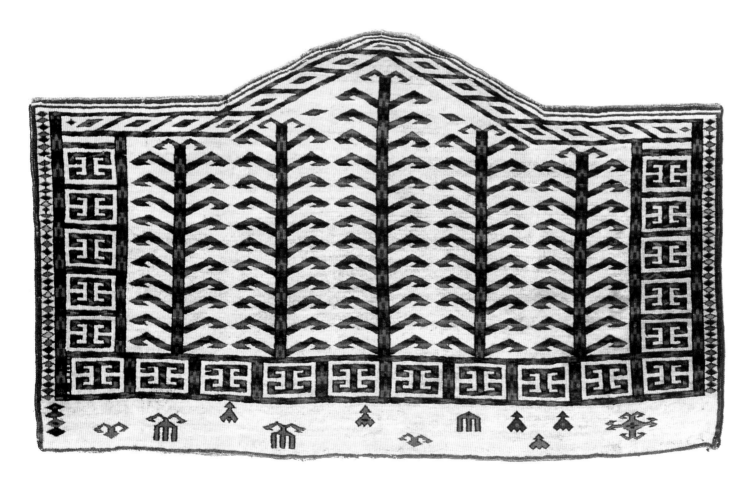

17.14 Yomud *asmalyk*, 4ft 1in × 2ft 9in (124cm × 84cm); nineteenth century.

17.15 Saryk *asmalyk*, 4ft 5in × 2ft 9in (135cm × 84cm); nineteenth century.

The exquisitely drawn *asmalyk* shown below could be regarded as *the* tribal weaving of the 1980s in the sense that its sale at Sotheby's in New York marked an important turning point in the rug market at that period. Until the sale of this piece, participants and observers in the market were uncertain whether the level of interest in rare tribal weavings, ascendant throughout the 1970s, was in danger of a serious decline. Dealers and collectors who followed this event will recall the great interest it generated. The sale of this *asmalyk* at a record sum confirmed the continued appreciation and demand for rare nomadic weavings. Aside from its unique place in the history of the market for tribal rugs, it is a rare object – and one of remarkable beauty.

Jon Thompson included this piece in *Oriental Carpets*. Concerning it, he observed:

Among the Turkmen it is the custom for the bride to ride to her wedding in a covered litter on a camel decorated with trappings she has made specially for the occasion. Naturally she devotes great care to making things for such an important event and the best Turkmen work is to be found in items made for the wedding tent and procession. Five-sided trappings are used in pairs to decorate the flanks of the camel. White is the colour for weddings among the Turkmen and the white ground blotched with red is associated in many cultures with the idea of fecundity in marriage.[16]

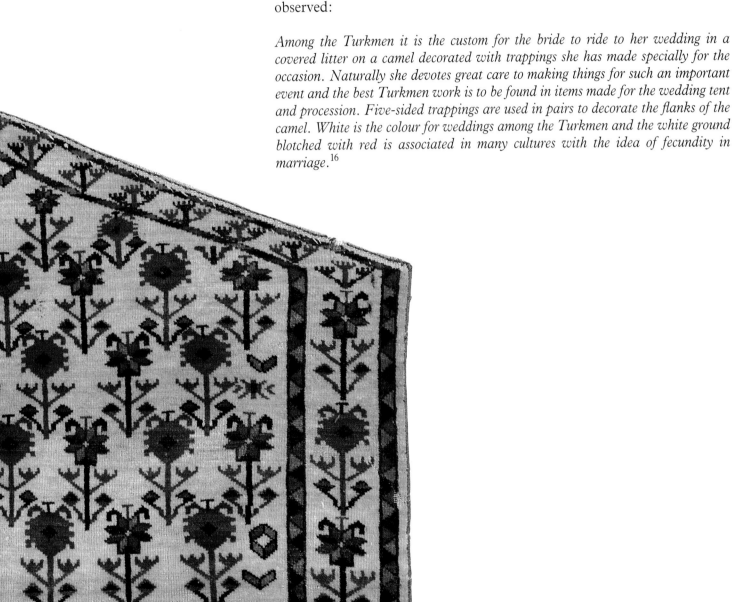

The origin and proper name for this style of prayer rug are still debated. The overall pattern suggests a design tradition only marginally related to nomadic Turkoman work. Unquestionably, many wealthy Turkoman families settled in cities and towns as comfortable members of the urban élite. Just as some Qashqa'i khan families preferred rugs with urban patterns, the wealthiest Turkoman families presumably had a role in encouraging the weaving of patterns that were foreign to nomadic traditions and habits. The patronage of tribal leaders may well have been a factor in the ceaseless evolution of rug designs since the time the Pazyryk rug was woven. This piece is a likely candidate for a relatively recent example of this process. It was probably woven in a town setting, if not in a major urban center such as Bukhara.[17] It may even have been made by non-tribal weavers who catered to the tastes of élite members of Turkoman society.

17.16 & 17.17 ''Beshir'', 3ft 6in × 4ft 4in (107cm × 131cm), and detail; second half of nineteenth century.

Turkoman rugs of the proportions seen on the right are known as *"engsi"*, a weaving type originally made as door pieces for Turkoman yurts. Indigenous as well as commercially motivated weavings of this type usually contain field patterns divided into four sections. The absence of this factor and the relaxed drawing of the repeating *kepse* guls make this piece exceptional. Although *kepse* guls are not native to Turkoman design repertoires,[18] this piece could be an authentic nomadic example. The irregularity of the piece and the presence of a human figure in the lower left-hand corner add to this impression.

Of direct interest to our study of traditional tribal motifs are those reproduced in Illustration 17.18, below, which appear in the *elem* (end panels). Note the correspondence between the basic shape of this motif and the Luristan two-headed form shown below. This design was presumably acquired through contacts with Iranian tribal culture and then altered to form a local *elem* pattern.

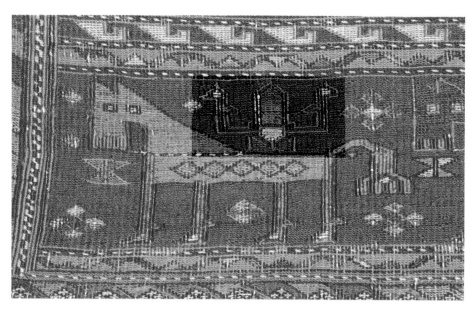

17.18 Detail from a Luri bag front shown on page 51.

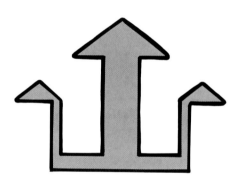

17.19 Detail from the Yomud rug, right.

17.20 Yomud, 4ft 5in × 4ft 10in (135cm × 147cm); second half of nineteenth century.

The Chodors were another powerful tribe within the large family of Turkoman peoples. A connection between Chodor designs in the *chuval* shown below and an Afshar pattern shown on page 216 makes historical ties between the two tribes likely. The spacing of medallions is more open in Chodor weavings, which, within the vast output of Turkoman tribes, are among the least influenced by commercial models from Iran, Anatolia, or the Caucasus. Tracing both Chodor and Afshar rugs of these types to an earlier source or influence is difficult, but ancient Iranian influences are a possibility. Animal-head elements are often a feature of older Chodor work.[19]

Turkoman weavings, though often derivative in terms of their designs, contain many surprises. The sale of a major Turkoman piece invariably causes excitement among dealers and connoisseurs of this tribe's work.

17.21 Chodor *chuval*, 2ft 9in × 3ft 11in (85cm × 120cm); nineteenth century.

17.22 Chodor, 6ft 7in × 13ft 3in (200cm × 403cm); nineteenth century.

The two rare rugs shown here represent the Karakalpak and Kirghiz groups. The octagons in the Karakalpak rug shown below immediately bring to mind repeating guls in Turkoman work. They could therefore demonstrate an additional step in the tribalization of patterns related to Tekke and Salor guls. The bold secondary design elements and two-headed animals suggest purely tribal elements.

The vase and floral forms in the Kirghiz rug shown opposite infer a Persian urban inspiration.[20] Such influences, far from the eastern borders of Iran, constitute one of the mysteries of Central Asian weaving. As I suggested in Chapters 2, 3, and 4, the sharing of geographically far-flung artistic styles dates to the first millennium B.C., if not earlier. From the viewpoint of western observers, Kirghizia is a remote and isolated part of the world. Nonetheless, it was always close to the flow of commerce along the old silk route.

17.23 Karakalpak, 5ft × 9ft 9in (152cm × 297cm); nineteenth century.

17.24 Kirghiz, 4ft 5in × 8ft 8in (135cm × 264cm); first half of nineteenth century.

Conclusions and Further Lines of Study

Bronze standard or finial from Luristan, eighth to seventh century B.C.

It is apparent that many designs that superficially appear to have arisen from tribal or village traditions were adapted from urban patterns. The task of sorting out and unwinding complicated networks of urban influences is a substantial but not impossible one. Several authors have laid the groundwork for this process – one that is important not only in advancing accurate work in tribal rug studies but also for a more general purpose. By studying the manner and speed with which urban designs altered after being introduced within tribal or village societies it may be possible to formulate broader principles concerning fundamental processes of change in textile arts as a whole.

It is considerably easier to trace urban influences within the past three or four hundred years than to track the origins of a much older body of what I call "traditional" tribal and village motifs and patterns. The latter have altered much more slowly, and we are left with only the final results of centuries-old and even millennia-old processes. The extreme difficulty of this undertaking explains the "confusion of tongues" characterizing many discussions in this area, complete with a spirit of "camps" and, in some cases, evidence that elicits merely belief or disbelief, rather than further study. This situation is not surprising. Uneven standards of scholarship are to be expected in young and undeveloped fields. Adding to the problem is the challenge of tracing designs that migrated considerable distances. Crowning our difficulties is the fact that textiles readily decay. The farther back this study is carried, the less tangible evidence remains, reducing the number of solid reference points. All these barriers set the stage for another problem in approaching ancient folk motifs: the temptation to decipher symbols before more fundamental questions are resolved.

Among these questions is the subject of which culture or cultures had the greatest impact on widely shared designs. Evidence presented in this book does not amount to iron-clad *proof* that a network of key designs originated among Iranian or related Indo-European peoples and gradually spread to outlying regions; however, in my opinion, this argument is supported by the ethnological and art-historical evidence now available to us. The complexity of early ethnic and linguistic histories in Asia and Europe lies beyond the scope of this book but will surely attract closer scrutiny in the future. In preparing the groundwork for an Iranian-origins thesis, I have emphasized relatively accessible design legacies among recognizable tribal groups, such as the Kurds and Baluchis, whose homelands once lay within present-day Iran but who expanded or moved in several directions, as well as Iranian tribes (Lurs, Iranian Kurds, and Bakhtiyaris) that remained in their traditional territories. The fact that Kurds spread mainly in one geographical area and the Baluch moved in another direction helps us to compare their motifs with those tribes who remained within their Iranian homelands.

An increasing body of opinion favors the conclusion that designs among native Anatolian and Iranian weavers were in place prior to both the coming of Islam in the seventh century and the arrival of Turkic-speaking groups in and following the ninth century. The quantity and variety of related motif traditions in Iran, Anatolia, the Caucasus, Afghanistan, and throughout Central Asia strongly suggest a long-term development of tribal and village weaving traditions in those areas. The discovery of pile weaving fragments in Iraq militates against the theory that Turkic-speaking groups brought basic pile-weaving techniques to western Asia.

An examination of motifs among Luri and Bakhtiyari weavings reveals a link with ancient forms found in the bronze art of the region, including two-headed animals. Illustrations 1 and 2 suggest correspondences between a Luristan bronze finial of the ninth to seventh centuries B.C. and a late-nineteenth-century Luri/Bakhtiyari animal-head column. In the absence of ancient textile evidence, however, the possibility of a direct connection remains only a working hypothesis. P. R. S. Moorey, Keeper of Antiquities at the Ashmolean Museum, Oxford, suggests that some of these ancient bronzes from disturbed graves had been available in Luristan from time to time since antiquity. According to this possibility, weavers may have copied motifs from the bronzes after these chance discoveries. If he is correct, the parallels I have noted would not be "ancient" in the same sense as advanced in my own comments.

A fundamental challenge of scholarship is to follow lines of inquiry wherever they may lead, sincerely and unconditionally. At the outset, it is all but impossible to experience a strong interest in a new field without, at the same time, having biases. However, these, too, can become a subject of investigation. To be useful to society at large and to oneself, an individual's scholarly efforts of necessity become an arrow with two points, one aimed at the outer material, the subject at hand, and the other toward oneself, including tendencies to interpret evidence in a manner that supports what one wishes to be true. The striving for impartiality in any endeavor calls for such a two-pointed study. As my own experiences often showed, one's biases are often more stubborn than the unyielding bodies of factual materials which mark the boundaries of scholarship. Our biases reflect a stage of interest in a discipline, but they also block the path to seeing unexpected relationships among facets of the subject under scrutiny. This difficulty is balanced, however, by an equally great potential for personal benefit. Prejudgments can relinquish some of their grip through the action of sincere questioning of what one knows. The loss of a precious preconception can be a fitful and even painful process, but the rewards are soon apparent.

Many subjects relating to tribal weavings remain unexplored. Beyond the factual level are questions of *meaning*. Scholarship becomes subjective, even polemical, if attempts to unravel meanings run far ahead of reasonably grounded facts. Yet, in order to be vital, scholarship needs to pursue inquiries related to the highest purposes of art, leading to the fundamental question: Why? Our effort to understand what was meaningful for other cultures helps to sustain their essential moral and psychological substance. Many of us, living in a culture that drowns us in factual information without clarifying its significance, find joy and solace in experiencing the emotional subtlety and intensity which, above all, attract us to this form of art.

The question of historical ties between Luri/Bakhtiyari animal-head columns and Luristan bronze art of the first millenium B.C. has yet to be resolved.

Notes

INTRODUCTION

1 Otis Mason, *Woman's Share in Primitive Society* (Macmillan, London and New York, 1898), p. 247.

CHAPTER 1

1 See Peter Andrews, "The Context of Flatweaves in Anatolia" in *Anatolische Kelims, Symposium Basel, Die Vorträge* (edited by J. Rageth, Basel, 1990), p. 73.

2 A number of contributions to this aspect of rug studies can be noted. Peter Andrews devoted special attention to the specific uses and names of weaving types in Anatolia. (See note 1, above.) Belkis Balpinar listed technical variations and a list of related literature in *Flatweaves of the Vakiflar Museum, Istanbul,* pp. 26-7 and 28-9.

John Wertime and Amedeo de Franchis discussed varieties of woven objects and local nomenclature in *Lori and Bakhtiyari Flatweaves,* pp.14-21. Elena Tzareva lists numerous local names for weaving types among Turkoman, Kirghiz and Uzbek tribes in *Rugs and Carpets from Central Asia,* pp. 23-4.

3 Turkic dialects are part of a larger language group known as "Altaic," which also includes "Mongolic." The distribution of Turkic-speaking peoples is quite broad, extending far beyond the confines of modern Turkey.

4 The term "Indo-European" refers to the broad distribution (first thought to encompass the area from India through Europe) of ethno-linguistic groups which speak an Indo-European language or reveal other primary cultural features of this grouping. "Indo-European" as used in this book follows this definition, referring to tribal groups whose language and history point to significant Indo-European ties. For discussions of topics related to Indo-European studies, see *In Search of the Indo-Europeans* by J. P. Mallory (Thames and Hudson, London, 1989) and *Indo-European Origins* by V. R. Curtis (Peter Lange, Bern, Switzerland, 1988). Indo-European languages are divided into two major divisions, the "satem" and "centum" branches, based on varying pronunciations of the word for "one hundred" and others related to it.

5 Sir Arnold Wilson, *S. W. Persia: A Political Officer's Diary, 1907-1914* (Oxford University Press, London, New York, Toronto, 1941), p. 145.

6 P. D. Ouspensky, *In Search of the Miraculous* (Harcourt, Brace and Company, New York, 1949), p. 35.

7 After moving to the West, some leading families adopted more practical western spellings such as "Ghashghai" or "Ghashgai," rather than the spelling devised by scholars, "Qashqa'i."

8 Conversation with author, November, 1991.

9 This is a key concept in *The Goddess from Anatolia,* by Balpinar, Hirsch, and Mellaart (John Eskenazi, Milan, 1989).

10 See William O. Douglas' report in *Strange Lands and Friendly People,* p. 142, and Lois Beck's remarks in *The Qashqa'i of Iran,* p. 144.

11 For an account of the final stage of Nassr Khan's struggle with the central government, see Beck, *The Qashqa'i of Iran,* Chapter 12.

12 See Jon Thompson's article on the DOBAG project, "A Return to Tradition," in *HALI,* issue 30, 1986.

CHAPTER 2

1 Marija Gimbutas, "Ancient Lithuanian Symbolism" in *Memoirs of the American Folklore Society,* volume 49 (Philadelphia, 1958).

2 Bunker, Chatwin and Farkas, *Animal Style Art from East to West,* pp. 147-51.

3 The term "animal-style" provokes some controversy among students of steppe cultures. Several scholars, including Emma Bunker, favor adopting a broader label, "zoomorphic style."

4 *The World Atlas of Archaeology,* p. 218.

5 The metal objects pictured in this chapter are related but not identical to pieces in this collection.

6 P. R. S. Moorey and other specialists often place "Luristan bronzes" in quotation marks, suggesting qualification for this term. One problem is that the region was not known by the name "Luristan" at the time the bronzes were made. Also, the stylistic diversity of bronzes made from the Bronze Age into the late Iron Age argues against a single label.

CHAPTER 3

1 For an account of Sergei Rudenko's work in the Pazyryk Valley and his analyses of objects found there, see his book, *Frozen Tombs of Siberia: The Pazyryk Burials of Iron-Age Horsemen.*

2 Asymmetrically knotted pile fragments found at Bashadar, a site about eighty miles west of the Pazyryk tombs, are older. John F. Haskins proposed that the ethnic group responsible for the Bashadar burials was probably the Massagetae, a predominantly Indo-European steppe-nomad group. See "China and the Altai" (*Bulletin of the Asia Institute,* New Series/volume 2, 1988), pp. 7-8.

3 The shifting cultures of Central Asia make dating an important and complex facet of this study. Current scholarship has arrived at a burial date somewhat at variance with the fifth century B.C. assessment often mentioned in earlier literature. Most scholars in this area now support a somewhat earlier date.

4 For a broad discussion of the sources of Pazyryk motifs, see Haskins, "Motives in Pazyryk Art." Also, Karen Rubinson, "The Textiles from Pazyryk, A Study in the Transfer and Transformation of Artistic Motifs" (*Expedition,* volume 32, no. 1). Related and more complete presentations by Annette L. Juliano, Emma Bunker, Trudy Kawami, and Judith Lerner appeared in *Source,* volume 10, no. 4, summer 1991.

5 Analyses of the red fibers in both the rug and a large and spectacular felt found at Pazyryk were addressed in a paper given by Jon Thompson and Harald Böhmer to the Sixth Conference on Oriental Carpets, San Francisco, November 1990. These findings led Thompson and Böhmer to conclude that both groups of fibers had been dyed with "Polish kermes" (Polish cochineal), available throughout the Central Asian steppe region, as opposed to "Ararat kermes" (Ararat cochineal), more readily available in Persia proper.

6 In the course of careful technical analyses, Jon Thompson observed that the rug has a remarkably consistent structure. Depressed knots and carefully regulated weft diameters permitted the weavers to maintain consistent shapes throughout the rug, with a minimum of horizontal or vertical distortions. As Thompson and Böhmer point out in "The Pazyryk Carpet: A Technical Discussion," the squares in the field are nearly square, and the animals around the major border are all the same size and shape. These consistencies differ from structures in the great majority of indigenous nomadic pile weavings and suggest that the Pazyryk was a workshop product rather than a truly nomadic one.

7 Haskins approaches the ethnological material in *The Fifth Pazyryk Kurgan and the "Animal Style"* and in "China and the Altai," cited in note 2, above. "The First Indo-Europeans in History" by W. B. Henning, in *Society and History, Essays in Honor of Karl August Wittfogel* contained proposals relating to possible eastward movements of centum-speaking Indo-Europeans from Iran. The presence of Indo-European-speaking groups in the vicinity of the Pazyryk Valley in the first millennium B.C. or earlier is well established.

8 See P. R. S. Moorey, *Catalogue of the Ancient Persian Bronzes in the Ashmolean Museum* (Oxford University Press, Oxford, 1971), figure 461, p. 241. The Pazyryk rug stag drawing is taken from p. 301 of Rudenko's *Frozen Tombs of Siberia.*

9 Ulrich Schurmann advanced the opinion that small circles (wheels) in one corner of the rug stem from an allegorical function related to burial rituals. (See *The Pazyryk, Its Use and Origin* by Ulrich Schurmann, Armenian Rug Society, 1982.)

10 I examined the rug collection of a Qashqa'i khan in Tehran in 1978. It included a number of Qashqa'i rugs with pronounced urban features.

11 The identity of nomadic burials is obscured by the fact that some grave goods in the Altai region and the eastern steppes were made in urban settings, including some distinctly nomadic-appearing metal objects. In her paper delivered to the 1991 University of Pittsburgh workshop, "The Chinese and Their Neighbors to the North," Emma Bunker discussed items from late first millennium B.C. nomadic burials made in Chinese urban settlements. Chinese writing found on the backs of some lost wax objects suggests that these examples of steppe-nomad art were made for nomadic clients by urban artisans, responding to nomadic tastes. Many other examples were surely made by nomads themselves or by village artisans in tribally-controlled territories.

CHAPTER 4

1 Seyyed Hossein Nasr, *Islamic Science, An Illustrated Study,* pp. 86-90.

2 The term *gabbeh* is easier to use than to define precisely. A loose weave with multiple wefts is usually, though not invariably, an identifying factor. Some rugs from southern Iran have simple geometric designs, another characteristic *gabbeh* feature, but reveal rather dense knotting. Most lion rugs from the Luri and Qashqa'i tribes are loosely-woven *gabbehs.*

3 See the comments of Willy Hartner and Richard Ettinghausen in "The Conquering Lion, the Life Cycle of a Symbol," in *Islamic Art and Archaeology, Richard Ettinghausen, Collected Papers* (Gebruder Mann Verlag, Berlin, 1984), pp. 693-711.

4 Tamara W. Hill, "A Himalayan Tantric Banner," *HALI,* issue 55, 1991, p. 109.

5 W. Eberhard, *A Dictionary of Chinese Symbols* (Routledge & Kegan Paul, London and New York, 1983), p. 281.

6 E. A. Speiser, "Closing the Gap at Teppe Gawra," in *Asia,* September 1938, p. 537.

7 After Francis Klingender, *Animals in Art and Thought,* (Routledge & Kegan Paul, London, 1971), p. 39.

8 Karl Jettmar, *The Art of the Steppes,* p. 226.

9 John F. Haskins, late Professor Emeritus at the University of Pittsburgh, advanced this opinion in conversation, pointing to the Massagetae as a predominantly Indo-European population which may have had ethnic ties to Celts or proto-Celts. He saw a close relationship between the Massagetae and the Yueh-Chih, proposing that the former name was applied by Greeks and the latter by the Chinese to factions of the same ethnic body. (See "China and the Altai," cited in note 2, Chapter 3).

Haskins' work involves highly complex studies, including one of the great ethnological and linguistic questions: who were the ancestors of the Tocharian-speakers in and near the Tarim basin. Tocharian is in the centum branch of Indo-European languages, the branch associated with western Indo-Europeans, including Celtic, Germanic, Italic, and Hellenic-speaking groups. Discovering evidence of centum-speakers so far to the east introduced a great puzzle into the study of Indo-European languages and their diffusion.

W. B. Henning saw the Guti tribe of the Zagros as "proto-Tocharians," centum-speakers who moved eastward from Iran after being driven from Babylonia at the close of the third millennium. (See "The First Indo-Europeans in History," in *Society and History, Essays in Honor of Karl August Wittfogel*.)

Henning did not go so far as to link Zagros tribes with the precursors of early Celts in Europe, except in a general way by proposing that they were centum-speakers. Haskins saw early ties to Celtic groups as a likely key to the "east-to-west" or "west-to-east" discussions.

The work of both Henning and Haskins represents extremely challenging proposals, ones which are supported by small minorities in their respective fields. The resolution of fundamental questions they addressed can come only with the discovery of more conclusive evidence.

At the time of writing, the origin of the endless-knot motif remains unknown. There are no endless-knots in Luristan bronze art, so any ties between Luristan metalwork and woven motifs could not apply in this case.

10 Count Bobrinskoy, *Peacock from Heaven, A Kurdish Yezidi Tale* (Two Rivers Press, Aurora, Oregon, 1983).

11 H. M. Raphaelian, *The Hidden Language of Symbols in Oriental Rugs* (Anatol Sivas Publications, New York, 1953), p. 161. (This reference is not an endorsement for the author's opinions regarding other aspects of symbolism. For carefully reasoned statements about symbolism in rugs, see *Kilims*, by Yanni Petsopoulos, pp. 46-8.)

12 Correspondence with author, 5 November, 1990.

13 Such studies could also focus on musical scales and other aspects of traditional songs and dances.

14 Unlike other weavings under discussion, a technical analysis of pieces of this type has not previously appeared in rug literature. The analysis of this piece is as follows:

Warps: wool, ivory with some light brown; 2 Z-spun yarns, S-plied.
Wefts in pile section (bottom): wool, dyed light orange; Z-spun yarns, two shoots. Foundation wefts in extra-weft wrapped section: wool, dyed orange and blue; some brown (possibly undyed). Fine single-ply Z-spun yarns. Extra weft wrapping: dyed wools, Z-spun, fine single-ply Z-spun yarns, 24 to 27 threads per vertical inch. Minor "countering". Sides: Multi-colored wrapping around a bundle of two threads, identical to warps. Minor evidence remains on the right side of simple wrapping of dyed plied yarns around two sets of adjacent warps.
End treatments: top band (alternative diamond and "x" shapes): reciprocal weft weave, based on three/three diamond twill. The bottom of the piece (pile) is incomplete.

An impressive feature of this altogether remarkable piece is the contrast between the coarse pile knotting of the bottom and quite fine extra-weft wrapping throughout the bulk of the object. The extreme care expended in its construction reveals itself in many details, including small lines under the eyes of three of the five horses in the lower horizontal band.

The use of dyed orange wefts in the pile section corresponds with those found in recent bags of the same design from the area of Khoramabad in Luristan. This contradicts the generalization that wefts in pile work from Luristan proper tend to be undyed brown or black woolen yarns. Evidently, some pile weavings in the eastern portion of Luristan resemble Luri weavings from Fars Province to the southeast in having wefts dyed red-orange.

15 I erroneously ascribed this two-headed "S" bronze to Luristan in part I of "Fragments of an Ancient Puzzle," *HALI*.

16 See note 9, above, for a discussion of possible lines of study extending to the early second

millennium B.C. For materials touching on the Sassanian period see "Iran and China: importation and influences," in *The World Atlas of Archaeology*, pp. 282-3.

17 Symbolic elements in both *The Bird Flower-Triller* and *Prince Hassan Pasha* are discussed by Marie Louise Von Franz in *Individuation in Fairy Tales* (Shambhala, Boston & London, 1990).

CHAPTER 5

1 Some of my previous writings on this subject gave greater emphasis to visual ties between woven column patterns and Luristan bronze finials. The proposal of Luristan origins for these woven designs is presented here as a hypothesis. See "Fragments of an Ancient Puzzle," *HALI*, and also the concluding chapter of this book.

2 Yanni Petsopoulos, *Kilims*, p. 53.

3 *The Goddess from Anatolia*, by Balpinar, Hirsch, and Mellaart (Eskenazi, Milan, 1989), created excitement with its claim that many Anatolian kilim designs owe their inspiration to 8,000-year-old Anatolian "goddess" motifs. It is important to note that many of Balpinar's contributions in this volume touch on themes that are not dependent on James Mellaart's portion of the Goddess theory. Elements in Mellaart's contributions are unacceptable as foundation stones in the study of design-origins. For discussion and criticism of Mellaart's evidence, see *Oriental Rug Review* articles by Marla Mallett and Murray Eiland in volume 10, no. 6, 1990, and Mary Voigt in volume 11, no. 2, 1991, and Dominique Collon in *HALI*, issue 53, 1990.

CHAPTER 6

1 Murray Eiland was among the first to challenge popular opinions in this area by emphasizing the urban basis of tribal designs in *Oriental Rugs: A New Comprehensive Guide*. My attention was first drawn to the analysis of the four-armed Qashqa'i medallion in the late 1970s, in conversation with Dr. Eiland. He developed the theme in subsequent articles, focussing on Timurid and Chinese influences in Turkoman guls ("Origins of Turkoman Guls," Oriental Rug Review). Jon Thompson contributed evidence in *Turkmen*, pp. 72-3 and 149-50. He also remarked on the impact of workshop designs on tribal motifs in *Oriental Carpets* and again in *Silk, Carpets and the Silk Road*. Jim Ford included examples related to Afshar and Kerman vase designs in *The Oriental Carpet*. Christine Klose carried the discussion into a review of popular Caucasian designs in "The Perepedil Enigma," *HALI*, issue 55, 1991.

2 According to Zoroastrian texts, the *Senmurv* lives in the "Tree of Seeds," has healing powers, and is able to cause rain to fall.

3 An eighteenth-century date would not undermine the thesis presented here.

CHAPTER 7

1 Curzon, 1892, volume II, p. 285.

2 P. R. S. Moorey, *Ancient Persian Bronzes in the Adam Collection* (Faber & Faber, London, 1974), pp. 23-4.

3 After a reign of one hundred and twenty-five years, the Guti were driven back into the Zagros and some elements may have been driven out of the region. The work of W. B. Henning in this area is mentioned in note 9 in Chapter 4. He proposed that, after being chased from the Zagros, Guti factions and sections of another Zagros tribe carried linguistic influences to the eastern steppe zone on the outskirts of northwestern China. Other scholars disagree with this proposal.

4 Henry Field, *Contributions to the Anthropology of Iran* (Field Museum of Natural History, Chicago, 1939), p. 175.

5 The sources of the two knot types (symmetrical and asymmetrical) will probably never be known. We do know that both were in use during the first millennium B.C. The

Pazyryk rug is symmetrically knotted and pile fragments found at Bashadar reveal asymmetrical knots. Symmetrically and asymmetrically knotted fragments were also found in the At-Tar caves, an Iraqi site dating from early in the Christian era. All of these weavings pre-date not only the period when Turkic groups dominated large portions of western Asia, but also their domination of the central Asian steppes. Consequently, the name "Turkish knot" has not helped the process of tracing the origin of motifs and weaving technologies. The knot was used in western Asia well before Turkic-speaking groups came there, and probably before they coalesced as a recognizable ethno-linguistic body.

Native Iranian tribes and other indigenous peoples in western Asia had no need to re-learn a technique which they already knew quite well.

6 Following publication of my first book, I recognized that Luri rug patterns shown on pages 113 and 115 of *Tribal Rugs of Southern Persia* are extremely tribalized "mina khani" designs.

7 For a personal account of the suffering which characterized this period, see chapter 12 of *Strange Lands and Friendly People* by William O. Douglas.

8 Parviz Tanavoli uses the Luri/Bakhtiyari label in this sense. He prefers the "Lori" spelling.

9 See *Gabbeh* by Tanavoli and Amanolahi, footnote 8, p. 29.

CHAPTER 8

1 Gene R. Garthwaite, *Khans and Shahs, A documentary analysis of the Bakhtiyari in Iran*, pp. 139-40.

2 See Ian Bennett's "Carpets of the Khans."

3 Merian C. Cooper, *Grass*, pp. 219-29.

4 Amadeo de Franchis and John Wertime, *Lori and Bakhtiyari Flatweaves*, plate 51; James Opie, *Tribal Rugs of Southern Persia*, p. 145. The latter illustration is the same kilim shown in this chapter.

CHAPTER 9

1 Arshak Safrastian, *Kurds and Kurdistan*, p. 16.

2 William Eagleton, *An Introduction to Kurdish Rugs*, p. 9. A rare combination of first-person reporting and careful scholarship.

3 Wilfried Stanzer, *Kordi*.

CHAPTER 10

1 Reported by C. Griffin Nelson and Heshmat Zomorrodian in their unpublished manuscript, *Qashqa'i Carpets from the Heshmat Zomorrodian Collection in Shiraz*, 1978.

2 The Bolvardi (Abivardi) *tireh* (clan) has lived in a Shiraz suburb for several centuries. Rugs labeled "Bolvardi" were popular in the Shiraz market throughout the 1970s.

3 See Kurt Erdmann's *Oriental Carpets*, p. 16 for a summary of the "Turkic origins" thesis. The Russian scholar Moshkova contributed the idea that Turkoman guls served totemic tribal functions, inherited from the distant past. Several writers subsequently adopted Erdmann's and Moshkova's theories, but weaknesses in these proposals had been identified and examined by the early 1980s.

4 For more typical samplings of Qashqa'i rugs, see James Opie, *Tribal Rugs of Southern Persia* or David Black and Clive Loveless, *Woven Gardens*.

5 Parviz Tanavoli and Sekandar Amanolahi, *Gabbeh*, pp. 15-17.

CHAPTER 11

1 Edwards acknowledged that he had not personally confirmed all the information on south Persian tribal weavings he reported. He was incorrectly advised on several key points relating to structure, including the statement that Khamseh rugs are single-wefted. Like Qashqa'i rugs, they are consistently double-wefted. His statement that Turkish knots predominate in Qashqa'i rugs is also inaccurate; most are asymmetrically (Persian) knotted.

2 Fredrik Barth, *Nomads of South Persia*, a landmark work which has long been regarded as the most informative academic study of daily life among pastoral nomads in Iran. Lois Beck added important volumes to this literature with *The Qashqa'i of Iran* and *Nomad: A Year in the Life of a Qashqa'i Tribesman in Iran*.

3 Fredrik Barth, *Nomads of South Persia*, p. 74.

4 *Ibid*, p. 77.

CHAPTER 12

1 Parviz Tanavoli, "The Afshars: A Tribal History," *HALI*.

2 Henry Field, *Contributions to the Anthropology of Iran* (Field Museum of Natural History, Chicago, 1939), p. 235.

3 See Murray L. Eiland, *Oriental Rugs from Pacific Collections* (San Francisco Bay Area Rug Society, San Francisco, 1990), p. 68.

4 A. Cecil Edwards, *The Persian Carpet*, pp. 212-13.

5 Anthony Smith, *Blind White Fish in Persia* (Readers Union, George Allen and Unwin, London, 1954). Like Edwards, Smith included first-hand reports on deceits and short-cuts practiced by male weavers in Kerman Province, pp. 149-151.

6 *Ibid*, p. 101.

7 Jenny Housego commented on the mixed origins of rugs labeled "Afshar" in her summary "Tribes of the Kirman District," in *Tribal Rugs: An Introduction to the Weaving of the Tribes of Iran*, pp. 16-17. She resisted use of the "Afshar" name.

8 Parviz Tanavoli provided useful information in this area in "The Afshars: A Tribal History" and "The Afshars, Part 2" in *HALI*.

9 Both knot types are found in rugs bearing the Afshar label. An unusual feature of asymmetrically knotted Afshars is that they are "open to the right." Other south Persian rugs with asymmetric knots are "open to the left."

CHAPTER 13

1 Jeff W. Boucher, *Baluchi Woven Treasures*, p. 13.

2 Over-simplified conclusions in this area served as a useful starting point but tended to block further enquiry. It may never be possible to achieve a complete understanding of the flow of motifs between Turkic-speaking and Indo-Iranian groups in and near Central Asia. The process may have involved distinct phases, including an early phase, prior to the presence of Baluch peoples in Afghanistan. In *Silk, Carpets and the Silk Road*, pp. 35-40, Jon Thompson offers a complex restatement of the role of Turkic groups in spreading pile weaving technologies. However, he also mentions the Massagetae (predominantly Indo-Europeans) in this analysis.

3 Siawosch Azadi, *Carpets in the Baluch Tradition*, p. 22.

4 This statement has been disputed by some students of design-origins. See "Some Anatolian Kilim Design Groups" in *The Goddess from Anatolia*, volume IV, by Belkis Balpinar, pp. 33-5. However, the use of hand images, an Islamic symbol, in association with Baluch *mihrabs* infers a concrete Islamic reference.

5 For reproductions of a wider sampling, see Michael Craycraft and Anne Halley, *Balouch Prayer Rugs*.

CHAPTER 14

1 Parviz Tanavoli, *Shahsavan*, p. 32. This book has greatly expanded our knowledge of the history and textiles of this group. Tanavoli examines a variety of weaving types, with special emphasis on *soumak* pieces. These vary in their structural details. *Shahsavan* includes only two pile-woven pieces. Jenny

Housego also referred to Kurdish elements within the Shahsavan in a contribution to *Yörük – The Nomadic Weaving Tradition of the Middle East*, p. 43. This catalog pictured weavings that were displayed at the Museum of Art, Carnegie Institute, in 1978.

2 In the essay cited in note 1, Jenny Housego broke new ground by suggesting that some rugs ascribed by dealers and collectors to the southern Caucasus may be Shahsavan work. Drawing on his own field work, Tanavoli reiterated the same conclusion in his article in *HALI*, "Shahsavan Pile Carpets," pp. 30-37.

3 Two of Parviz Tanavoli's articles in *HALI* include pile weavings, "Shahsavan Scissor Bags" and "Shashsavan Pile Carpets."

4 Parviz Tanavoli, *Shahsavan*, p. 23.

CHAPTER 15

1 For discussion related to the proposal that kilim design and kilim weaving represent an eight-thousand-year-old tradition in Anatolia, see *The Goddess from Anatolia* by Mellaart, Hirsch and Balpinar, published in four volumes by John Eskenazi, Milan, 1989. Key elements in James Mellaart's portion of the case came under special challenge in articles in *Oriental Rug Review* (Murray Eiland, book review, and Marla Mallett, "A Weaver's View of the Çatal Hüyük Controversy"). Both authors raised the question of misrepresented and possibly invented evidence. Mellaart responded in a letter published in *HALI* (February 1991, pp. 86-7), which addressed some criticisms but ignored others. Debate may continue for some years on a fundamental question: is some of Mellaart's evidence in *The Goddess from Anatolia* a hoax?

2 Dr. Peter Andrews focuses attention on the tangle of ethnic mixtures in Anatolia in *Ethnic Groups in the Republic of Turkey*.

3 I am indebted to Murray Eiland for many observations which influenced my commentary on ethnic clusters within nomadic and semi-nomadic elements in Anatolia and on related aspects of modern Turkish history.

4 Peter Andrews, "The Context of Flatweaves in Anatolia," *Anatolische Kelims*, Basel, 1990, p. 80.

5 More thorough attempts to understand the art-historical background of these objects would require an exploration of regional history from the linguistic, ethnic, economic, and political perspectives. Turkish, European, and American scholars working in the field have contributed a great deal to this end. Writings by Kurt Erdmann, Werner Brüggemann and Harald Böhmer, Belkis Balpinar, Udo Hirsch, Yanni Petsopoulos, Serare Yetkin, Peter Andrews, Michael Franses, Josephine Powell, Marla Mallett, Walter Denny, Oktay Aslanapa and many others have helped lay a foundation. Further steps can be made when subjects related to ethnicity become less sensitive in Turkey and when studies focusing on design origins gain a more secure footing.

6 Michael Franses and Ian Bennett suggested in *HALI*, issue 38, 1988, p. 33, that the piece shown on p. 271 may date from the seventeenth century.

CHAPTER 17

1 See Murray Eiland's comments in *Chinese and Exotic Rugs* (New York Graphic Society, Boston, 1979), pp. 4-5.

2 G. I. Gurdjieff described the arrival of Western culture in this region in *Meetings with Remarkable Men* (E. P. Dutton & Co Inc., New York, 1963) pp. 257-9.

3 Some longstanding names of so-called "autonomous" republics in the Soviet Union were revised in 1991 and 1992. At the time this book was completed, Turkmenistan had declared its independence.

4 The title of the landmark book, *Turkmen*, edited by Louise Mackie and Jon Thompson, is based on this preference.

5 G. I. Gurdjieff mentioned urbanized Turkomans in *Meetings with Remarkable Men*,

p. 254.

6 J. B. Fraser, *Narrative of a Journey into Khorasan* (London, 1825), p. 281.

7 Edmond O'Donovan, *The Merv Oasis* (London, 1882), volume II, p. 352.

8 See Lawrence Kearney, "Whither Turkomania?", *Oriental Rug Review*, 1982, volume I, no. 10, p. 8.

9 Thompson coined the term "S-group" after recognizing a group of Turkoman pieces with consistent structures that were distinguishable from identified work of specific Turkoman tribes, but of uncertain origin. See his note in connection with plate 6 in *Carpets of Central Asia* by A. A. Bogolyubov.

10 Eiland was the first to comment on this feature of "S-group" weavings.

11 See "The Origins of Turkoman Guls" by Murray Eiland in *Oriental Rug Review*. Robert Pinner referred to related materials in a paper tracing design origins delivered at the 6th International Design Conference on Oriental Carpets, San Francisco, 1990.

12 Several motifs deserve separate commentary. The possibility that two-headed animal figures originated among Turkomans or other Turkic tribes is remote, given that metal or clay objects with this form are not found in early Turkic archeological sites.

Evidence that some weavings labeled "Seljuk" contain what are here called "animal-head medallions" led some observers to conclude that these forms were brought to western Asia by Turkic groups. (See Aktay Aslanapa, *One Thousand Years of Turkish Carpets*, Eren, Istanbul, 1988, pp. 16-26 for an expression of this point of view.) By repetition, this outlook became a truism, but one that neglected the possibility that these designs were already a part of Iranian and Anatolian folk design vocabularies before Turkic groups entered the scene.

The challenge of deciding proper labels is also involved. "Seljuk" may have to be reconsidered with regard to some weavings.

13 This point is also controversial. See Murray Eiland, "The Origin of Turkoman Guls," in *Oriental Rug Review*, pp. 1-6. For a contrary opinion, see Hans Wilfling, *Antique Oriental Carpets in Austrian Collections*, 1983, volume II, p. 18.

14 Jon Thompson referred to roundels in early textiles in *Turkmen*, p. 138. See also the Eiland article, "The Origins of Turkoman Guls," mentioned in notes 11 and 13.

15 Robert Pinner and Michael Franses, *Turkoman Studies I*, chapter 19, p. 244. This chapter contains a wealth of mythological images from widespread cultures, many of which relate to zoomorphic themes in rugs and other weavings.

16 Jon Thompson, *Oriental Carpets*, p. 100.

17 Thompson proposed in *Turkmen* that designs of this type were developed in Bukhara and were not true Turkoman weavings.

18 See Thompson's comments in *Turkmen*, p. 150.

19 Michael Craycraft was the first to comment on shared features of Chodor guls and certain Afshar medallions.

20 For other opinions, see commentary with plate 46 in *Oriental Rugs of the Hajji Babas* (The Asia Society and Harry N. Abrams, New York, 1982).

Glossary

abrash Term used to describe the shifts in tone within a particular color in a weaving, which usually occur as a result of the use of different dye lots.

Achaemenian A dynastic period in early Persian history, extending from the sixth to the fourth centuries B.C. Also used to describe architecture or art objects made during the period, or related in artistic style.

Afshars A group of Turkic-speaking nomads whose primary habitat is in Kerman Province in southeastern Iran. Clusters of Afshars also live in Khorasan, near Bidjar, in western Iran, and in several sites in eastern Anatolia. Many rugs labeled "Afshar" are actually the work of the ethnically diverse villagers in Kerman Province.

asmalyk A type of weaving, usually pile and commonly five-sided, woven to decorate the leading camel in a Turkoman wedding procession.

asymmetrical knot One of the two main knotting types found in pile rugs. Also known as the "Persian knot."

Bakhtiyari (*bakh-tee-YAR-ee*) A tribal confederacy of peoples in the central-eastern part of the Zagros Mountains in Iran, including those living in villages in the Chahar Mahal district, west of Isfahan. From the linguistic and ethnological viewpoints, the Bakhtiyaris are part of the Luri group.

balisht A type of cushion cover produced by the Baluch or other closely related tribes.

Baluch (sometimes spelt "**Belouch**") A Persian-speaking tribal group in eastern Iran, portions of western Afghanistan and Pakistan. Most Baluch peoples in Iran are village dwellers, while those in Afghanistan and Pakistan are nomads.

boteh A tear-drop or leaf-shaped form with a curved top, commonly arranged in infinitely repeating patterns in the field of pile rugs.

Boyer-Ahmadi A major Luri group in Fars, neighbors of both Mamasani Lurs and Quashqa'i tribes.

Chahar Mahal A district mainly peopled by Bakhtiyari villagers in the foothills of the Zagros Mountains, west of Isfahan.

chanteh Small, single Iranian tribal bags.

Chodor A Turkoman tribe. Chodor weavings, more than the products of other Turkomans, consistently feature traditional folk patterns, rather than those with urban influences.

Coptic Term used in referring to early Egyptian Christian communities and their art.

DOBAG Acronym for "*Dogal Boya Arastirma ve Gelistirme Projesi*," a substantial weaving and dyeing project in Turkey, which promotes the use of vegetable dyes and traditional patterns among village weavers.

elem An end panel in a variety of Turkoman and other Central Asian pile weavings.

engsi A type of weaving which serves as a door in Turkoman yurts. The term is also applied to related weavings of similar design and shape.

Fars Province Southern Iran's most important administrative province, home to the Quashqa'i and Khamseh Confederacies, Lurs, Leks, and other Iranian tribes.

Farsi The family of languages also known as Persian.

gabbeh A term used by Lurs, Quashqa'i and other south Persian tribes to describe a style of pile rug, usually loosely woven and decorated with bold, primitive patterns.

gul Term derived from the Persian word for "flower," and traditionally applied to repeating patterns in Turkoman weavings.

Huns The name applied to a collection of steppe-nomad Turko-Mongolian tribes, including the Hsiung-nu, who invaded and conquered vast regions in Asia in the fourth century B.C., and had extended their influence into Europe by the fourth and fifth centuries A.D.

Jaffs A Kurdish tribe located in parts of western Iran, eastern Iraq, and southeastern Turkey.

jajim (sometimes spelt "**djidjim**") A type of thin flatweave from Iran or the Caucasus, often decorated with repeating stripes.

kadkhuda (sometimes spelt "**khadkhoda**") A leadership position or rank among clans in several Iranian tribes.

Kashkuli A Qashqa'i tribe, well known for their weavings, most of which reveal strong urban influences.

Kazak A generic name applied to a group of weavings from the southern Caucasus.

Kazakh The dominant tribal population of Kazakhstan and neighboring regions in China. Their closest ethnic kin in the region are Uzbeks, from whom they became divided in the fifteenth century.

kepse gul A particular style of *gul*, descended from forms used in commercial rug patterns and modified by generations of Yomud weavers.

Khamseh (*hahm-say*) **Confederacy** Formerly a collection of five ethnically diverse tribes in southern Iran, mostly migratory, but with some settled members. They lived in the area to the west of the Afshars and east of the Quashqa'i territories. They were the source of many south Persian rugs in highly traditional patterns.

khan A tribal chief.

Khorasan A large district in northeastern Iran, the capital of which is the shrine city of Mashad.

khorjeen The Farsi term for saddlebags.

kilim (sometimes spelt "**gelim**") A flatwoven carpet.

Kuhgilu Term used to refer to Kurdish nomads or village-dwellers in western Iran, eastern Iraq, Syria, eastern Anatolia, northwestern Iran, and the southern Caucasus; also to their Indo-European language and their long-established culture.

Lurs A native Iranian tribe which incorporates both nomadic and settled elements, spread over Luristan Province in western Iran, in territories to the south in Fars Province, and in some other parts of Iran. Luri people are found in both the Quashqa'i and Khamseh Confederacies and in Afshar-dominated districts south of Kerman. "Luri" refers to the Persian dialect spoken by both Lurs and Bakhtiyaris.

mafrash Turkish name for a large, box-like textile container, either pile or flatwoven, made by Turkic-speaking tribes in Iran, the southern Caucasus and eastern Anatolia, for the transport of bedding and clothes. In Central Asia, the same name is used to refer to much smaller pile weavings.

malband A long, narrow strip of flatweave from Iran, used to tie loads onto pack animals, and tribal in origin.

Mamasani A major Luri group living in and near Fars Province in southern Iran.

mihrab The area within a prayer rug which contains a pointed arch form. In use, the arch is pointed towards Mecca.

mina khani A floral pattern comprised of a large flower-head with four smaller flowers, arranged in an infinitely repeating pattern. Tribal and village weavers from western Iran to Central Asia have copied this popular design.

Mohammed Reza Pahlavi (1919-1981) Son of Reza Shah, and second and last shah of the twentieth-century Pahlavi dynasty of Iran.

Nadir Shah The royal name of Nadir Quli, an Afshar leader who, after a series of military successes, deposed Shah Tahmasp in 1731 and ascended the throne of Persia in 1736. He was assassinated in 1747.

Pazyryk (*pazz-er-ik*) **Valley** Site in the Altai Mountains of southern Siberia, location of important tombs dating to the second half of the first millenium B.C.

Qashqa'i (*ghash-ga-EE*) **Confederacy** Southern Iran's largest tribal confederacy, composed mostly of Turkic-speaking peoples, although also including some Lurs and other native Iranians.

rakhtekhab-pich The Persian term for a box-like woven container of the type called *mafrash* by Turkic-speaking tribes in Iran.

Reza Shah (1878-1944) Founder of the Pahlavi dynasty in Iran. Father of Mohammed Reza Pahlavi.

Safavid A dynastic period of Persian history, covering the sixteenth and seventeenth centuries. The term is used to refer to a whole network of artistic styles.

Salor A Turkoman tribe, prominent until the mid-nineteenth century, when it was defeated by the neighboring tribes. Its people were famous for the refinement of their pile rugs and bags.

Sassanian A dynastic period of Persian history, lasting from the third to the early seventh century. The term is also used to refer to the artistic styles associated with the period.

Scythians A collection of Indo-European tribes, both settled and nomadic, of the first millenium B.C., based in locations north of the Black Sea, but active at various times in a much wider area, extending from the Central Asian steppes, south to Persia and west as far as Greece. The generic term "Scythian" has been popularly applied to all artistic styles of various steppe tribes, many of whom were not Scythian in a stricter sense.

Seljuks Turkic-speaking tribes and their leaders who dominated the area between the Bosphorus and the western borders of China during the late eleventh and early to mid-twelfth centuries.

Shahsavan (*shah-sah-VAN*) **Confederacy** A Turkic-speaking tribal confederacy of mixed ethnic origin in northwestern Iran, formerly inhabiting parts of the southern Caucasus.

Shiraz The capital of Fars Province, and a major center for the sale of south Persian tribal rugs.

sofre A type of tribal flatweave from Iran or the Caucasus, often used as a ground cloth during meals.

soumak A type of flatweave in which the patterns are formed by extra weft threads, which may be wrapped horizontally, vertically, or diagonally.

symmetrical knot One of the two main knotting types found in pile rugs. Also known as the "Turkish knot."

Tamerlane Name used in the West for Timur, a Central Asian Turkic warlord who led Turko-Mongolian warriors out of the steppes in the fourteenth century, conquering a vast area stretching from Mongolia as far as the Mediterranean, and including parts of India. The name "Timurid" was subsequently applied to his successors, and is also used to describe a network of artistic styles that were strongly influenced by Persian aesthetic traditions.

Tekke The largest and most powerful tribe within the Turkoman group during the nineteenth and early twentieth centuries; the source of great numbers of rugs and other weavings.

torba A shallow Turkoman bag, hung inside the yurt and used for storage.

Turkoman (alternatively, **Turkmen**) A broad collection of Turkic-speaking tribes in Central Asia, northern Iran, and in scattered enclaves in Turkey.

Turks Term for a broad ethno-linguistic grouping, encompassing Turkic-speaking residents of Anatolia and neighboring regions, Turkic-speaking tribes on the steppes, and earlier Turko-Mongolian tribes.

Uzbek Turkic-speaking nomadic tribe, dominant in Uzbekistan in Central Asia.

wagireh A sample rug, woven either to familiarize weavers with a new pattern or to provide training for novice weavers.

warps Longitudinal threads which, when stabilized by wefts, comprise an essential element in any woven structure. In a pile weaving, portions of the warp threads are visible in the fringe.

wefts (sometimes also known as **woof**) Latitudinal threads which are woven in a variety of configurations at right angles to warp threads, therefore an essential part of any woven structure. Except in extremely worn examples, weft threads are invisible from the front of a pile weaving, but visible on the back. In flatwoven rugs, patterns are controlled by changing the color of weft threads.

yastic (sometimes spelt *"yaztik"*) A type of Turkish cushion cover, or very small rug.

Yezidi Term for followers of an ancient religion, surviving among scattered Kurdish communities in western Iran, eastern Iraq, and, to a lesser extent, the southern Caucasus. Yezidis were often persecuted by neighboring populations, in the belief that they were devil-worshippers.

Yomud (sometimes spelt **"Yomut"**) A Turkoman tribe living in Turkestan and Iran.

yurt A circular nomad home, made by draping felt coverings over a portable framework.

Yürük Term used to refer to small groups of nomads in eastern Anatolia. It is a generic label rather than a concrete ethnic identity. The word "Yürük" appears to derive from the word "yurumek," meaning "to walk," and is also applied to the weavings these peoples produce.

Zagros Mountains A mountain chain in western Iran, home to a variety of native Iranian and Turkic-speaking nomadic tribes.

Bibliography

Articles in periodicals are shown chronologically. Wherever possible, volume and issue numbers have been given in addition to the date.

Acar (Balpinar), Belkis, "Yucu Nomad Weaving in the Balikesir Region of Western Turkey" in *Yörük: The Nomadic Weaving Tradition of the Middle East*, Carnegie Institute, Pittsburgh, 1978.

Andrews, Peter A. and Andrews, Mugul, *The Turcoman of Iran*, Abbot Hall Art Gallery, Kendall, England, 1971.

Andrews, Peter A., "The Turkmen Tent" in *Turkmen*, edited by Louise Mackie and Jon Thompson, The Textile Museum, Washington D. C., 1980.

– "Felt Tents in Anatolia" in *Sosyal Antropoloji ve Etnoloji Dergisi*, Ayri Basim, 1986.

– "Tent Screens to Kilims: Argument against Argument", *HALI*, issue 33, London 1987.

Azadi, Siawosch, *Carpets in the Baluch Tradition*, Klinkhardt and Biermann, Munich, 1986.

– and Andrews, Peter A., *Mafrash*, Dietrich Riemer Verlag, Berlin, 1985.

Balpinar, Belkis, *Kilim–Cicim–Zili–Soumak: Turkish Flatweaves*, Eren Yayin Lari, Istanbul, 1985.

– and Hirsch, Udo, *Carpets of the Vakiflar Museum, Istanbul*, Uta Hulsey, Wesel, 1982.

– and Hirsch, Udo, *Flatweaves of the Vakiflar Museum, Istanbul*, Uta Hulsey, Wesel, 1988.

Barth, Fredrik, *Nomads of South Persia*, Oslo University Press, Oslo, and Humanities Press, New York, 1961.

Bausback, Peter, *Kelim*, Klinkhardt & Biermann, Munich, 1983.

Beck, Lois, *Nomad: A Year in the Life of a Qashqa'i Tribesman in Iran*, University of California Press, Berkeley, 1991.

– *The Qashqa'i of Iran*, Yale University Press, New Haven and London, 1986.

Bennett, Ian, "Carpets of the Khans," parts I and II, *HALI*, issues 43 and 44, London, 1989.

Black, David, and Loveless, Clive, *Rugs of the Wandering Baluchi*, David Black, London, 1976.

– *Woven Gardens*, David Black, London, 1979.

Bogolyubov, A.A., *Carpets of Central Asia* (edited by Jon Thompson), Crosby Press, Hampshire, England, 1973.

Boucher, Jeff W., *Baluchi Woven Treasures*, Jeff W. Boucher, Alexandria, Virginia, 1989.

Brüggemann, W., and Böhmer, H., *Rugs of the Peasants and Nomads of Anatolia*, Verlag Kunst und Antiquitaten GMBH, Munich, 1983.

Bunker, E., Chatwin, B., and Farkas, A., *Animal Style Art from East to West*, The Asian Society Inc., New York, 1970.

Burns, James D., *The Caucasus: Traditions in Weaving*, Court Street Press, Seattle, 1987.

Cameron, George G., *History of Early Iran*, Greenwood Press, New York, 1936.

Cammann, Schuyler, "Paradox' in Persian Carpet Patterns," *HALI*, issue 3, London, 1978.

Campbell, Joseph, *The Hero With A Thousand Faces*, Pantheon Books, New York, 1949.

Collins, John J., Jr., *Flowers of the Desert*, The Walrus Press, Newburyport, Massachusetts, 1989.

– *Shiraz*, The Walrus Press, Newburyport, Massachusetts, 1987.

Collon, Dominique, "Subjective Reconstruction? The Çatal Hüyük Wall-paintings," *HALI*, issue 53, London, 1990.

Cooper, Merian C., *Grass*, G. P. Putnam and Sons, New York and London, 1925.

Craycraft, Michael and Halley, Anne, *Balouch Prayer Rugs*, Adraskand Gallery, Point Reyes Station, California, 1982.

Crowther, Margaret, and Pichon, Elizabeth (eds.), *The World Atlas of Archaeology*, Portland House, Mitchell Beazley International Ltd., New York, 1985.

d'Alviella, Count Goblet, *The Migration of Symbols*, University Books, New York, 1956.

de Franchis, Amadeo, and Wertime, John T., *Lori and Bakhtiyari Flatweaves*, Tehran Rug Society, Tehran 1976.

de Franchis, Amadeo, "Kurdish Rugs from Northeastern Iran," *Discoveries from Kurdish Looms*, Northwestern University, Evanston, Illinois, 1983.

Denny, Walter, "Anatolian Rugs: An Essay on Method," *Textile Museum Journal*, volume 3, no.3, Washington D.C., 1973.

Douglas, William O., *Strange Lands and Friendly People*, Harper and Brothers, New York, 1951.

Eagleton, William, *An Introduction to Kurdish Rugs*, Interlink Books, New York, 1988.

– "The Weavings of Iraqi Kurdistan," in *Discoveries from Kurdish Looms*, Northwestern University, Evanston, Illinois, 1983.

Edwards, A. Cecil, *The Persian Carpet*, Duckworth, London, 1953.

Eiland, Murray, *Oriental Rugs: A New Comprehensive Guide*, Little Brown and Company, Boston, 1981.

– "Origins of Turkoman Guls," *Oriental Rug Review*, volume 2, no.4, New Hampshire, 1982

– "Development of Village and Nomad Rug Designs," *HALI*, volume 4, no. 4, London, 1982.

– "The Kurdish Rugs of Iran," *Discoveries from Kurdish Looms*, Northwestern University, Evanston, Illinois, 1983.

– book review, "The Goddess from Anatolia," *Oriental Rug Review*, volume 10, no. 6, New Hampshire, 1990.

– and Opie, James, "Barriers to Productive Scholarship in Rug Studies," *Oriental Rug Review*, volume 12, no. 2, New Hampshire, 1992.

Ford, P. R. J., *The Oriental Carpet*, Portland House, New York, 1989.

– "Flatweaves of Kerman Province," *Oriental Rug Review*, volume 12, no. 2, New Hampshire, 1992.

Franses, Michael and Pinner, Robert, *Turkoman Studies I: Aspects of the Weaving and Decorative Arts of Central Asia*, Oguz Press, London, 1980.

– "The Turkoman Collection in the Victoria and Albert Museum," *HALI*, volume 2, no. 4, London, 1980.

Garthwaite, Gene R., *Khans and Shahs: A Documentary Analysis of the Bakhtiyari in Iran*, Cambridge University Press, Cambridge, 1983.

Ghirshman, Roman, *The Art of Ancient Iran* (translated by Stuart Gilbert and James Emmons), Golden Press, New York, 1964.

Grigg, Jocelyn, "Sassanian Influence in the Silks of T'ang China," *HALI*, volume 2, no.2, London, 1979.

Grousset, René, *The Empire of the Steppes* (translated by Naomi Walford), Rutgers University Press, New Brunswick, New Jersey, 1970.

Haskins, John F., "Motives in Pazyryk Art," in *The Fifth Pazyryk Kurgan and the "Animal Style,"* dissertation, Department of Fine Arts, New York University, 1961.

Henning, W. B., "The First Indo-Europeans in History," in *Society and History, Essays in Honor of Karl August Wittfogel* (edited by G. L. Ulman), Mouton Publishers, The Hague, undated.

Herrmann, Eberhart, *Asiatische Teppich- und Textilkunst* (3 volumes, volume 1 with English text supplement), Munich, volume 1, 1989; volume 2, 1990; volume 3, 1991.

– *Seltene Orientteppiche*, (10 volumes), Munich, published annually between 1978 and 1988.

Hirsh, Udo, "A contribution to the study of Anatolian tribal groups and their kilims," in *Anatolian Kilims*, John Eskenazi, Milan, 1984.

Housego, Jenny, *Tribal Rugs: An Introduction to the Weaving of the Tribes of Iran*, Scorpion Publications, London, 1978.

– "Northwestern Iran and Caucasus, Part 1," in *Yörük*, Carnegie Institute, Pittsburgh, 1978.

Irwin, John, *The Kashmir Shawl*, Victoria and Albert Museum, London, 1973.

Ittig, Annette, "A Group of Inscribed Carpets from Persian Kurdistan," *HALI*, volume 4, no. 2, London 1981.

Janata, Alfred, "The So-called Herat Baluch Rugs and their Weavers," in *Oriental Carpet and Textile Studies I*, edited by Robert Pinner and Walter Denny, *HALI*, London, 1985.

Jettmar, Karl, *The Art of the Steppes*, Greystone Press, New York, 1967.

Juliano, A., Bunker, E., Kawami, T., and Lerner, J., series of articles pertaining to the Pazyryk burials in *Source*, volume 10, no.4, 1991.

Kinnane, Derk, *The Kurds and Kurdistan*, Oxford University Press, Oxford, 1964.

Lambton, Ann, "Ilat," in the *Encyclopedia of Islam* (second edition), E. J. Brill, Leiden.

Lamm, Carl Johan, *Carpet Fragments*, Uddevalla, Nationalmuseum, Sweden, 1985.

Landreau, Anthony N., "Kurdish Kilim Weaving in the Van-Hakkari District of Eastern Turkey," *Textile Museum Journal*, volume 3, no. 4, Washington D. C., 1973.

Laszlo, Gyula, *The Art of the Migration Period*, University of Miami Press, Coral Gables, Florida, 1974.

Mackie, Louise W. and Thompson, Jon (eds.), *Turkmen*, The Textile Museum, Washington D. C., 1980.

Maenchen-Helfen, Otto J., *The World of the Huns*, University of California Press, Berkeley, Los Angeles and London, 1973.

Mallett, Marla, "A Weaver's View of the Çatal Hüyük Controversy," *Oriental Rug Review*, volume 10, no. 6, New Hampshire, 1990.

Moorey, P. R. S., "The Art of Ancient Iran," in *Ancient Bronzes, Ceramics and Seals*, Los Angeles County Museum of Art, 1981.

Mushak, Paul, "Scientific Approaches to the Study of Oriental Rugs, Trappings, and Textiles," *Oriental Rug Review*, volume 5, New Hampshire, 1986.

– and O'Bannon, George, "Chemical analysis of a Turkoman Chuval," *Oriental Rug Review*, volume 2, no. 9, New Hampshire, 1982.

– and Opie, James, "Trappings of the Luri," *Oriental Rug Review*, volume 6, pages 126-8 and 162-5, New Hampshire, 1986.

Nasr, Seyyed Hossein, *Islamic Science, An Illustrated Study*, World of Islam Festival Publishing Company Ltd., 1976.

O'Bannon, George, *Kazakh and Uzbek Rugs from Afghanistan*, Pittsburgh, 1979.

– "The Nomenclature of Baluch Rugs," *Oriental Rug Review*, volume 3, no. 5, 1983.

Opie, James. *Tribal Rugs of Southern Persia*, James Opie Oriental Rugs, Inc., Portland, Oregon, 1981.

– "Smaller Weavings of the Qashqa'i," parts I and II, *Oriental Rug Auction Review*, volume 1, no. 2, and volume 1, no. 3, New Hampshire, 1981.

– "Buying Tribal Rugs in Shiraz," in *Oriental Rug Auction Review*, volume 1, no. 3, New Hampshire, 1981.

– "Bargaining with a Bakhtiyari," *Oriental Rug Auction Review*, volume 1, no. 4, New Hampshire, 1981.

– "Afghanistan Reflections," parts I – V *Oriental Rug Auction Review*, volume 2, no. 1 – no. 6, New Hampshire, 1982.

– "The Tribal Road," *HALI*, issue 29, London, 1986.

– "Bird Rugs of South Persia," *Oriental Rug Review*, volume 8, no. 4, New Hampshire, 1987.

– "Did Anatolian Kilim Designs Descend from Iranian Tribal Traditions?" *Oriental Rug Review*, volume 10, no. 5, New Hampshire, 1990.

– "Fragments of An Ancient Puzzle," parts I and II, *HALI*, issues 53 and 54, London, 1990.

Petsopoulos, Yanni, *Kilims*, Rizzoli, New York, 1991.

Pinner, Robert, "The Animal Tree and the Great Bird in Myth and Folklore," in *Turkoman Studies I*, edited by Robert Pinner and Michael Franses, Oguz Press, London,

1980.

Pope, Arthur Upham (ed.), *A Survey of Persian Art from Prehistoric Times to the Present*, Oxford University Press, 6 volumes, 1938, with subsequent additional volumes.

Porada, Edith, *The Art of Ancient Iran: Pre-Islamic Cultures*, Holle Verlag GMBH. Baden-Baden, 1965.

Rudenko, Sergei, *Frozen Tombs of Siberia: The Pazyryk Burials of Iron-Age Horsemen*, University of California Press, Berkeley, 1970.

Ryder, Michael L., "Felt: Man's Earliest Fabric," *HALI*, issue 29, 1986.

Sabahi, Taher, *Qashqai, Tappeto Tribali Persiani*, Instituto Geografico de Agostini, Novara, 1990.

Safrastian, Arshak, *Kurds and Kurdistan*, The Harvill Press, London, 1948.

Schlamminger, Karl and Wilson, Peter L., *Weaver of Tales*, Callway Verlag, Munich, 1980.

Schurmann, Ulrich, *Caucasian Rugs*, Ulrich Schurmann, K. G., Cologne, 1964.

Shaffer, Daniel, "Persian Collection," in *HALI*, issue 34, 1987.

Stanzer, Wilfried, *Kordi*, Collection Adil Besim, Vienna, 1988.

Tanavoli, Parviz, *Lion Rugs: The Lion in the Art and Culture of Iran*, Wepf & Co. AG Publishers, Basel, 1985.

– *Shahsavan*, Rizzoli, New York, 1985.

– "The Afshars: A Tribal History," *HALI*, issue 37, 1988.

– "Too Good to be True," *HALI*, issue 40, 1988.

– "Shahsavan Scissor Bags," *HALI*, issue 40, 1988.

– "Shahsavan Pile Carpets," *HALI*, issue 45, 1989.

– "The Afshars, Part 2," in *HALI*, issue 57, 1991.

– and Amanolahi, Sekandar, *Gabbeh*, George D. Bornet, Zurich, 1990.

Thompson, Jon, *Oriental Carpets: From the Tents, Cottages and Workshops of Asia*, E. P. Dutton, New York, 1983.

– "Continuity and Change in the Language of Art," in *Von Uschak bis Yarkand: Seltene Orientteppiche*, Eberhart Herrmann, Munich, 1979.

– "Centralised Designs," in *Rare Oriental Carpets*, Eberhart Herrmann, Munich, 1980.

– "A Return to Tradition," *HALI*, issue 30, 1986.

– *Silk, Carpets and The Silk Road*, NKH Culture Centre, Tokyo, 1988.

– and Böhmer, H., "The Pazyryk Carpet: A Technical Discussion," *Source*, volume 10, no. 4, 1991.

Trapper, Richard, introduction to *The Conflict of Tribe and State in Iran and Afghanistan*, St. Martin's Press, New York, 1983.

– "The Tribes in Eighteenth- and Nineteenth-Century Iran," in *The Cambridge History of Iran, The Afshars, Zands and Quajars*, volume 7, edited by P. Avery and G. Hambly, Cambridge University Press, 1992.

Trilling, James, *The Roman Heritage: Textiles from Egypt and the Eastern Mediterranean 300 to 600 A.D.*, The Textile Museum, Washington D.C., 1982.

Tzareva, Elena, *Rugs and Carpets from Central Asia*, Aurora Art Publishers, Leningrad, 1984.

Weber, George W. Jr., *The Ornaments of Late Chou Bronzes*, Rutgers University Press, New Brunswick, New Jersey, 1973.

Wertime, John T., "The Lors and Bakhtiyaris," in *Yörük: The Nomadic Weaving Tradition of the Middle East*, Carnegie Institute, Pittsburgh, 1978.

– "Salt Bags from Iran," *HALI*, no. 1, 1978 and no. 3, 1979.

– "The Names, Types and Functions of Nomadic Weaving in Iran," in *Yörük: The Nomadic Weaving Tradition of the Middle East*, Carnegie Institute, Pittsburgh, 1978.

– "Flat-Woven Structures Found in Nomadic and Village Weavings from the Near East and Central Asia," *Textile Museum Journal*, volume 18, Washington D. C., 1979.

– "Weft-wrapping in Nomadic and Village Flat-woven Textiles from the Near East and Central Asia," in *Flat-Woven Textiles in the Arthur D. Jenkins Collection*, volume 1, edited by Cathryn Cootner. The Textile Museum, Washington D. C., 1981.

– "The Principal Types and Woven Structures of Kurdish Weavings in Norrtheastern Iran," in *Discoveries from Kurdish Looms* Northwestern University, Evanston, Illinois, 1983.

– "The Classification and Description of Fabric Structures in Near Eastern Textiles: Another Example of Weft-Wrapping," in *Oriental Carpet and Textile Studies*, volume 1, edited by Robert Pinner and Walter Denny, *HALI*, London, 1985.

– "The Shahsavans in Oriental Rug Literature: A Personal Perspective," five-part series in *Oriental Rug Review*, volume 6, New Hampshire, 1986.

– "The Weavings of the Lors and Bakhtiyaris: A Fifteen-Year Retrospective," *Oriental Rug Review*, volume 12, no. 2, New Hampshire, 1992.

Whiting, Mark C., "Dyes of Turkoman Rugs," *HALI*, volume 1, no. 3, London, 1978.

– "Progress in the Analysis of Dyes of Old Oriental Carpets," *HALI*, volume 2, no. 1, London, 1979.

– "A Report on the Dyes of the Pazyryk Carpet," in *Oriental Carpet and Textile Studies I*, edited by Robert Pinner and Walter Denny, *HALI*, London, 1985.

Wilber, Donald L., *A Descriptive Catalogue of Dated Rugs and of Inscribed Rugs*, The Near Eastern Art Research Center, 1989.

Yohe, Ralph S., "Rugs of the Yörük Triangle: A Family of Rugs of Eastern Turkey," *HALI*, volume 2, no. 2, London, 1979.

Picture Credits

Title spread, Hutchison Library
page 7, James Opie

CHAPTER 1

1.1 Robert Harding
1.2 Ernest Schoedsack, in *Grass*
1.3 Hutchison Library
1.4 Rippon Boswell, Germany
1.5 Hutchison Library
1.6 Morteza Ghashghai
1.7 Hutchison Library

CHAPTER 2

2.1 Hermitage Museum, St. Petersburg
2.2 Metropolitan Museum of Art, New York, Joseph Pulitzer Fund, 1955
2.3 Drawing after Rudenko
2.4 Hermitage Museum, St. Petersburg
2.5 Hermitage Museum, St. Petersburg
2.6 British Museum
2.7 Adam Collection
2.8 Robert and Mary Balam
2.9 James Opie

CHAPTER 3

3.1 Trillium Studios
3.3 Trillium Studios
3.5 Trillium Studios
3.6 Drawing after Moorey
3.7 Drawing after Rudenko

CHAPTER 4

4.2 Parviz Tanavoli
4.2 Metropolitan Museum of Art, New York
4.4 Bennie Norris
4.9 Al Berreth
4.10 Private collection
4.12 Drawing after Weber
4.19 Clive Loveless
4.20, 4.21 Robert and Mary Balsam
4.22 Robert Harding
4.23 Private collection
4.25 Drawing after Gimbutas
4.27 Private collection
4.29 Private collection
4.33 Sergei Rudenko
4.35 James Opie
4.37 Islamische Museum, Berlin
4.39 Private collection
4.40 After Balpinar, Hirsch and Mellaart
4.43 Los Angeles County Museum of Art
4.44 Private collection
4.45 Mr and Mrs Richard L. Clements

CHAPTER 5

5.1 Bennie Norris
5.3 Private collection
5.4 James Opie
5.6 James Opie
5.8 Eberhart Herrmann
5.10 Rosalie and Mitchell Rudnick
5.15 Christie's, London
5.16 Private collection
5.17 Eberhart Herrmann
5.18 Franz Bauback
5.19 John Eskenazi
5.22 Private collection
5.24 George O'Bannon
5.27 Eberhart Herrmann
5.29 Robert and Mary Balsam
5.32 Private collection
5.35 John Eskenazi
5.36 David Opie

CHAPTER 6

6.1 Franz Bausback
6.2 Christie's, London
6.4 Rippon Boswell, Germany
6.5 Eberhart Herrmann
6.7 John Leach
6.8 Clive Loveless
6.11 Sotheby's, New York
6.17 Eberhart Herrmann

CHAPTER 7

7.8 James Opie
7.9 James Opie
7.10 James Opie
7.11 Private collection
7.12 James Opie
7.13 James Opie
7.14 Charles Lave
7.15 James Opie
7.16 L. A. Bibler
7.18 Timothy and Betsy String
7.19 Thomas Cook
7.22 Janos Ferago
7.23 Eric Keller
7.25 Timothy and Betsy String
7.26 Joseph Throop
7.27 Private collection
7.28 John and Caroline Gilbert
7.29 Dr. and Mrs. Ralph Nottingham
7.30 Joseph Throop

CHAPTER 8

8.2 James Opie
8.3 James Opie
8.4 Ernest Schoedsack, in *Grass*
8.5 Ernest Schoedsack, in *Grass*
8.7 James Opie
8.9 Private collection
8.10 Fred Mushkat
8.12 Private collection
8.14 Private collection
8.16 Timothy and Betsy String
8.17 Gallery Zadah
8.18 Gallerie Theo Haberli
8.21 Timothy and Betsy String

CHAPTER 9

9.3 Robert Harding
9.4 James Opie
9.5 (top) Robert Harding (bottom) James Opie
9.7 Ernst Holtzer
9.8 Alexandra Opie
9.9 Joanna Kline
9.11 Mercante d'Orient, Verona
9.12 Steven Maeck
9.13 William Moore
9.14 Private collection, photograph courtesy of John Collins
9.15 Jim Klingner
9.16 Franz Bausback
9.17 Derek and Anita Stables
9.18 Rippon Boswell, Germany
9.19, 9.20 Jan Melgaardsbakken
9.21 Bernheimer Fine Arts Ltd., London

CHAPTER 10

10.2 James Opie
10.3 James Opie
10.4 James Opie
10.5 Robert Harding
10.7 Christie's, London
10.8 Timothy and Betsy String
10.10 Private collection
10.12 Private collection
10.13 Thomas Cook
10.15 J. B. Henderson
10.17 Private collection
10.18 Don Nakonechny
10.19 Eberhart Herrmann
10.20 Rosalind Rustigan
10.21 Galerie Neiriz, Berlin
10.22 James Opie
10.23 Private collection
10.24 Gil McDonald
10.25 Robert Harding
10.26 Timothy and Betsy String

CHAPTER 11

11.2 Fredrik Barth, Oslo University Press
11.3 Fredrik Barth, Oslo University Press
11.4 Fredrik Barth, Oslo University Press
11.6 Timothy and Betsy String
11.7 Private collection

11.8 Private collection
11.9 Private collection
11.10 Timothy and Betsy String
11.11 Paul Ryan
11.12 Timothy and Betsy String
11.13 Private collection
11.14 Private collection
11.16 Joseph Throop
11.18 John and Caroline Gilbert
11.19 Private collection
11.20 Rippon Boswell

CHAPTER 12

12.3 John Wertime
12.6 John Corwin
12.8 J. B. Henderson
12.9 Private collection
12.10 Private collection
12.11 Herbert Bieler
12.13 Private collection
12.14 Sotheby's, New York
12.15 Richard Purdon

CHAPTER 13

13.3 Hutchison Library
13.4 Hutchison Library
13.5 James Opie
13.7 Joyce Ware: photograph by Gayle Garrett
13.8 Eberhart Herrmann
13.9 Hazara Gallery
13.12 Randy Wells
13.15 Joseph Throop
13.17 Adraskand Gallery
13.18 Adraskand Gallery
13.20 Danny Shaffer
13.21 Dennis R. Dodds, Philadelphia
13.22 Clive Loveless and Arkie Robins
13.24 Clive Loveless
13.25 Franz Bausback
13.26 Franz Bausback
13.27 Eberhart Herrmann
13.28 Eberhart Herrmann

CHAPTER 14

14.2 Parviz Tanavoli
14.3 Parviz Tanavoli
14.4 Parviz Tanavoli
14.5 Guy Gehling
14.6 Richard Purdon
14.7 Danny Shaffer
14.9 Eberhart Herrmann
14.10 James Opie
14.11 Wendel Swan
14.12 Wendel Swan
14.13 Private collection
14.14 Private collection
14.16 George and Loretta O'Leary

CHAPTER 15

15.2 Dr. Peter Andrews
15.3 Gayle Garrett
15.4 Gayle Garrett
15.5 Gayle Garrett
15.6 Vakiflar Museum, Istanbul
15.7 Museum of National Antiquities, Stockholm
15.10 Metropolitan Museum of Art, New York
15.11 Jim Klingner
15.12 Mark Hopkins
15.13 John and Donna Sommer
15.14 The Textile Museum, Washington D. C., gift of John and Donna Sommer
15.16 Private collection, photograph courtesy of Wilfried Stanzer
15.17 Sotheby's, New York
15.18 Adraskand Gallery

CHAPTER 16

16.2 Robert Haring
16.3 Rosalie and Mitchell Rudnick
16.4 Rosalie and Mitchell Rudnick
16.5 Skinner's

16.6 Eberhart Herrmann
16.7 Private collection
16.8 Private collection
16.9 Rosalie and Mitchell Rudnick
16.10 Rosalie and Mitchell Rudnick
16.11 Private collection
16.12 The Markarian Collection

CHAPTER 17

17.2 James Opie
17.3 James Opie
17.4 James Opie
17.5 Hutchison Library
17.6 Hutchison Library
17.7 Private collection, photograph courtesy of Sotheby's, New York
17.9 Franz Bausback
17.11 Rippon Boswell, Germany
17.12 Rippon Boswell, Germany
17.13 Christie's, London
17.14 Christie's, London
17.15 *Hali* Publications Ltd
17.17 Adil Besim
17.20 Timothy and Betsy String
17.21 Franz Bausback
17.22 Adil Besim
17.23 Skinner's
17.24 The Textile Museum, Washington D. C.; no. R37.9./. Acquired by George Hewitt Myers in 1914.

CONCLUSION

1 Los Angeles County Museum of Art

Index